PENGUIN BOOKS

RAPT

Winifred Gallagher's books include *House Thinking*, *Just the Way You Are* (a *New York Times* Notable Book), *Working on God*, and *The Power of Place*. She has written for numerous publications, such as *Atlantic Monthly*, *Rolling Stone*, and *The New York Times*. She lives in Manhattan and Dubois, Wyoming.

RAPT

Attention and the Focused Life

Winifred Gallagher

PENGUIN BOOKS

PENGUIN BOOKS

Published by the Penguin Group

Penguin Group (USA) Inc., 375 Hudson Street, New York, New York 10014, U.S.A.

Penguin Group (Canada), 90 Eglinton Avenue East, Suite 700, Toronto,
Ontario, Canada M4P 2Y3 (a division of Pearson Penguin Canada Inc.)

Penguin Books Ltd, 80 Strand, London WC2R 0RL, England

Penguin Ireland, 25 St Stephen's Green, Dublin 2, Ireland (a division of Penguin Books Ltd)

Penguin Group (Australia), 250 Camberwell Road, Camberwell,
Victoria 3124, Australia (a division of Pearson Australia Group Pty Ltd)

Penguin Books India Pvt Ltd, 11 Community Centre, Panchsheel Park, New Delhi – 110 017, India

Penguin Group (NZ), 67 Apollo Drive, Rosedale, North Shore 0632,
New Zealand (a division of Pearson New Zealand Ltd)

Penguin Books (South Africa) (Pty) Ltd, 24 Sturdee Avenue,
Rosebank, Johannesburg 2196, South Africa

Penguin Books Ltd, Registered Offices:
80 Strand, London WC2R 0RL, England

First published in the United States of America by The Penguin Press,
a member of Penguin Group (USA) Inc. 2009
Published in Penguin Books 2010

1 3 5 7 9 10 8 6 4 2

Grateful acknowledgment is made for permission to reprint
excerpts from the following copyrighted works:

"The Skaters" from *Rivers and Mountains* by John Ashbery. Copyright © 1962, 1963, 1964, 1966, 1997
by John Ashbery. Reprinted by permission of Georges Borchardt, Inc., on behalf of the author.
"The soul selects her own society" from *The Poems of Emily Dickinson: Variorum Edition*, Ralph W. Franklin, ed.,
Cambridge, Mass.: The Belknap Press of Harvard University Press. Copyright © 1998 by the President and
Fellows of Harvard College. Copyright © 1951, 1955, 1979, 1983 by the President and Fellows of Harvard College.
Reprinted by permission of the publishers and the Trustees of Amherst College.

THE LIBRARY OF CONGRESS HAS CATALOGED THE HARDCOVER EDITION AS FOLLOWS:
Gallagher, Winifred.
Rapt : attention and the focused life / Winifred Gallagher.
p. cm.
Includes bibliographical references and index.
ISBN 978-1-59420-210-0 (hc.)
ISBN 978-0-14-311690-5 (pbk.)
1. Attention. I. Title.
BF321.G25 2009
153.7'33—dc22   2009002633

Printed in the United States of America
Designed by Jennifer Ann Daddio

CONTENTS

"My experience is what I agree to attend to."

—William James

RAPT

Attention and the Focused Life

INTRODUCTION:

Choosing the Focused Life

We're all amateur psychologists who run private experiments on how best to live. Some of us specialize in relationships and mostly explore bonding. Others concentrate on work and test ways to be more productive and creative. Still others look to philosophy or religion and investigate the big picture: the ultimate way things are. Five years ago, a common-enough crisis plunged me into a study of the nature of experience. More important, this experiment led me to cutting-edge scientific research and a psychological version of what physicists trying to explain the universe call a "grand unified theory" or "theory of everything": your life—who you are, what you think, feel, and do, what you love—is the sum of what you focus on.

That your experience largely depends on the material objects and mental subjects that you choose to pay attention to or ignore is not an imaginative notion, but a physiological fact. When you focus on a STOP sign or a sonnet, a waft of perfume or a stock-market tip, your brain registers that "target," which enables it to affect your behavior. In contrast, the things that you don't attend to in a sense don't exist, at least for you. All day long, you are selectively paying attention to *something*, and much more often than you may suspect, you can take charge of this process to good effect. Indeed, your ability to focus on *this* and suppress *that* is the key to controlling your experience and, ultimately, your well-being.

Attention is commonly understood as "the concentration of the mental powers" or "the direction or application of the mind to any object of sense or thought." Recently, however, a rare convergence of insights from both neuroscience and psychology suggests a paradigm shift in how to think about this cranial laser and its role in behavior: thoughts, feelings, and actions. Like fingers pointing to the moon, other diverse disciplines from anthropology to education, behavioral economics to family counseling, similarly suggest that the skillful management of attention is the sine qua non of the good life and the key to improving virtually every aspect of your experience, from mood to productivity to relationships.

If you could look backward at your years thus far, you'd see that your life has been fashioned from what you've paid attention to and what you haven't. You'd observe that of the myriad sights and sounds, thoughts and feelings that you *could* have focused on, you selected a relative few, which became what you've confidently called "reality." You'd also be struck by the fact that if you had paid attention to other things, your reality and your life would be very different.

Attention has created the experience and, significantly, the self stored in your memory, but looking ahead, what you focus on from this moment will create the life and person yet to be. Since Sigmund Freud, psychology has mostly examined our pasts to explain and improve our lives. If you think in terms of the present and future instead, you might encounter an intuition lurking in the back of your mind, as it was in mine: if you could just stay focused on the right things, your life would stop feeling like a reaction to stuff that happens to you and become something that you create: not a series of accidents, but a work of art.

MY INTEREST IN attention goes back to childhood, when I ran the usual experiments on its effects on behavior. I saw that by focusing on one thing, you could ignore another. If you concentrated on some enjoyable activity, you could make time simultaneously race and stand still. Staying focused on a goal over time might not guarantee you'd achieve it but was a crucial step in that direction.

In midlife, an attention experiment of a different magnitude set me on the path that led to this book. Walking away from the hospital after the biopsy from hell—not just cancer, but a particularly nasty, fairly advanced kind—I had an intuition of a highly unusual blue-white clarity. This disease wanted to monopolize my attention, but as much as possible, I would focus on my life instead.

As Samuel Johnson observed, the prospect of hanging wonderfully concentrates the mind. Right from the start, my attention experiment went well. Through many months of chemo, surgery, more chemo, and daily radiation, I mostly stayed focused on taking care of business in the present—suddenly all I could count on—and on the things that matter most and make me feel best: big ones like my family and friends, spiritual life, and work, and smaller ones like movies, walks, and a 6:30 p.m. martini. As a result, I spent very little time and energy on the past or future or on the suddenly very many things that seemed unimportant or negative. I began to relish corny admonitions to "Have a good day!" and my husband started referring to our house as "Harmonia."

That's not to say that cancer was the proverbial "best thing that ever happened to me," or that I'm glad I had it: it wasn't, and I'm not. Nor was my focusing strategy 100 percent effective 24/7. There are moments in life—when someone hands you a pink slip, perhaps, or can't find your "good" chemo vein—when you just can't immediately shift your attention to what to have for dinner, much less to the music of the spheres. Then too, stimuli that you don't consciously focus on, such as a scowling face in a crowd or an unpleasant noise, can sometimes sneak into your brain and influence your behavior, albeit weakly.

Nevertheless, throughout a long, grueling ordeal, I cleaved to the principle that your life is the creation of what you focus on—and what you don't. Whenever possible, I looked toward whatever seemed meaningful, productive, or energizing and away from the destructive, or dispiriting. I found that I could pretty much carry on with business as usual and stay in pretty good spirits, too. No doubt partly because I was really present in the moments we shared, kind people appeared to enjoy my seemingly sepulchral, bald-headed company. Although that year was not my easiest, neither was it the hardest. Certainly, it was my most focused.

A psychological theory—your life consists of what you focus on—is one thing in your mind or on paper, and something else again when you test-drive it over rough terrain. I was impressed enough to start thinking seriously about attention not just personally but also professionally, as someone who writes about behavior. I began with some questions:

What *is* attention, exactly? What happens in your brain when you focus on something? Does the same process apply to thoughts and feelings as to sights and sounds? How does your characteristic way of focusing affect who you are? Why do certain things "grab" your attention? How come bad stuff, like the site of a car crash or an overheard insult, is more riveting than good stuff, like pretty scenery or a direct compliment? Is the difference between common glitches such as mind-wandering and serious problems such as ADHD one of quality or quantity? How do you "pay attention" to something over long periods of time, as you do to your career or health?

After some reporting in pursuit of answers, I learned that attention is now a hot subject in both neuroscientific and behavioral research, which increasingly reveals its importance to functions from the simplest learning to *Homo sapiens*' distinctive search for meaning. I found that my small-scale experiment simply illustrates what a tremendous amount of eclectic science proves: you cannot always be happy, but you can almost always be focused, which is the next best thing. As the poet says in *Beowulf*, "Every life has more than enough sadness and more than enough joy." By skillfully managing your attention, you're able to experience both in a balanced way and stay oriented in a positive, productive direction. John Milton might have been thinking of the power of focus when he wrote: "The mind is its own place, and in itself / Can make a heav'n of hell, a hell of heav'n."

THEY LACKED THE tools to explore it fully, but even back in the nineteenth century, scientists, including Freud, were intrigued by attention. The human brain was still a mysterious "black box" that couldn't be studied directly in an ethical way, so their insights were largely descriptive and limited to inferences from brain-injured patients and observations of their own and others' behavior. The formal "discovery" of attention is often credited to the German physician Wilhelm Wundt, but William James (1842–1910), his great contemporary and fellow founder of psychology, remains its philosopher king.

Just as modern cognitive psychology is a response to the recent revolutions in communications and information, the behavioral science of James's era was shaped by its important cultural developments, including the theory of evolution and the growing conflict between reason and religion. A philosopher before he became a psychologist, James broke with the rationalism of the influential Germans Immanuel Kant and Georg Hegel to become a "pragmatist," who rejected abstract verities that conflict with the individual's own "feeling of reality" and experience of the way things are. Thus, he accepted evolution but not the implication that nature rigidly determines your behavior, making you a ghastly biological robot. As he wrote, "The whole sting and excitement of our voluntary life depends on our sense that in it things are *really being decided* from one moment to another, and that it is not the dull rattling off of a chain that was forged innumerable ages ago."

Attention is woven into the warp and woof of James's defense of your freedom, individuality, and ability to create your own unique experience. Because your mind is profoundly shaped by what it imposes on itself, he argued, where you choose to focus it is vitally important. This conviction underlies many of his best maxims, such as "The greatest weapon against stress is our ability to choose one thought over another."

In his masterwork *The Principles of Psychology* (1890), James offered one of the earliest scientific definitions of attention, which is still admired for both substance and style. With an opening flourish as bold as it is disingenuous, he wrote, "Everyone knows what attention is. It is the taking possession of the mind, in clear and vivid form, of one out of what seem several simultaneously possible objects or trains of thought. Focalisation, concentration, of consciousness are of its essence. It implies a withdrawal from some things in order to deal effectively with others."

On a certain level, everyone *does* know what attention is. We can even feel it in our bones. The legendary mime Marcel Marceau specialized in wordlessly conveying the profound concentration of an athlete or artist poised for action. When the drill sergeant barks, "Atten-hut!" soldiers instantly snap into the alert, erect position that conveys intense focus. For me, the word evokes what I think of as the "cobra feeling": an almost muscular albeit mental bearing-down on a subject or object, which you rise above, hood flaring to block distractions, and hold steady in your unblinking focus. Despite this kind of gut-level understanding, however, until recently, scientists agreed with a turn-of-the-twentieth-century predecessor who compared the investigation of attention to "the discovery of a hornet's nest: the first touch brought out a whole swarm of insistent problems."

The first modern efforts to explore that hornet's nest began a half-century after James, when World War II made attention a life-or-death matter for the radar operators and combat pilots who had to monitor multiple signals on screens and in cockpits. (Anyone who has tried to drive a car in fast-moving heavy traffic while talking on a cell phone knows something of the challenge.) Still unable to penetrate the black box, psychologists kept trying to probe attention from the outside in. In a typical experiment, subjects wearing headphones that played different words into the right and left ear were told to listen to just one side; then, to see what had "gotten through" anyway, they were tested on material from both sources.

In the 1950s, researchers investigated attention in peacetime situations, such as the settings that created the "cocktail party effect." At a noisy gathering, they wondered, how do you screen out the din and attend to your companion's voice? When someone in a nearby cluster mentions you, why do your ears prick up, even though you hadn't been listening to their chatter? Some theories stressed the stimulus's physical characteristics, such as a voice's volume or proximity, others its content, such as your own name or a sexy remark, and still others both.

Despite accumulating research, however, well into the twentieth century, psychologists were hard pressed to improve on James's definition of attention. Their efforts were so vague and various—"the will to see," "psychic energy," "the mental condition or physiological precondition of certain experiences"—that some feared the field was destined to remain "a hodgepodge."

By the 1960s, however, neuroscience began to transform the study of behavior in general and attention in particular with new technology that revealed much more of what goes on inside the black box. At the National Institutes of Health, researchers recorded electrical signals from the brains of primates as they performed focusing tasks. Over the past twenty years, this process has been accelerated by increasingly sophisticated tools, such as functional magnetic resonance imaging (fMRI) and magnetoencephalography (MEG), that allow scientists to see parts of the brain activate and appear to light up and turn different colors when people think, feel, and act.

Researchers now have a good grasp of the brain's sensory, perceptual, and motor processes, but their understanding of the high-flying mental acrobatics of emotion and cognition is less well developed. Indeed, the "mind/brain problem" complicates all efforts to comprehend how a neurological event, such as an electrochemical shift, gets translated into a human experience, such as a sudden insight or a rush of desire. Nevertheless, one picture is indeed worth a thousand words, and neuroscience's inside-out physiological facts now constrain psychology's hitherto outside-in theories about behavior.

Where attention is concerned, most experiments involve vision and hearing, because those systems are most amenable to measurement and study. There's no single, widely accepted way to measure attention, which involves lots of mental processes, but many tests can measure the efficiency of its different aspects by analyzing how you perform various tasks. In a "visual search" experiment, for example, scientists measure how long it takes you to find a particular target among distractions. The basic insights derived from these studies generally apply to the other senses as well as to focusing on thoughts and feelings.

Research now suggests that like *consciousness* or *mind*, *attention* is a term for a complex neurological and behavioral business that seems like more than the sum of its parts. There's no tidy "attention center" in the brain. Instead, an ensemble of alerting, orienting, and executive networks collaborate to attune you to what's going on in your inner or outer world in a coherent way that points you toward an appropriate response. The brain's parietal and frontal cortexes are especially important to this process, but the sensory systems and many other structures are also involved; indeed, every neuron, or nerve cell, shows some sort of attentional modulation.

Neuroscience's truly groundbreaking insight into attention is the discovery that its basic mechanism is a process of selection. This two-part neurological sorting operation allows you to focus by enhancing the most compelling, or "salient," physical object or "high-value" mental subject in your ken and suppressing the rest. Outside an elite scientific circle, however, this finding's implications for everyday life have been stunningly unremarked.

As the expression *paying attention* suggests, when you focus, you're spending limited cognitive currency that should be wisely invested, because the stakes are high. At any one moment, your world contains too much information, whether objects, subjects, or both, for your brain to "represent," or depict clearly for you. Your attentional system selects a certain chunk of what's there, which gets valuable cerebral real estate and, therefore, the chance to affect your behavior. Moreover, this thin slice of life becomes part of your reality, and the rest is consigned to the shadows or oblivion.

Attention's selective nature confers tremendous benefits, chief of which is enabling you to comprehend what would otherwise be chaos. You couldn't take in the totality of your own experience, even for a moment, much less the whole world. Whether it's noise on the street, ideas at the office, or feelings in a relationship, you're potentially bombarded with stimuli vying for your attention. New electronic information and communications technology continually add to the overload. By helping you to focus on some things and filter out others, attention distills *the* universe into *your* universe.

Along with performing the Apollonian task of organizing your world, attention enables you to have the kind of Dionysian experience beautifully described by the old-fashioned term *"rapt"*—completely absorbed, engrossed, fascinated, perhaps even "carried away"—that underlies life's deepest pleasures, from the scholar's study to the carpenter's craft to the lover's obsession. Some individuals slip into it more readily, but research increasingly shows that with some reflection, experimentation, and practice, all of us can cultivate this profoundly attentive state and experience it more often. Paying rapt attention, whether to a trout stream or a novel, a do-it-yourself project or a prayer, increases your capacity for concentration, expands your inner boundaries, and lifts your spirits, but more important, it simply makes you feel that life is worth living.

Your ability to screen and select your experience, create order from chaos, and delight in fascination are attention's great benefits, but they exact a price. That little piece of reality that you tune in on is literally and figuratively far sketchier and more subjective than you assume. This underappreciated discovery has particularly important implications for your relationships and other social exchanges. Because different people focus on different things—even different aspects of the same thing—to say that someone else "lives in a different world" is to speak the plain truth.

STAYING FOCUSED IS an excellent strategy for well-being but not necessarily an easy one at first. Just grasping attention's role in determining your experience can be a challenge, because it requires seeing the forest instead of the trees. As psychology increasingly investigates what makes people feel and function well rather than poorly, it's ever more clear that the skillful management of attention is the first step toward any behavioral change and covers most self-improvement approaches like a vast umbrella.

Then, too, the mastery of focus is a skill, which like any other takes discipline and effort to develop. Considering attention's importance, it's surprising that until recently, science has come up with few strategies to improve it. Since the Arab world first discovered coffee's bracing effects, pharmacology has produced attention-boosting stimulants such as Ritalin and its variations and newer agents such as modafinil, but all have side effects and the potential to be abused. Where behavioral approaches are concerned, James suggested various tricks, such as taking a fresh perspective on your target or elaborating on its various aspects. Some of his modern heirs are experimenting with computerized workouts to improve focusing ability. However, most new strategies have a "back to the future" quality derived from their origin in meditation, secularized and made amenable to scientific study. These cognitive regimens can strengthen attention and improve well-being and are both free and safe, all of which must appeal to the 75 million baby boomers and their aging children, who are equally concerned about maintaining both their mental and their physical health.

The focused life requires not just a robust capacity for paying attention but also the discerning choice of targets that will invite the best possible experience. Much is made of the fact that human beings are the only creatures to know that they must die, but they're also the only ones to know that they must find something engaging to focus on in order to pass the time—increasingly, a lot of time. As Ralph Waldo Emerson, who was William James's godfather, put it, "To fill the hour—that is happiness."

Deciding what to pay attention to for this hour, day, week, or year, much less a lifetime, is a peculiarly human predicament, and your quality of life largely depends on how you handle it. Moses got his focus from God, and Picasso from his nearly supernatural creativity. We have other motivations and gifts, and most of us have to go through a more complicated process to find the right things to focus on. We must resist the temptation to drift along, reacting to whatever happens to us next, and deliberately select targets, from activities to relationships, that are worthy of our finite supplies of time and attention.

Some decisions about what to focus on, such as which profession to pursue or person to live with, automatically receive serious attention. Other choices may be less obvious but are just as important to the tenor of your daily experience: deciding to concentrate on your hopes rather than your fears; to attend to the present instead of the past; to appreciate that just because something upsetting happens, you don't have to fixate on it. Still other targets may seem inconsequential: focusing on a book or guitar instead of a rerun; a chat instead of an e-mail; an apple instead of a doughnut. Yet the difference between "passing the time" and "time well spent" depends on making smart decisions about what to attend to in matters large and small, then doing so as if your life depended on it. As far as its quality is concerned, it does.

Abundant research shows that most of the rich and famous, brainy and beautiful are little or no happier than individuals of ordinary means and gifts, because no matter who you are, your joie de vivre mostly derives from paying attention to someone or something that interests you. Even in the hell of the Nazi death camps, many inmates avoided depression because they took charge of and concentrated on the one thing that was left to them: their inner experience. The rates of psychological problems as well as mortality among people in extreme situations such as shipwrecks and plane crashes in remote areas are surprisingly low—often lower than in normal settings. Vicissitudes notwithstanding, these people are not sitting around brooding about the past or killing time by channel surfing but are living the focused life.

It's not a coincidence that the term *distracted* once referred not just to a loss or dilution of attention but also to confusion, mental imbalance, and even madness. It's all too easy to spend much of your life in such an unfocused, mixed-up condition, rushing toward the chimera of a better time and place to tune in and, well, be alive. It's the fashion to blame the Internet and computers, cell phones and cable TV for this diffused, fragmented state of mind, but our seductive machines are not at fault. The real

problem is that we don't appreciate our own ability to use attention to select and create truly satisfying experience. Instead of exercising this potential, we too often take the lazy way out, settle for less, and squander
our mental money and precious time on whatever captures our awareness
willy-nilly, no matter how disappointing the consequences.

Where the quality of your life is concerned, focus is not everything,
but it is a great deal. The question is: If all the world's a stage, as Shakespeare puts it, where do you shine the spotlight of your attention?

THIS BOOK FOLLOWS a loose time line of paying attention over frac-
tions of seconds to moments, days, weeks, months, years, and even a
whole life. First, we'll look at some basic operating principles that apply
whenever you become aware of something in your world—a changing
traffic signal, a sudden stab of jealousy—focus on it, and prepare to respond. Next, we'll explore the two-way relationship between how you feel
and what you attend to. We'll consider different styles of paying attention,
which are as unique as fingerprints, and the evidence that just as who you
are affects how you focus, what you focus on affects who you are. Then
we'll consider attention's role in major aspects of life, including learning,
memory, emotion, relationships, work, decision making, and creativity.
After looking at some normal attentional glitches and more serious
problems, we'll take the long view and examine the role of focus in motivation, health, and the quest for life's meaning.

Five years of reporting on attention have confirmed some home
truths. "The idle mind is the devil's workshop" conveys the fact that
when you lose focus, your mind tends to fix on what could be wrong with
your life instead of what's right, putting you in a bad frame of mind. As
"look for the silver lining" suggests, focusing on the productive aspects of
difficult situations does indeed lead to a more satisfying experience.

Common wisdom aside, attention research is full of surprises. Focusing on upbeat emotions such as hope and kindness literally, not just figuratively, expands your world, just as dwelling on negative feelings shrinks it. Contrary to the messages from our wired, workaholic culture, multitasking is a myth. Not just individuals but also cultures have characteristic ways of attending that create different realities. The reason you can't remember the name of the person you just met isn't impending Alzheimer's, but because you didn't pay attention to it in the first place. Even very smart people can make dumb decisions about important matters if they focus on the wrong things. Despite its prevalence, shockingly little is known about attention-deficit/hyperactivity disorder.

Perhaps the most important things I've learned are that it shouldn't take a crisis to show you that your life is the sum total of what you focus on or to make you question the notion that your well-being depends on what happens to happen to you. After running that tough experiment, however, I have a plan for living the rest of my life. I'll choose my targets with care—writing a book or making a stew, visiting a friend or looking out a window—then give them my rapt attention. In short, I'll live the focused life, because it's the best kind there is.

CHAPTER 1

Pay Attention:
Your Life Depends on It

F ar more than you may realize, your experience, your world, and
even your self are the creations of what you focus on. From distressing sights to soothing sounds, protean thoughts to roiling emotions, the
targets of your attention are the building blocks of your life. Sometimes
your focus is captured by a compelling stimulus—a bee sting or a fender
bender—but much of the time it's potentially under your control. Like
other forms of energy, this mental sort is used most effectively by those
who understand how it works.

Rapidly developing neuroscience of which many psychologists still
aren't aware shows that, as the terms *in focus* and *out of focus* suggest,
attention shapes your experience by selecting and clearly depicting something in your external or internal world, leaving the rest in a blur. This
two-part neurophysiological process basically functions in the same way
whether you're zeroing in on a cat or a concept, a fragrance or a feeling,
but it's easier to grasp in the sensory world.

You have only to walk down a city street or a country lane to notice
that the environment contains approximately a zillion more things, from

traffic and buildings to flora and fauna, than your three-pound brain can process for you at any given moment. Your ability to focus on just a few of those things and screen out the rest allows you to experience a more or less orderly world. (Indeed, the terrifying "bad trips" associated with large doses of LSD are partly attributed to the drug's release of the brain's attentional brakes, which flood the user with way, way too much information.) By filtering your experience, however, attention also assembles a reality that's far more partial and individual than you think.

Let's say that you decide to take a stroll in New York City's Central Park. Surprisingly, this oasis of green in a desert of concrete is one of America's ten best spots for bird-watching. Within minutes of your arrival, a splendid red cardinal zooms into a crowd of less charismatic wrens and sparrows pecking at the ground and immediately "grabs your attention."

This common expression captures the essence of one of the two basic ways of focusing that enable you to tune in on what is most interesting in your world: involuntary "bottom-up" attention. This passive process is not driven by you, but by whatever thing in your environment is most salient, or obviously compelling, such as that arresting scarlet cardinal.

Thanks to evolution, bottom-up attention has hard-wired you to zoom in on brightly colored flowers, startle at a snake's hiss, wrinkle your nose at the smell of spoiled meat, and otherwise detect and react to things that could threaten or advance your survival. Whether it concerns a crouching predator to dodge or a tasty bit of prey to stalk, the potentially life-or-death information that attracts your involuntary focus is likelier to come from something new or different in your environment than from something old and familiar. That's why you, like your prehistoric ancestors, are particularly drawn to "novel" stimuli. Because you're especially attuned to new things that suggest danger or reward, you'll instantly notice the angry growl that warns you to fight or flee and the honking that signals a possible dinner on the wing.

Bottom-up attention automatically keeps you in touch with what's going on in the world, but this great benefit comes with a drawback, particularly for postindustrial folk who live in metropolitan areas and work at desks rather than on the savannah: lots of fruitless, unwelcome distractions. Maybe you want to focus on your book or computer instead of the fly that keeps landing on your arm or that ambulance's siren, but just like your evolutionary forebears, you're stuck with attending to those insistent stimuli.

IF BOTTOM-UP ATTENTION asks, "What's the obvious thing to home in on here?" top-down attention asks, "What do *you* want to concentrate on?" Because this active, voluntary form of focusing takes effort, the harder you concentrate, the better you'll attend, but the longer you persist, the likelier you'll fade. If you were to spend a few hours identifying Central Park's birds in May, when perhaps eighty species flit through the trees, you'd eventually get glassy-eyed and woolly-brained and have to stop for a rest.

Like bottom-up attention, the top-down sort has advanced our species, particularly by enabling us to choose to pursue difficult goals, such as nurturing the young for extended periods or building and operating cities. Where the individual is concerned, this deliberate process is the key to designing your daily experience, because it lets *you* decide what to focus on and what to suppress.

Many extraordinary achievers are distinguished by their ability to pay rapt attention. David Lykken, the University of Minnesota's late, great personality psychologist, observed that these individuals have vast stores of "mental energy," which he defined as the capacity "to focus attention, to shut out distractions, to persist in search of a solution" for a challenging problem over long periods without tiring. Among his exemplars is the slightly built, one-eyed, one-armed Vice-Admiral Horatio Nelson, who helped save Britain from Napoleon. In one diary entry, he observed: "I have been 5 nights without sleep (at work) and never felt an inconvenience." Another such attentional Olympian was the mathematician Srinivasa Ramanujan. After a colleague idly remarked that he had just ridden in a taxi identified as #1729, which seemed like dull digits, the genius immediately took exception: "No, it is a very interesting number. It is the smallest number expressible as a sum of two cubes in two different ways." His peers attributed such mind-boggling feats to Ramanujan's way of regarding numbers as "friends" and focusing on them "all the time."

In the summer of 2008, after winning his fourth U.S. Open tournament despite a severe, painful knee injury, the golfer Tiger Woods's imperturbable top-down focus on his game brought him near godlike status in our increasingly distractible culture. (According to his father, by the age of six months, little Tiger could settle into his bouncy chair and focus on watching golf for two hours.) Even the *New York Times*'s psychologically savvy political columnist David Brooks took a break from election-year commentary to enthuse about the hero's mental energy: "In a period that has brought us instant messaging, multitasking, wireless distractions and attention deficit disorder, Woods has become the exemplar of mental discipline." Like all great athletes, he has superb physical skills, but as Brooks points out, "It is his ability to enter the cocoon of concentration that is written about and admired most."

Attention à la Tiger's offers the great advantage of sharpening your focus on your target, but the nearest and dearest of such top-down champs can attest to its drawback: shrinking your larger experience. Perhaps reflecting on his own home life and that of his extended family— the novelist Henry was his brother—William James acknowledges that a Nelson, Ramanujan, or Woods more than likely "breaks his engagements, leaves his letters unanswered, neglects his family duties incorrigibly, because he is powerless to turn his attention down and back from those more interesting trains of imagery with which his genius constantly occupies his mind."

An amusing experiment on "change blindness" illustrates the stunning intensity of top-down focus. First, some inventive psychologists filmed volunteers passing a basketball back and forth in a gym; at a certain point, a large "gorilla" walked by the group and even stopped to beat its chest. Next, the researchers showed their movie to an audience that had simply been instructed to track the ball's movement by counting the number of passes made. Some were told to attend to the team wearing white shirts and others to the black shirts.

So powerful is deliberate, voluntary attention that half of the participants didn't even notice the appearance of the outrageous ape. Moreover, viewers who tracked the white shirts were much likelier to miss the black gorilla. Many other studies of change blindness confirm that once you're familiar with a situation, your top-down conviction that you know what's going on can cause you to miss even dramatic alterations to it, such as the substitution of a horse's head for a human one. It's hard to overstate the implications for daily life, from finding fresh solutions to problems at work to keeping the zest in marriage.

ALL DAY LONG, your reality develops from the shifting targets of your automatic and deliberate attention. As you wander through Central Park, a crow's loud, insistent call has the most bottom-up salience. However, those raucous squawks become mere background noise when you choose to tune in to an operatic cluster of Hollywood finches.

Like your either/or, bottom-up visual focus on the glamorous cardinal, which turned its less-colorful peers into dull little blobs, your top-down auditory fix on the melodic finches and suppression of the crow illustrates attention's fundamental mechanism: the enhancement of one target, which wins nice, clear representation, or depiction, in your brain, and the suppression of the also-rans, which are consigned to negligible status, if not oblivion. A little knowledge about this neurological "biased competition," which was discovered by the neuroscientists John Duncan of Cambridge University and Robert Desimone of MIT, underscores the importance of your choices about what to attend to in constructing your daily experience.

Near Central Park's Strawberry Fields, some bird lovers have scattered lots of seed in a clearing, creating an avian mosh pit that's a natural laboratory for experimenting with biased competition. Because we assume that "seeing is believing" and because sight lends itself to measurement, which is science's gold standard, research on vision provides the clearest demonstration of what happens in your brain when you focus on a target and of how selective your ability to process reality actually is.

According to the Johns Hopkins neuroscientist Steve Yantis, who researches attention and vision, when you first come upon the feeding area and its array of winged life-forms, you glance randomly at the bustling tableau, which allows passive, stimulus-driven bottom-up attention to take over. Your eye gathers some surprisingly scanty information about the scene—mostly its light intensities, edges, and color—which is transmitted to your brain's visual-processing regions, where a huge population of neurons can portray colors, shapes, sizes, and other features.

Left to their own bottom-up devices, these neurons will be biased toward the scene's most salient object, which is that big blue jay, whose sharp edges and bright color they "like" more than, say, the wrens' and sparrows' drab hues and pouchlike little forms. The nerve cells translate your eyes' incoming information into an explicit representation that's supported by your previous knowledge of the world—in this case, regarding ornithology—and bingo! The eye-popping jay wins the competition for the kind of strong brain representation that makes you go, "Some bird!"

Things change upstairs when you decide to use active, goal-oriented top-down attention to scan the busy feeding area for a *particular* target, such as a little woodpecker called the yellow-bellied sapsucker. The mere anticipation of spotting this not-so-rara avis immediately intensifies your attentional capacity for doing so. If you're told to concentrate on a spot where something will soon appear, simply having this deliberate objective ramps up activity in your visual cortex, which will further increase when the object finally manifests. In other words, just *thinking* about paying attention affects your brain, revving it up for the actual experience.

Instantly, your top-down objective biases the competition for your attention in favor of any birds that might be sapsuckers. In a still mysterious process, the activity level of many nerve cells that were depicting the blue jay changes in a way that both suppresses it and other probable losers, like robins and doves, and enhances possible winners, such as woodpeckers and birds with black-and-white mottling, red spots, or lemony wings. Thus stacked, the battle for your focus ensues, ending when you locate your target as if it were spotlighted amid its horde of rivals. In this "zero-sum game," says Yantis, the sapsucker's winnings equal the jay's losses: "Your neuron populations can represent pretty much anything, but not everything at once. You have to choose—or they do."

The big lesson from this little experiment is that depending on how the competition for your attention is biased, whether by you or your neurons, you can have very different experiences of the same scene. All day long, you focus on what seems most important—the blue jay and the sapsucker—and suppress what doesn't, such as the drab little gray birds. If you happen to gaze idly at your backyard, bottom-up attention makes sure you won't miss that salient blazing red maple tree and leaves the rest in a greenish blur. However, if you peer out with a top-down aim, such as checking on your dog, you'll see Rex but might not even notice the maple.

Of course, vision is just one of five sensory systems that collaborate with your attentional networks to construct your physical world. By way of illustration, Yantis draws an analogy to a control panel whose dials you can twiddle as you go from one activity to another. By turning the volume knob up or down on smell, say, or by switching from the touch to the taste circuit, you can tune in the information you want and tune out competing stimuli.

"If I ask, 'What does your chair's pressure feel like on your back?' you'll instantly access that information," says Yantis. "That tactile input was present all along, but when you turn up its volume, you permit it to come up to the level of your awareness." Similarly, when you drive a car, everything framed by the windshield is technically visible. If you become engrossed in the news on the radio or a conversation with a passenger, however, you're unaware of most of that scenery. As Yantis says, "You've turned down the sight dial and allowed audition to capture your attention."

ATTENTION'S SELECTIVE MECHANISM of biased competition boosts your efficiency by allowing you to fashion a coherent world, but it also imposes boundaries on that construct, making it more idiosyncratic and fragmented than you assume. For verification, you have only to note the honest differences in perspective that surface in your next disagreement with friends or family. Renowned as a poetic treatment of memory, the classic Japanese film *Rashomon*, which portrays four characters' very different accounts of the same event, is also a documentary on attention.

You get a chance to experiment with attention's subjective, piecemeal dimension near Central Park's Bethesda Fountain, where a crowd is gathered around a magician who's performing tricks for donations. He's dressed as an Edwardian gent in a tuxedo and top hat, and when he lets his old-fashioned monocle fall, your gaze follows the plummeting eyepiece. By creating this bottom-up distraction, however, the magician can "make a steal" of a billiard ball from under his jacket. The trick takes place right in front of you, yet because it goes unattended, it's undetected and, as far as you're concerned, never happened.

The magician has many other ways to misdirect your attention and fool you about the reality of what's going on. If he looks you in the eye, chances are that you'll look right back at him, allowing him to do whatever he wants with his hands. To produce cards from thin air, he could wave his iconic wand above his head. When your focus moves up too, he'd pull the cards from his other sleeve, held low along his thigh, then bring the wand—and your gaze—back down. In short, magic is what happens when you're paying attention to something else.

As it is in magic, so it is—at least more often than we like to imagine—in life. To condense the vast, encyclopedic world down to a comprehensible pocket edition, your attentional system, like the magician, focuses you on some things at the expense of others. As you continue your stroll, you realize that although you vividly recall that top-hatted trickster, with the exception of a woman in a bright violet jacket who stood right beside him, you only fuzzily recall the rest of the scene.

Whether your hazy processing of the larger setting at Bethesda Fountain even merits the official label of "attention" is debatable. However, research shows that "implicit" information, or material that you don't explicitly attend to, can slip into your brain without quite reaching your conscious awareness yet weakly affect your memory and experience. Unlike peers who see a dichotomy between attended and unattended things, the Carnegie Mellon neuroscientist Marlene Behrmann sees more of a continuum. To describe her nuanced view of how attention works, she tells a little story about looking for your keys on your cluttered desk. (She throws in a nifty trick that you can try at home: as you search for them, hold your eyes still and "just move your attention around.") When you spot the keys, the competition for your focus would seem to be over, but to Behrmann, it's not so simple, because even the losers in the battle get some points for just being there.

Like the woman in the violet jacket beside the magician, the objects that are closest to the winning keys—perhaps your glasses and cell phone—get a little "boost" by virtue of their mere proximity to your top-down goal. Attention's spotlight is so powerful that when you pass your desk later on, you're likelier to notice the specs and phone that benefited from the peripheral glow than you would if you hadn't searched for your keys earlier. Thus, says Behrmann, "it's not so clear to me that your life is really constructed only from the material of attention. There are influences outside of that penumbra as well."

To many other researchers, however, such implicit influences are too fleeting and feeble to be called "attention" and muddy the traditional understanding of the term as a conscious phenomenon. They argue that stable, goal-directed selective attention gives the winner the kind of strong representation that supports conscious experience in a way that a loser's weak representation cannot. In one experiment, for example, subjects who focused on a task while researchers flashed images of faces in the periphery knew the pictures were there but couldn't tell much about them, even their gender.

In short, scientists agree that stimuli can activate parts of your brain and even influence your experience without your conscious awareness, but most won't dignify a phenomenon of such weak intensity, duration, and effect with the term *attention*. Taking a stance to be applauded by English majors everywhere, their position is: "Subconscious information? Okay. Subconscious attention? No way."

ATTENTION'S SELECTIVE NATURE is an important reason why your reality is quirkier and less complete than you assume, but not the only one. As the poet John Ashbery observes, "Calling attention to / Isn't the same thing as explaining . . ." Once out of your cradle, you don't focus on the world in the abstract, perceiving things for the first time, but in synchrony with your accumulated knowledge, which enriches and helps define your experience, as well as ensuring its uniqueness.

As you pause at one of Central Park's small ponds, an ebullient old birder in steel-rimmed specs bounds up the trail and gives you an exciting top-down goal to focus on. "There's a woodcock just over the rise, by the little rill!" he says. "He's hard to see, though." Fortunately, you know just enough about birds to realize that the man is talking about a small, shy, brown-speckled bird with an extraordinarily long bill. Your attentional apparatus processes his tip in the context of your existing command of avian species, and you spot the elusive creature with dispatch.

The efficiency with which attention integrates new information with previous knowledge suggests that there's something like *2001*'s HAL or a medieval homunculus in your head: a supervisory agent that takes in bits and pieces of information, analyzes them, then tells you, "That funny little dappled bird over there is a woodcock." You have no need for such a cranial wizard, however. As research on the "beauty bias" shows, your attentional system doesn't just focus you on sensory stimuli but also helps you to turn them into a coherent event. You can gauge a stranger's attractiveness in as little as one hundred milliseconds because you don't process facial features abstractly, but filtered through your previous knowledge of comely eyes, noses, and mouths. Your "Ugh!" or "Ooh-la-la!" doesn't just depend on the stranger's visuals per se, but on whether they jibe with the concept of beauty you've acquired.

The evolving understanding of attention's role in how you learn (acquire knowledge and skills) and remember (store and retrieve information) is complicated but crucial to the management of the focused life. To make a long story short: if you want to master and retain certain material, from a bird's name to your *Speak French Like a Native* tapes, you'd best really pay attention to it in the first place.

That's easy enough to do in simple, leisurely situations, when you can indulge in the close concentration required for serial "binding," or integrating your target's different features, such as shape, color, and motion. You focus on that bird improbably traveling upside down on a branch, take in its bill shape, size, call, and body form, then conclude: "A white-breasted nuthatch!" Because you took the time to focus closely on it, the little creature gets clearly represented and securely stored in your brain.

After much research on binding and attention's interaction with experience, the Princeton cognitive psychologist Anne Treisman distinguishes between the slow, "narrow" attention that you paid to the nuthatch and the "broad" sort required when you must rapidly take in a complex new scene, such as the path that bisects the Central Park Zoo. As you stride briskly past the seals and sea lions cavorting in their pool, you blithely assume you're taking in the entire milieu. However, your eyes see sharply and in full color only a tiny area around your focal point, which happens to be the shiny black beast that's catching a fish tossed by its keeper. Your brain quickly blends this new sensory information with your previous knowledge of zoos in general and seals in particular to "fill in the blanks." What you perceive, however, is not a kind of photograph of the marine playground but a mental model that your attentional system has produced for you.

Like narrow attention, the quick and dirty broad sort has advantages—notably, the rapidly acquired big picture—and drawbacks, starting with sketchiness. Just as it binds lots of stuff into a coherent experience a.s.a.p., an expansive focus also reduces certain things to averages. If Treisman showed you a display of circles of different diameters, you'd be very good at guessing the average size, but not at knowing if you'd seen a *particular* size—a bias toward the least common denominator that's handy in real life. Were she to ask you to look for and identify "an animal" in scenes that were shown very quickly, you'd do so easily but loosely, answering "bird" or

"fish," rather than "magpie" or "trout." If she rapidly flashed colored letters at you, then asked you what you'd seen, sometimes you'd get it right—
a red O and a green T—but you might also make an "illusory conjunction"
and perhaps say, with equal conviction, "a red T." Attention's unpredictable, fractured, subjective aspects incline Treisman to describe your experience as being "at one remove from the physical stimuli": a collage of
objective reality rather than a blueprint.

AFTER CONSIDERING THE idea that your life is the sum of what you
focus on, Steve Yantis says, "I like that. I like the notion that attention is
the key to awareness, the essence or center of our mental life as we go
through time. That makes all kinds of sense." Where attending to ideas
and emotions rather than sights and sounds is concerned, he says, "To the
degree that you can control what enters your awareness, you have to be
able to focus on some things, let other things go, and move on, or your
thoughts can control you."

Even an allegorical meander through Central Park illustrates the
neurological basics of how attention helps you to take charge of your experience in two different ways. The stimulus-driven bottom-up sort automatically attunes you to compelling events, and the deliberate top-down
kind lets you direct your focus. Thus, you can concentrate on birds as you
walk, confident that you'd immediately detect any information, such as the
smell of food or the rumble of thunder, that signals promise or peril.

Attention's selective, this-or-that nature enables you to create a coherent but also custom-tailored reality. The things that you focus on, such
as that physically salient blue jay and psychologically high-value sapsucker, will win turf in your brain and influence over your experience,
while the losers, like the grayish-brownish avian hoi polloi, for your purposes don't exist. Reinforcing this subjectivity, your attentional system

combines new information with your previous knowledge to invest what you focus on with certain meanings. Thus, you could identify that eremitical woodcock that most strollers would have missed.

Most important where the quality of your life is concerned, this imaginary ramble shows that by choosing to focus on something specific—birds, and certain ones at that—you had a very particular experience in the park. If you had paid rapt attention to flora rather than fauna, or to thinking over a personal problem or chatting with a companion, your time there would have been very different. Moreover, by attending to any of these deliberately selected targets, or even making a conscious decision to "veg out" for a spell, you would have had a far better experience than many of us have much of the time, captured by whatever flotsam and jetsam happens to wash up on our mental shores. In short, to enjoy the kind of experience you want rather than enduring the kind that you feel stuck with, you have to take charge of your attention.

CHAPTER 2

Inside Out: Feelings Frame Focus

Just as it orders your experience of the physical world, attention organizes your ideas and emotions, giving you an inner reality that's comprehensible but also limited. *Homo sapiens* has evolved to focus not only on howling coyotes, flickering flames, sugary tastes, and other salient sensory signals, but also on compelling thoughts ("Get to work on time" or "All men are created equal") and feelings ("I love you" or "I wish you were dead"). Moreover, these mental stimuli not only attract your attention but also affect how it operates.

The inextricability of thought and emotion is one of contemporary psychology's most important discoveries. Until recently, like Western academe in general, the field accepted Greek philosophy's major distinction between supposedly lofty cognition, which focuses on reason and absolute truth, and funky emotion, which centers on subjective value judgments. Over the past ten years, however, scientists have discovered that thinking and feeling often have a chicken-or-the-egg relationship and are hard to tease apart. Speculating about the complicated relationship between focus and the yoked capacities of emotion and cognition, Leslie

Ungerleider, the National Institute of Mental Health's attention expert, says, "You have to prioritize your options in life, because you simply can't do everything. Depending on where you put value, those are the possibilities you'll tend to select. Being a good mother, for example, is highly valued, so you'll be motivated to attend to all the cues that are wrapped up in that process and to expend energy on it. You'll organize your day around that focus and see other things in that context."

It's the business of great artists to focus on intangible thoughts and emotions and give them form, and within moments of entering the Frick Collection, a jewel box of a Manhattan museum, you're drawn to a prime example of that skill, hanging in an exhibit of the works of George Stubbs. The eighteenth-century British painter is famed for his pictures, really portraits, of horses, which in his day were considered to be the creatures closest to man in grandeur, virtue, and beauty. Most of his noble thoroughbreds appear remarkably composed in their tranquil manorial settings. Any feelings they harbor seem to be along the complacent lines of "How lucky to be me."

Horse Frightened by a Lion depicts a majestic stallion in a very different situation. Stubbs painted this magnetic masterpiece to illustrate the nature of the sublime, which was one of his era's most popular philosophical concepts, and its relation to a timelessly riveting feeling: fear. The magnificent horse galloping through a vast wilderness encounters the bottom-up stimulus of a crouching predator and responds with a dramatic display of what psychologists mildly call "negative emotion." The equine superstar's arched neck, dilated eyes, and flared nostrils are in fact the very picture of overwhelming dread. The painting's subject matter reflects the philosopher Edmund Burke's widely circulated *Philosophical Enquiry into the Origin of Our Ideas of the Sublime and Beautiful*, which asserts that because "terror" is unparalleled in commanding "astonishment," or total, single-pointed—indeed, rapt—attention, it is "the ruling principle of the sublime."

Just as the horse is completely focused on the lion, you and the other museumgoers are totally focused on this pair of animals, compressed into the painting's lower right corner. Like these glorious beasts, you barely notice the landscape that takes up three-quarters of the big canvas. As Stubbs and Burke knew, what psychologists call a high-value idea or emotion is as compelling as a flash of lightning or volley of thunder, and it biases the competition for your attention so thoroughly that everything else fades into the background.

SCIENTISTS AS WELL as artists have documented emotion's influence on attention, starting with those early "cocktail party" experiments that showed that despite the din, you're apt to overhear your own name or a risqué remark. If you take an "attentional blink" test, in which you're asked to focus on a certain word in a list, you'll spot its first appearance, but probably not the second—unless it happens to be an emotional word. The so-called Stroop effect predicts that if you're given a list of words such as red, blue, and green that are respectively printed in blue, green, and red ink, and are then asked to name each word's color, the anxiety caused by the conflicting input will interfere with your concentration on the task. The reason you have such a vivid memory of your circumstances when you heard that the World Trade Center had been destroyed is that the intense emotion you felt riveted your focus and heightened your perception.

Just as you're primed to attend to swarming insects and snarling dogs, you're strongly wired to focus on the negative ideas and emotions that signal threats of a different kind. Indeed, whenever it's not otherwise occupied, your mind is apt to start scanning for what could be amiss, allowing unpleasant thoughts along the lines of "I feel fat" or "Maybe it's malignant" to grab your attention.

Like physical discomfort, the psychological sort is meant to focus you on a possible problem and motivate you to solve it. If you're camping in grizzly bear habitat, for example, a frisson of fear keeps you alert and reminds you to be careful about food storage. The desolation or anger you feel at the loss of a relative, friend, or lover testifies to our highly social species' crucial dependence on such ties for survival.

As Charles Darwin wrote, "Pain is increased by attending to it." In August 2007, the National Public Radio show *This American Life* aired an episode called "Break-Up," which explored just how hard it can be to stop focusing on the pain of a lost love. The British pop star Phil Collins and the writer Starlee Kine discussed their own melancholic fixations and the sad lyrics they inspired. "The Three of Us," co-written with Joe McGinty and Julia Greenberg, stresses Kine's inability to shift her attention from her tragic target, despite understanding the effects on her life. Judging by the responses posted on the show's website, many listeners have experienced a similar dark obsession.

According to psychology's "negativity bias theory," we pay more attention to unpleasant feelings such as fear, anger, and sadness because they're simply more powerful than the agreeable sort. (This would have come as no surprise to Freud, who saw life as a struggle filled with conflict, guilt, grief, anger, and fear.) An all-too-abundant body of evidence attests to psychological pain's bottom-up grip on your attention. In a survey of which topics we spend the most time thinking about, problematic relationships and troubled projects topped the list. You'll work harder to avoid losing money than you will to gain the same amount. If you hear both something positive and something negative about a stranger, you'll take the negative view. If something bad happens, even if something good does too, you'll still feel dispirited. You're likelier to notice threats than opportunities or signs that all's well.

The grim testimony to a dark emotion's way of grabbing your attention goes on and on. You'll spot an angry face in a crowd of cheery people much faster than a cheery one in an angry crowd. You'll process and remember negative material better than the positive sort. You'll spend more time looking at photographs depicting nasty rather than nice behavior and react to critical words more slowly and with more eye blinks—signs of greater cogitation—than to flattering ones. Asked to focus on printed adjectives that describe personality, such as *sadistic* and *honest*, and then to name each word's ink color, you'll take longer to answer for words referring to a nasty trait. You'll listen longer to complaints about yourself than to compliments. Even when you sleep, most of your dreams are the bad kind. Here's the icing on the cake: on your birthday, you're up to 20 percent likelier to have a heart attack, perhaps prompted by stress caused by fears of aging or disappointed hopes.

For the species in general and the individual in particular, the main advantage of paying attention to an unhappy emotion is that it attunes you to potential threat or loss and pressures you to avoid or relieve the pain by solving the associated problem. Thus, your fear of becoming ill induces you to get a flu shot. Your guilt over a divorce pushes you to give extra consideration to the children. Your shame at being fired hardens your resolve to go out there and get an even better job.

Then too, a pessimistic, warts-and-all focus is helpful when you're stuck in a tough, let's-get-to-the-bottom-of-this situation. Looking at the dark side of things can also confer a certain objectivity; indeed, according to one school of thought, the depressed person's bleak focus on life tends to be more realistic than the sanguine person's upbeat view. After all, it took a grim, paranoid Richard Nixon to open relations with Communist China, because no one could suspect *him* of too much optimism or altruism.

Notwithstanding the flinty advantages, focusing on negative emotions, particularly when they don't serve their primary purpose of promoting problem solving, exacts a high cost: you spend a lot of time feeling crummy even if your life is pretty good.

. . .

CITIZENS OF THE twenty-first century are likelier than were Stubbs and Burke to apply such terms as *sublime* and *rapt* to romantic passion than to terror, but the two feelings are just extreme examples of the kind of intense emotion, positive as well as negative, that can command your bottom-up attention. After some somber contemplation of *Horse Frightened by a Lion*, it's pleasant to adjourn to one of the Frick's grandest rooms, which is devoted to the masterwork of Jean-Honoré Fragonard, Stubbs's French contemporary.

A supreme expression of amorous delight, *The Progress of Love* is a series of eleven painted panels commissioned by Madame du Barry, a mistress of Louis XV. Beginning with *The Pursuit*, the pictures portray stages in the rapturous romance of a pair of beautiful, young, dressed-to-the-nines aristocrats. Perhaps the most captivating is *The Meeting*, which shows the moment when the ardent young lover scales a low wall to focus on his beloved as she intently searches for him in the opposite direction.

Just as we evolved to attend to negative thoughts and emotions that could promote survival, we're also drawn to the positive sort that serve the same purpose in a different way. If fear and sadness warn us of danger and loss, joy, curiosity, and contentment invite us to reach out and explore the world. Summarizing passion's riveting effect on attention, the French dramatist Jean Racine compares it to "Venus entire and whole fastening on her prey." Love's intense, other-directed focus is essential for a species that must form lasting bonds to nurture the young for prolonged periods and cooperate to prosper.

Where the individual is concerned, good feelings such as affection, pride at a promotion, and enthusiasm for a new project are the carrots on the stick that keep you moving smartly along life's up-and-down road. The Bible puts it this way: "A woman when she is in travail hath sorrow, because her hour is come: but as soon as she is delivered of the child, she remembereth no more the anguish, for joy that a man is born into the world."

Countering the baleful negativity bias theory, the cheery "positivity offset" thesis allows that nasty stuff more readily snags your immediate focus but in the end, you spend more time attending to nice things. In fact, some research asserts that most people feel "mildly pleased" most of the time. According to complementary studies, you'll tend to put a positive spin on even neutral situations, focus hard on upsets because they're relatively rare, and forget unhappy events faster than pleasant ones. From this upbeat perspective, barring a profound blow such as losing a loved one or getting fired, whether you get a flat tire or a raise today, you'll soon revert to feeling pretty good.

Theories about the power of positive versus negative emotion inspire research papers with droll titles such as "Bad Is Stronger Than Good" and "Being Bad Isn't Always Good." Where real life is concerned, however, the Swiss psychologist Carl Jung makes an important point that's often overlooked: "There are as many nights as days, and the one is just as long as the other in the year's course. Even a happy life cannot be without a measure of darkness, and the word *happy* would lose its meaning if it were not balanced by sadness."

SOME EXCITING NEW research examines the surprising relationships between attention and pleasant or painful feelings and suggests how to exploit those connections to improve the quality of your life. Based on objective lab tests that measure vision, Barbara Fredrickson, a psychologist at the University of North Carolina at Chapel Hill, shows that paying attention to positive emotions literally expands your world, while focusing on negative feelings shrinks it—a fact that has important implications for your daily experience.

In one type of experiment on emotion's effect on focus, subjects are first prompted to entertain good feelings by watching short film clips that have uplifting themes. Then they're told to look at complex, abstract computerized visual displays. Compared to control subjects who are in a neutral or negative emotional state, these benignly disposed people are far likelier to attend to an image's larger, global configuration than to its small details.

In complementary research, subjects in so-called eye-tracking experiments are first asked to look at a visual display's central object. However, if they're then prompted to feel a positive emotion, such as gratitude, they proceed to take in significant peripheral material, despite the earlier instruction. In contrast, subjects who remain in a neutral or negative state continue to focus on the display's central element and tune out the surrounding stimuli. Like the similarly disposed participants who were asked to look at the complex visual displays, they just don't take in the big picture. These findings shed light on a well-documented phenomenon called the "weapons effect." Caught at a violent crime scene, a frightened spectator's attention often narrows to the point that all he or she can accurately recall is the knife or the gun, which makes much vaunted "eyewitness testimony" notoriously unreliable.

These inventive experiments on emotion's effects on attention confirm something that you've often experienced, most recently perhaps when you focused on Stubbs's terrified horse and suppressed the expanse of surrounding scenery. When you feel frightened, angry, or sad, reality contracts until whatever is upsetting you takes up the whole world—at least the one between your ears. Life seems like a vale of tears, the future looks bleak, and the only memories that come to mind are unpleasant. The best explanation for why bad feelings shrink your focus is that in a potentially ominous situation, homing in on and reacting to any trouble quickly is more important than taking your time to get the big picture.

Just as bad feelings constrict your attention so you can focus on dealing with danger or loss, good feelings widen it, so you can expand into new territory—not just regarding your visual field, but also your mind-set. This broader, more generous cognitive context helps you to think more flexibly and creatively and to take in a situation's larger implications. Offering an example, Fredrickson says that when you feel upbeat, you're much likelier to recognize a near-stranger of another race—something that most people usually fail to do. "Good feelings widen the lens through which you see the world," she says. "You think more in terms of relationship and connect more dots. That sense of oneness helps you feel in harmony, whether with nature, your family, or your neighborhood."

RESEARCH ON the relationship of attention to affect and cognition distinguishes between positive and negative emotions, but life is often more complicated than scientific journals suggest, and the two sorts of feelings aren't always easy to tell apart. Here's Prince Andrei in *War and Peace*, focusing on his beloved:

> [He] looked at the singing Natasha and something new and happy occurred in his soul. He was happy, but at the same time he felt sad . . . About what? . . . The main thing he wanted to weep about was a sudden, vivid awareness of the terrible opposition between something infinitely great and indefinable that was in him, and something narrow and fleshly that he himself, and she, was. This opposition tormented him and gladdened him while she sang.

The type of complex inner experience that cascades from Andrei's focus on Natasha is of particular interest to the Northwestern University cognitive scientist Don Norman. According to his conceptual model, the brain has three major parts, which focus on very different things and sometimes conflict. The "reactive" component, which handles the brain's visceral, automatic functions, concentrates on stuff that elicits biologically determined responses, such as dizzying heights and sweet tastes. The "behavioral," or routine, component attends to well-learned skills, such as riding a bike or typing. According to Norman, these two "lower" modes of brain functioning handle most of what you do, and mostly without requiring your conscious attention. He's not alone in taking this seemingly iconoclastic view. The influential Dutch psychologist Ap Dijksterhuis, a coauthor of "Of Men and Mackerels: Attention and Automatic Behavior," boldly states on his website: "My research basically highlights the automatic and unconscious side of behavior and although I do sometimes investigate conscious processes, I'm more and more inclined to draw the conclusion that consciousness is a pretty unimportant thing."

Consciousness, which is the "reflective" element of Norman's conceptual brain, handles the "higher" functions at the metaphorical tip of the very top of that complicated organ. Because consciousness pays a lot of attention to your thoughts, you tend to identify it with cognition. However, if you try to figure out exactly how you run your business or care for your family, you soon realize that you can't grasp that process just by thinking about it. As Norman puts it, "Consciousness also has a qualitative, sensory feel. If I say, 'I'm afraid,' it's not just my mind talking. My stomach also knots up."

The brain's reactive, behavioral, and reflective elements pursue their own agendas, yet they also constantly communicate with one another. When your alarm triggers an argument over whether to roll over or get up and go to the gym, you experience a mild version of the kind of conflict that occurs when two or more of these networks insist that you focus on different things. Offering a more complicated example, Norman says, "Take jumping out of an airplane." On the reactive level, your brain attends to the bottom-up imperative of the earth far, far below and goes, "What the hell are you doing?" In order to proceed, you have to pay top-down attention to messages from its behavioral component, where you've stored your routine skydiving skills, and to the reflective voice that says, "You'll be okay, and think of how much you'll enjoy this experience afterward."

Drawing on his fascinating research on our emotional relationships with everyday things, from can openers to MacBooks, Norman offers a potentially costly example of how your feelings can affect what you attend to and vice versa. When you first decide to buy a car, you focus earnestly on the reflective level. You do lots of research and analysis to figure out which auto best meets your needs and offers the most value, and you settle on a medium-priced Toyota. Then, says Norman, "You go to the dealer and drive away in something else."

Once you leave home, your spouse's admonitions, and your well-thumbed copies of *Consumer Reports* and head to the glittering showroom, redolent of new-car smell, your attention shifts from the brain's sober, cerebral, reflective voice to the reactive, sexy, visceral one. As Norman says, "If you buy a white Camry instead of a red BMW, that says something about you, and you're aware of that." Your focus moves from gas mileage and child safety to that hot little convertible's sensual upholstery, high-status brand, and other emotional payoffs. The same affective-attentional dynamic explains why clean, shiny used cars sell better than dirty ones and why a salesman trying to close the deal doesn't ask "Do you want the car?" but "What color?"

SPEAKING OF THE proverbial shifty car salesman, you might not be entirely surprised if you heard that he tries to manipulate his customers' attention with more unscrupulous appeals to their emotions. After all, in the 1950s and '60s, amid anxieties about Cold War brainwashing and extraterrestrials from increasingly accessible outer space, some major companies were accused of focusing an unsuspecting public on "subliminal advertising." These emotionally arousing images or cues to Drink, Eat, or Smoke Brand X were supposedly flashed so quickly on movie and TV screens that viewers were not consciously aware of, yet were somehow influenced by, them.

Claims that such covert signals could snare your attention, subvert your free will, and turn you into a kind of zombie who followed corporate orders were never proved. Nevertheless, the Federal Communications Commission banned subliminal advertising in the 1970s, but its specter lingers on. In 2006, the California Milk Processor Board hung some "Got milk?" advertising posters that emitted the smell of chocolate chip cookies at San Francisco bus stops, and protesters complained of an underhanded scheme to snag their attention and lighten their wallets.

Although "attention" implies "conscious experience," you can sometimes take in subliminal information that flies under the radar of awareness yet influences your behavior—especially when the material carries an emotional charge. Research on a fascinating group of brain-injured patients, some of whom have been studied by the Carnegie Mellon neuroscientist Marlene Behrmann, supplies some particularly intriguing evidence of attention paid to seemingly unattended information.

Usually following a stroke that causes a lesion in one hemisphere of the brain, patients afflicted with "hemispheric neglect" can attend to only half of the world. If the lesion is in the right hemisphere, the person eats only from the left side of the plate and sees only the numerals 1 through 6 on a clock. One such was Federico Fellini, an artist as well as a filmmaker, who did some drawings that illustrate this hemi-demi reality. In one of his sketches, a ghostly figure represented by a left shoulder and arm waters a daisy. In another, half of a woman rides half of a bicycle.

Despite their apparent inability to focus on half the world, however, hemispheric neglect patients seem to absorb some sort of information from it, especially if the stimulus is freighted with emotion. In one much-cited experiment, a man is shown a picture of a normal house and another whose left side is on fire. Asked to describe what he's looking at, the man, who doesn't consciously see the fire, simply says, "Two houses." When asked which house he'd prefer to live in, however, he chooses the one that's not ablaze, because he somehow feels uneasy about the dangerous one.

If you took part in an experiment in which you saw images of faces wearing a neutral expression as well as some angry ones that were followed by a so-called masking stimulus, like the man who couldn't see the flames, you wouldn't know you'd seen the vexed visages. Nevertheless, just as the invisible fire made him uncomfortable, physiological monitoring would probably reveal that the negative images elicited a galvanic skin response from you, which indicates that you experienced stress. Because a stimulus you weren't aware of could affect what you *are* aware of, when you leave the lab, some trivial matter might upset you or you might feel on edge without understanding why.

It's unclear how your brain could react to something that's beneath the level of conscious attention yet is capable of influencing your behavior. Certain low-flying information, particularly the affective sort, may not have to be handled by the brain's cortex, as attended material is, but could be processed automatically by the amygdala. This interesting structure, which is involved in regulating fear and other emotions, could mediate a kind of subconscious awareness of an event and a weak learning response of the sort that could account for your vague uneasiness as you leave the psych lab.

To FUNCTION IN the external world of the senses, you often don't need to spend much energy on directing your attention. You'll involuntarily focus on the ringing phone, the stinky garbage, the red-hot pepper. To hear your companion in a noisy restaurant, you'll automatically home in on her voice and damp down the chatter from nearby tables. Waiting to cross the street, you'll focus on the traffic signal and let the surroundings blur.

Where operating in the internal world of thoughts and feelings is concerned, however, staying focused on the optimal target requires more effort, beginning with your mindfulness of attention's either/or dynamics. Just as you're geared to attend to loud crashes and lovely smells, you'll home in on very pleasant or unpleasant ideas and emotions. For evolutionary, self-protective reasons, however, you're apt to focus more on the latter. Nevertheless, to protect the quality of your experience, you must shift your focus from dull or dispiriting ideas and feelings that serve no useful, problem-solving purpose, as many if not most don't, and concentrate as much as possible on the productive, life-enhancing sort.

Thus, the first step toward getting on with your work despite a financial setback or repairing a relationship after a nasty quarrel is to direct—perhaps yank—your attention away from fear or anger toward courage or forgiveness. Thanks to positive emotion's expansive effect on attention, your immediate reward for that effort is not just a more comfortable, satisfying affective state, but also a bigger, better worldview. Where the long-term benefits are concerned, you've come closer to making a habit of the focused life.

CHAPTER 3

Outside In: What You See Is What You Get

An arousing target such as Stubbs's lion or Fragonard's lover can capture your rapt attention and roil your emotions, but you often deliberately employ the reverse dynamic: you shift your focus to change how you feel. Capitalizing on attention's selective nature, you deliberately spotlight something in your external or internal world and suppress the rest, thereby customizing your experience. As the poet W. H. Auden put it, "Choice of attention—to pay attention to this and ignore that—is to the inner life what choice of action is to the outer. In both cases, a man is responsible for his choice and must accept the consequences, whatever they may be."

As you travel to your next destination after leaving the celestial Frick Collection, attending to the interior of a rush-hour bus during flu season brings you back down to earth with a thud. In response, you take responsibility for your choice of focus, wrest your bottom-up attention from the chorus of coughs, microbial air, and recent history of the sticky pole you're clutching, and fervently concentrate on a top-down target: the audiobook stored on the iPod you carry for just such moments. The zeal with which many of your fellow passengers focus on their newspapers, books, or MP3 players attests to a similar strategy of using attention to regulate their emotional state, albeit at the cost of tuning out a lot of wild and woolly reality.

Your ability to deal with *Homo sapiens'* universal fear of contamination is a good example of the way you use attention to control your experience and function smoothly in everyday life. Because public transportation rubs your nose in a highly unpleasant universal reality—you live in a filthy world—it's an ideal laboratory for proving that although controllable top-down attention isn't "better" than the involuntary bottom-up sort, it's the key to managing your experience.

Stuck in a germy, jam-packed bus or subway, you have two choices. You can allow a compelling bottom-up target—the hacking, sneezing seatmate who's spraying you with a viral mist—to hold your attention and generate stress, or you can direct your top-down attention to your paperback or music. Most of us are able to shift focus in that comfortable way most of the time. Those who can't stop concentrating on the awful truth are said to suffer from obsessive-compulsive disorder.

The irony, of course, is that psychiatric diagnosis notwithstanding, these tormented attenders are "the rational ones," says the Penn psychologist Paul Rozin. "The rest of us live in a disgusting world, too, yet to function, we somehow don't concentrate on that. We focus on something else, unless the contamination is overtly called to our attention." As he tells his students, they happily accept small change in a shop, but they wouldn't think of taking a coin from a grubby, smelly derelict: "*That's disgusting*—but you're getting his quarter in the store!" Fortunately, all cultures try to help you bias the competition for your focus on what's clean and what's dirty in a way that helps you cope with the unpleasant reality. Indeed, this observation leads Rozin to a stunning conclusion: "Disgust is the basic emotion of civilization."

In a dirty world, by focusing on certain stuff as particularly disgusting, we reduce the number of things to worry about and avoid. We also assert that we are people, not animals—despite the fact that the things that most offend us are those we share with other creatures, including our bodies, waste products, and especially death. Unlike them, we regard the smell of decay as the most revolting odor—a distinction that is, as Rozin says, "partly a way of thinking that we're immune to mortality, which is an 'animal problem.'"

To help you manage the dread of contamination, every society designates certain places, such as parlors and offices, as "clean," and assigns others, such as bathrooms and kitchens, for focusing on worrisome stuff. Should a complication arise, however, the world's ubiquitous filth easily recaptures your attention. Offering an example, Rozin says that you accept that it's okay, if not ideal, to attend to body wastes in a public restroom. Yet if someone before you fails to flush or wash up before leaving, the lapse draws your attention to the room's inherent pollution. In response, you might avoid touching the door handle as you leave.

From a Freudian perspective, even in the bathroom of your officially clean home, you may choose to focus on a top-down target—that handy reading material again—to distract yourself from what you're *really* doing there. However, as Rozin points out, the things that disgust us often have "an ambivalent, yes-and-no quality, because there's also a fascination with what we do in the bathroom." When we want to be entertained, as the commercial success of *Borat*, *Animal House*, and other intentionally gross films proves, we may decide to pay attention to offensive stuff from a safe distance. As Rozin says, "Someone else stepping in dog dirt is funny."

Like elimination, eating is animalistic, and to distract ourselves from what our talons and fangs are doing, we focus on crooking our pinkies and making polite conversation. (Freud notwithstanding, Rozin argues that most of us pay far more attention to food than sex, which is one reason why he studies eating.) To differentiate ourselves from critters red in tooth and claw, we dine with fancy utensils, sit erect at tables, chew with closed mouths, and socialize at meals. Noting a hallmark of civilization, Rozin says, "We can even *talk* while chewing with the mouth almost closed, which is really quite a remarkable feat."

Different cultures offer different top-down approaches to diverting attention from our ravening jaws and gurgling guts. The French famously concentrate on the taste and quality of the food and the whole experience of the meal. In contrast, says Rozin, "Americans focus on food in the body and what it's going to do to us. We're very concerned with its content of fiber or anti-oxidants." With their fixation on food as calories, anorexics and bulimics are just extreme examples of this pervasive cultural bias.

The number of people who have severe eating disorders is relatively small, but many if not most Americans focus on the purity of drinking water. That attention underlies the recent bottled-water boom comes through loud and clear in the rallying cry of Californians who battle against consuming recycled water: "From Toilet to Tap!" As Rozin points out, the consumer craze is a true marketing triumph, considering that most packaged water is neither tastier nor more healthful than the free stuff. Indeed, he says, "All water goes through something like a toilet at some point or other." Nevertheless, the silly slogan focuses you on something you usually manage not to think about: the history of what comes out of the faucet. "The battle isn't over water quality," says Rozin, "but over what you attend to."

A similar attentional-emotional dynamic kicks in when you think about your body image. You can get more accurate information about how men and women really look—their girth of middle and depth of thigh—from old masters' paintings in a museum than from contemporary media. Thanks to the latter, however, thin is in, and both American women of all ages and older men tend to think they're too heavy. As a result, many women seem to be either on the latest diet or planning to start soon. Men, however, respond very differently. Unlike women, they often don't focus on their weight, which therefore doesn't affect their behavior. As Rozin says, "In terms of attention, there's a gender difference both in the perception of body image and the desire to change it." Similarly, he finds that some obese people feel that fat is just the way they are, and they focus on other things. Other heavyweights react much like people afflicted with obsessive-compulsive disorder and can't stop concentrating on something that makes them miserable.

Just as different individuals focus on their physical appearance in different ways, we vary in how much attention we pay to the gap between the beau-ideal self and the all-too-real one. Being the best you can be is a major top-down focus for saints, workaholics, and others who continually strive to improve; some may decide to listen to Prozac to help ensure that they're functioning at 110 percent of normal. Others figure that hey, nobody's perfect, and easily suppress comparisons between themselves and Nelson Mandela or Hillary Clinton. As Rozin says, "How much do you attend to your desire to be a certain way? How much of a disparity between your real and ideal self is there? As a focus, it may or may not be important to you, but it's an attentional issue."

The particular ways in which you direct your focus to cope with your mixed emotions about dirt, food, body image, and ego illustrate your ability to use attention to shape and improve your experience in general. Offering a modest personal example, Rozin says, "My home has a beautiful view. Many people would have stopped noticing it, but I enjoy it as much now as fifteen years ago." At first glance, choosing to assign a few moments each day for stopping to smell a fine vista's literal or figurative roses may not seem like a big deal. However, it's just such efforts to pay rapt attention to things that give you pleasure and help you feel and function well that make the difference between the good life and the kind that William James described as feeling like "the dull rattling off of a chain."

. . .

As the abundance of vaguely annoying sayings such as "When life gives you lemons, make lemonade" proves, the idea of restoring emotional equilibrium by refocusing on a problem in a different way is not new. What *is* is the impressive research that increasingly shows that Pollyanna's insistence on "looking at the bright side," even in tough situations, is a powerful predictor of a longer, happier, healthier life. In one large, rigorous study of 941 Dutch subjects over ten years, for example, the most upbeat individuals, who agreed with statements such as "I often feel that life is full of promise," were 45 percent less likely to die of all causes during the long experiment than were the most pessimistic. They surely had more fun, too.

If a snowstorm prevents a trip to the store for groceries, one person curses the weather and has a rotten day, while another quickly focuses on what a good thing it is to be snug inside and to have that nice leftover meatloaf. Research on the so-called cognitive appraisal of emotions, pioneered by the psychologists Magda Arnold and Richard Lazarus, confirms that what happens to you, from a blizzard to a pregnancy to a job transfer, is less important to your well-being than how you respond to it. Because your reaction to any event is at least partly a matter of interpretation, the aspects you concentrate on become what the UNC psychologist Barbara Fredrickson calls "leverage points" for a simple attentional-attitudinal adjustment that works as an emotional "reset button." If you want to get over a bad feeling, she says, "focusing on something positive seems to be the quickest way to usher out the unwanted emotion."

That's not to say that when something upsetting happens, you immediately try to force yourself to "be happy." First, says Fredrickson, you examine "the seed of emotion," or how you honestly feel about what occurred. Then you direct your attention to some element of the situation that frames things in a more helpful light. After a big blowup over an equitable sharing of the housework, rather than continuing to concentrate on your partner's selfishness and sloth, you might focus on the fact that at least a festering conflict has been aired, which is the first step toward a solution to the problem, and to your improved mood. Interestingly, people who are depressed and anhedonic—unable to feel pleasure—have particular trouble using this venerable attentional self-help tactic. This difficulty suggests to Fredrickson that they suffer from a dearth of happiness rather than a surfeit of sadness: "It's as if the person's positive emotional systems have been zapped or disabled."

Of course, it's one thing for a jilted lover or tournament loser to stop focusing on rejection or defeat and start thinking about new possibilities, but quite another for the victim of a devastating natural catastrophe or a fatal illness. On the other hand, even such dire situations can afford various targets for attention. By way of illustration, one psychologist recalls the experience of his mother-in-law, who had just been told that she had only a few months to live: "She got up the next morning and said to herself, 'I'm dying.' Then she realized that she actually still felt pretty good." The woman decided that she'd concentrate on living well for as long as possible, then deal with dying at the appropriate time. This ability to direct her focus to the present moment and its rewards and away from fears of the future immediately made her feel more in control—a powerful influence on well-being—and her tough situation became more comfortable.

It's a hard thing to accept, but as Fredrickson says, "Very few circumstances are one hundred percent bad." Even in very difficult situations, she finds, it's often possible to find something to be grateful for, such as others' loving support, good medical care, or even your own values, thoughts, and feelings. Focusing on such a benign emotion isn't just a "nice thing to do," but a proven way to expand your view of reality and lift your spirits, thus improving your ability to cope.

. . .

IN OUR YOUTH-CRAZED media and popular culture, one situation that's generally regarded as very unfortunate indeed is old age. The assumption is that, considering the wrinkles, aches and pains, and unchic footwear, old people must be unhappy with life, but new research shows that by and large, barring some crisis, they're not. Despite certain obvious declines, elders' emotional well-being is as good as, if not better than, that of younger people. One major reason for their surprisingly upbeat attitude is their increased skill in focusing on things that foster feelings of contentment.

Chances are that your grandmother didn't need a psychologist to tell her to try to see the proverbial glass as half-full. When you were acting droopy, she listened to your tale of woe—your teacher gave you a D in math or your father docked your allowance—then reframed your reality by pointing out that you were *lucky* to be taught by someone who wanted you to realize your true potential or to have a parent who cared about your character development. Think of all the poor children who have neither!

Research shows that it's no accident that many grandparents are experts in making such empowering attentional adjustments. Indeed, seeing that glass as *at least* half-full may be aging's greatest underremarked benefit. Compared with the young, the old experience fewer unpleasant emotions and just as many delightful ones. They're also more satisfied with their relationships and better at solving problems that crop up in them. Elders who have a particularly positive focus tend to be healthier as well as happier: according to the Ohio Longitudinal Study, they live 7.5 years longer.

To William James, wisdom was "the art of knowing what to overlook," and many elders master this way of focusing. Lots of studies show that younger adults pay as much or more attention to negative information as to the positive sort. By middle age, however, their focus starts to shift, until in old age, they're likely to have a strong positive bias in what they both attend to and remember.

The differences in what young and old people focus on and in their emotional well-being may have more to do with chronological changes in motivation rather than age per se. In her studies of "socioemotional selectivity," the Stanford psychologist Laura Carstensen finds that when your lifespan seems open-ended, as it typically does in youth, you focus on the future and on acquiring information—expanding your horizons and seeking new experiences. When your lifespan seems limited, as it does among elders, your attention sensibly shifts to emotional satisfaction in the here-and-now and to worthwhile "sure things" rather than novelty. Interestingly, when young people are thrust into situations that highlight life's fragility, such as war or serious illness, they too tend to focus on fulfilling experiences in the present moment. As Carstensen puts it, "Age does not entail the relentless pursuit of happiness, but rather the satisfaction of emotionally meaningful goals, which involves far more than simply 'feeling good.'"

As elders' more benign outlook suggests, older brains attend to and remember emotional stimuli differently from younger ones. In one study, compared to younger people, they remembered nearly twice as many positive images as the negative or neutral sort. Moreover, when the experiment was repeated using fMRI brain scans, the tests showed that in younger adults, the amygdala, an emotional center, reacted to both positive and negative images, but in older adults, only in response to the positive cues. Perhaps because elders use the "smart" prefrontal cortex to dampen activity in the more volatile amygdala, their brains actually encode less negative information, which naturally reduces their recall of it and its impact on their behavior.

FACED WITH A DIFFICULT situation, your grandmother and hers knew that sometimes the best strategy is to "grin and bear it," or to "look for the silver lining." However, the appreciation of such attentional-attitudinal coping tactics is a recent development in Western psychology. Since Freud, most forms of therapy have maintained that the best way to deal with a problem or trauma is to concentrate on it. Through this "processing," the theory goes, you'll eventually gain insight and feel wiser, and hopefully better. Accordingly, most people who've taken Psych 101 think they're more or less obliged to chew over a breakup or career reversal, alone or with a friend or therapist, or maybe all of the above.

This common wisdom notwithstanding, some eclectic research suggests that rather than being helpful, focusing top-down attention on a psychic wound can make you feel worse. Debriefing-style counseling after a trauma often aggravates the victim's stress-related symptoms, for example, and 4 in 10 bereaved people do better without grief therapy.

Directing your attention away from a negative experience not only is not as maladaptive as many of his peers think but, according to the Columbia psychologist George Bonanno, can be a superior coping strategy. Indeed, he finds that in the wake of an upsetting event, "self-deception and emotional avoidance are consistently and robustly linked to a better outcome."

Even when you're reeling from a severe blow, such as a loved one's death, diverting your focus from your grief can boost your resilience. Bonanno interviewed and tested people who had lost a spouse or a child, at four months and eighteen months after the deaths. When he asked them to perform a difficult lab task, their physiological stress responses predictably increased. This evidence notwithstanding, some individuals reported that they weren't upset by the challenging chore—an indication that they weren't fully attending to the stressor. Accordingly, these tended to be the same people who were coping better with bereavement. The idea that directing your attention away from negative events can be adaptive is supported by a complementary study in China, where the culture's mourning rituals focus the grief-stricken person outward toward the community, rather than inward on the solitary processing of loss.

Individuals of sanguine temperament, such as certain politicians, CEOs, and salesmen, seem naturally to excel at directing their focus away from negative targets. Research shows that when they confront a potentially unpleasant situation, such as some unfriendly faces at a gathering, these extraverts are apt to shift their attention rapidly around the room and zero in on amiable or neutral visages, thus short-circuiting the distressing images before they can get stored in memory.

Whatever your temperament, living the focused life is not about trying to feel happy all the time, which would be both futile and grotesque. Rather, it's about treating your mind as you would a private garden and being as careful as possible about what you introduce and allow to grow there. Your ability to function comfortably in a dirty, germy world is just one illustration of your powerful capacity to put mind over matter and control your experience by shifting your focus from counterproductive to adaptive thoughts and feelings. In this regard, one reason why certain cultures venerate the aged for their wisdom is that elders tend to maximize opportunities to attend to the meaningful and serene, and to the possibility that, as E. M. Forster put it in *A Room With a View*, ". . . by the side of the everlasting Why there is a Yes—a transitory Yes if you like, but a Yes."

CHAPTER 4

Nature: Born to Focus

Your characteristic way of focusing is an important factor in making you who you are. Attention is a basic human capacity, like memory or intelligence, not a personality trait, like shyness or thrill-seeking. Yet a person's individuality and experience are much affected by his or her attentional style.

Consider the role of focus in the character and daily life of Bill Brown, who's the director of the Surveillance Camera Players, a group that opposes the use of these security devices in public places. As he puts it, "I am observant about things that are observant." To illustrate his assertion, he points out that he has personally detected six thousand of the perhaps fifteen thousand such cameras in Manhattan alone, despite the fact that many are just fist-sized and cleverly embedded inside lamps and moldings or affixed to the edges of buildings. The particular way Brown uses attention to organize yet limit his world by enhancing certain targets—hidden cameras—and suppressing competing stimuli is just one example of the complex relationship between identity and attention, from Martha Stewart's focus on the home to Barack Obama's concentration on politics.

When discussing his favorite targets, Brown also describes the two expressions of the quintessential personality trait—often called "extraversion"—and the different attentional styles that tend to complement them. At one end of this continuum lies the introverted disposition and inward concentration typical of many "knowledge workers" drawn to the big cities where surveillance cameras abound. As Brown says, "Most of them are not really in the world. They're just hooked into themselves, paying attention to their own thoughts and fears, as well as their cell phones, iPods, and BlackBerries. They walk very, very quickly with their eyes down diagonally, towards people's shoes. They tunnel through urban space."

A person who has an extraverted personality and an outward focus behaves very differently when out and about. Like Brown, who founded as well as leads his activist group, such an individual engages with the physical and social environments rather than burrowing through them. As he puts it, "There is an important reason why I notice these cameras while others do not. I tend to walk slowly and look up. I pay attention to the architectural details, and once you start, you begin to find other details." Practice makes perfect, and after a civil rights group in Boston failed to find any cameras in a particular neighborhood, Brown retraced their steps and located more than a hundred.

Whether you're an extravert, who mostly directs attention outward to the great world, or an introvert, who tends to focus inward on your own thoughts and feelings, your disposition inclines you to home in on the very aspects of your experience and environment that reinforce it. Thus, the outgoing person gravitates to the situations, such as leading a group tour of a stimulus-packed city, that make him even more focused on and engaged with the world. In contrast, the introvert is drawn to the quiet, familiar settings, such as home or office, that protect his sensitivity and shyness.

Just as it interacts with an outward- or inward-looking disposition, attention is bound up with an individual's temperamental orientation toward positive or negative emotionality. At one end of this affective spectrum are people whose innately cheerful, optimistic nature inclines them to focus on the world through rose-colored glasses and to pick up numerous cues to feel upbeat. At the other end are people whose dark, pessimistic dispositions incline them to regard the world as bleak or threatening and to search for signals of potential danger or loss. Even when focusing on neutral situations, they can often find reasons to be worried, mad, or sad.

Among these temperamentally unhappy campers are "reactant" personalities, who focus on what they often wrongly perceive as others' attempts to control them. In one experiment, some of these touchy individuals were asked to think of two people they knew: a bossy sort who advocated hard work and a mellow type who preached la dolce vita. Then, one of the names was flashed before the subjects too briefly to register in their conscious awareness. Next, the subjects were given a task to perform. Those who had been exposed to the hard-driving name performed markedly worse than those exposed to the easygoing name. Even this weak, subliminal attention to an emotional cue that suggested control was enough to get their reactant backs up and cause them to act to their own disadvantage. All relationships involve give-and-take and cooperation, so a person who habitually attends to ordinary requests or suggestions like a bull to a red flag is in for big trouble in both home and workplace.

A particularly interesting example of how the dynamic between attention and personality can affect daily experience pops out of an exhaustive survey of 9,211 employees and managers. Analysis showed that a worker's tendency toward perfectionism, manifested by a persistent focus on small, inconsequential details and errors, correlated with an inability to distinguish between what is or isn't doable and with being unsuited for risky tasks. Because they consistently pay too much attention to the wrong things, these hardworking but anxious zealots end up reducing their productivity.

. . .

ARGUABLY THE MOST intriguing characteristic assessed by the Multidimensional Personality Questionnaire (MPQ), a widely used test developed
by the University of Minnesota's eminent psychologist Auke Tellegen, is
"absorption," which describes a particular *style* of focusing. If you get a high
score in this trait, you're naturally inclined toward what he calls a "respon-
dent" or "experiential" way of focusing. As did Vincent van Gogh, Virginia
Woolf, and Glenn Gould, you tend to become totally engrossed in what
you're doing and in "experiencing the moment." Prone toward deep,
effortless states of rapt attention, you might, for example, weep spontaneously at the sound of beautiful music—a reaction that Tellegen calls
"the involuntary response of your being to a stimulus, as opposed to the
kind of concentration shown by a rat learning a maze." It's not possible to
break down nature's and nurture's contributions to a single individual's
identity, but among a group, genes account for 50 percent of the variation
in this trait.

At its extreme, a habitually experiential mode of attending produces
true space cadets who have trouble focusing on and coping with practical
realities. However, more moderate exemplars often prosper as artists, academics, actors, writers, musicians, or advertising whizzes. Then too, in
daily life, the ability to pay rapt attention to the matter at hand is a good
strategy for increasing well-being. "Absolutely!" says the Northwestern
neurologist Marsel Mesulam. "It's that wonderful Eastern approach. Instead of wolfing down your dinner, if you could savor every bite, reflecting on how wonderful it is to be eating, you'd be ecstatic, but life doesn't
always work out that way."

Some individuals, however, including certain epileptics as well as
some celebrated saints and gurus, are prone to experiences that go beyond
rapt attention to a prolonged state of rapture. The Hindu mystic Ramana
Maharshi, the model for the sage in Somerset Maugham's *The Razor's Edge*,

had a kind of near-death experience in his teens. Suddenly, he experienced the "cosmic consciousness" that, according to his Advaita Vedanta tradition, is all that there is. For his remaining fifty-odd years, Ramana stayed focused on it in a state of apparent bliss: the elusive goal that would later draw the Beatles and hordes of Western hippies to Indian ashrams. Their quest reminds Mesulam of Faust's search for the true essence of life *("was die Welt im Innersten zusammenhaelt")*. "The wish to attend to and extend the present moment is certainly a wonderful idea, a beautiful literary conclusion," he says. "Whether it's the definition of happiness . . ."

A person's attentional style doesn't operate in a vacuum, but in the larger context of his or her other traits. For an individual who has an upbeat personality, such as Walt Whitman, a state of profound experiential absorption can be what Tellegen calls "a very positive stretching of the self's boundaries." For someone whose sense of self is fragmented or whose temperament has an angry, depressive, alienated cast, such a responsive state can be overwhelmingly unpleasant, frightening, or even disintegrative, as it often is for the seriously mentally ill. As Tellegen says, "Deep absorption is not always a 'peak experience.'"

If your MPQ results show a low score in absorption, you don't tend toward the deep, experiential, expansive attentional style that can turn listening to a bubbling brook or watching a sunset into a quasi-mystical experience. If your personality is also goal-oriented and controlled, you may be inclined toward the "instrumental," take-care-of-business way of focusing that helps a traveler find a hotel in a strange city or a householder put together those "some assembly required" furnishings from Target or IKEA. Everyone has some capacity for this practical, down-to-earth attention— if you didn't, you couldn't insert flap A into slot B—but it ideally suits individuals who mostly function in realistic frames of reference, from an operating room to a bridge game.

Certain individuals excel at paying both experiential and instrumental attention. They can focus in a very pragmatic, goal-oriented manner and also be "carried away" by thoughts, feelings, and sensory stimuli. Tellegen describes a visit that Mozart made to Leipzig, where he stopped at the church where Bach had been cantor. Apparently, he hadn't yet heard Bach's music, so someone obligingly played one of the master's cantatas. After a few seconds, Mozart shot up and said, "What's this?" Rapt, he focused intently on the glorious sound, then declared, "This is someone a fellow can learn from!" Savoring this anecdote of one incomprehensible genius attending to another, Tellegen says, "Mozart would have listened to Bach in experiential fascination, but also instrumentally, so that afterward he could have reproduced the whole cantata from beginning to end."

This lovely vignette reminds Tellegen of other exceptional experiences of deeply absorbed attention that resemble the effortlessly focused state often called "flow." There's a certain opera singer who, when she finally masters an extremely difficult aria, is so totally focused on singing it that when she's finished, she doesn't even remember performing. "It's almost as if an experiential mind-set has replaced the instrumental one required to learn the piece," he says, "so that her singing no longer requires effortful attention. A talented cellist might play a Bach sonata the way an average person can relax his frontalis muscle. The high-level instrumental skill has become so well assimilated that it happens automatically."

Where visual artists are concerned, the Baroque sculptor and architect Bernini and the painter and sculptor Picasso were clearly adept at both experiential and instrumental attending, says Tellegen, as is the modern architect Frank Gehry. Choosing a literary example, he says that F. Scott Fitzgerald once admitted to "wrapping one of his romantic flings in cellophane" for later artistic use and notes that "this kind of heartless but honest professionalism is not uncommon among creative people."

Colorful artistic types are by no means the only people who excel in paying both pragmatic and experiential attention. Turning to politicians,

Tellegen points out that when asked how he could focus on his duties during the huge distraction of impeachment, President Bill Clinton described an extremely practical, feet-on-the-ground response to the stressor: "It's simple. I go to work, look at my calendar, and do what I'm supposed to do!" Yet whether erupting in rage at a hapless journalist or eloquently eulogizing Coretta Scott King, the political virtuoso is also known for being captured by emotion. As Tellegen says, "Bill—see, I call him Bill—feels my pain, but the next moment, when we are both still teary-eyed, he is twisting my arm. He's genuinely experiential, but he also uses that capacity in the service of 'getting the job done,' which comes across as manipulative to the more refined. If you can attend in both highly experiential and pragmatic modes, then the question is whether you can integrate these dispositions in a way that works."

Your attentional style is shaped not just by your personality traits but also by your other capacities, such as intellectual ability. Referring to his research on different kinds of intelligence, the Harvard psychologist Howard Gardner says that someone who's particularly strong in one area—music, say—might very well focus there, and thus have a very different experience at a Bach concert than someone who's tone-deaf or has musical talent but lacks familiarity with the classical idiom. He recalls that when he took his own three children to *Cats*, each saw the same show yet interpreted its narrative, characters, dances, visuals, and songs in very different ways. "No doubt," says Gardner, "what you focus on is determined in significant part by the strengths of your intelligences, which channel your attention."

Different styles of attending are also complemented by different physical and social environments. In one experiment, some experientially prone subjects were asked to relax while listening to music; they quickly and effortlessly complied. However, when they were asked to monitor feedback about whether their muscles were relaxing—a structured, goal-oriented task—the same people found it harder to "just let go." In contrast, pragmatically inclined subjects felt uncomfortable when they were told to relax and simply listen, but they did better in the feedback situation. As Tellegen says, "The attentional trait interacts with the circumstances."

Neither the instrumental nor the experiential attentional style is good or bad per se, and both have benefits and drawbacks. We delight in the imagination and fantasy of a Roz Chwast or a George Balanchine, but we don't want our airline pilots and accountants to get lost in contemplation of the starry heavens or the complexities of our tax returns. From personal experience, Tellegen finds that the propensity for abstract thought that's prized in academe is unhelpful in the supermarket: "When I go to the store to buy a certain item, I might end up coming home with something else altogether."

If you're prone neither to habitual states of laserlike problem-solving nor to flights of fantasy, you have lots of company. As is the case with capacities such as intelligence and memory or personality traits such as boldness and conscientiousness, most people fall somewhere in between the extreme ends of the spectrum. Where your attentional style or any other deeply rooted characteristic is concerned, the real trick is to figure out how to make it work for you.

By the age of eighteen, the West Virginia farm boy Chuck Yeager was an aircraft mechanic in the army, where he already manifested the bold temperament, 20/10 vision, and raptor's instrumental focus that underlie "the right stuff." By twenty, the country kid was a fighter pilot who went on to become a highly decorated flying ace in World War II. As a test pilot, he once flew an experimental aircraft that dropped 51,000 feet in fifty-one seconds before he righted it and landed safely. Of his many exploits, Yeager is best known for being the first to break the sound barrier in a plane and for penetrating space without a spacecraft. Although he is the epitome of temperamental derring-do, Yeager modestly credits his success more to his careful, pragmatic, instrumental attentional style than to machismo: "It was my fear that made me learn everything I could about my airplane and my emergency equipment, and kept me flying respectful of my machine and always alert in the cockpit."

Just as some instrumental little boys become fighter pilots who pay rapt attention to high-flying mechanics, others who are naturally engrossed in the rapt contemplation of truth or beauty become artists. Despite their impoverished circumstances in the grim Soviet industrial town of Ufa, the mother of scrawny little Rudolf Nureyev managed to sneak him into a ballet performance at the age of seven. Mesmerized by this new world, "Rudik" was soon performing in local folk dances. Despite his sketchy training, Nureyev's naturally experiential focus helped to make him the perfect vehicle to express the divine frenzy of the dance. The young provincial made it all the way to Leningrad's famed Kirov ballet school, where he concentrated on acquiring ballet's formal instrumental skills before leaping to astounding artistic heights. As if describing the two ways of focusing, he said, "Technique is what you fall back on when you run out of inspiration."

As WITH PERSONALITY or intelligence, attentional capacity is the creation of both nature and nurture, which account for our individual differences. For reasons of biology, for example, a color-blind person focuses on a different world than someone who has normal vision. Similarly, physiological differences in tongues and taste buds mean that people eating from the same bowl of Brussels sprouts may attend to very different gustatory experiences. So-called supertasters find the sprouts and certain other strongly flavored vegetables very bitter and hate them. "Tasters" perceive some astringency but find the veggies palatable enough. Those who ask for seconds are "nontasters," who detect no bitterness.

Anyone who has an intact brain can pay attention, but brains differ, and so do their focusing capacities. Over his long career—"William

James is not around anymore, so I've been working on it longest!"—the University of Oregon neuroscientist Michael Posner has developed a well-known three-part model of the brain's attentional system. He describes its alerting, orienting, and executive networks, each with its own neurophysiology and function, as nothing short of "the mechanisms through which we have experience and control the sequence of our ideas."

With the University of Oregon psychologist Mary Rothbart, who's known for her research on temperament, Posner has recently been looking at how the attentional networks get organized in early life. He finds significant neurophysiological differences among children that shape their different ways of focusing and aspects of their identities, from the capacity for learning to the control of thoughts and emotions.

If you took Posner's computerized Attention Network Test, which is meant to gauge the strength of an individual's three networks, you might find that you're especially strong in orienting. Therefore, you're adept at getting your bearings in your internal or external environment and directing your attention to a particular target. This skill has obvious benefits if you're a hunter, say, or Bill Brown. More surprisingly, Rothbart finds that you'll also be inclined to notice and appreciate the little things in life that make it worth living, which she winningly calls "low pleasures." (In *Delta Wedding*, Eudora Welty describes just such a child in the character of the bride's younger sister: "Bluet was a gentle little thing . . . filled with attention, quick to show admiration and innumerable kinds of small pleasures.") This tendency to focus on the seemingly minor delights of a good, crisp apple or your favorite song on the radio is an important element in the construction of an optimistic, upbeat personality and corresponds with a greater overall satisfaction with life. Conversely, a chronic inability to focus on small opportunities to cheer up and enjoy yourself correlates with depression and its dour worldview.

If your attentional system has a strong executive network, you can easily direct your focus despite distractions and respond to your target swiftly and appropriately. When you spot that piece of cake on the kitchen counter, you remember your waistline and seamlessly switch your attention back to your objective of washing the dishes. This capacity, which old-fashioned report cards called "self-control" and psychologists now call "self-regulation," often figures in the high achiever's personality, just as its opposite trait of impulsiveness often appears in a self-defeating person's profile. Moreover, a well-developed executive network makes it easier to shift your attention from unproductive thoughts and feelings to the energizing, generative sort, which is a big advantage in the pursuit of the focused life.

Biological differences in brains can account for different attentional and temperamental profiles, but nurture as well as nature plays an important role. In Rothbart's research on cultural differences in executive attention and self-regulation, she finds that the capacity for effortful control is a very good thing for both American and Chinese children. However, in the United States, kids who have this ability focus on keeping a lid on feelings like anger, fear, and frustration—an important skill in our up-tempo, gregarious society. In China, on the other hand, self-regulating kids concentrate on curbing their exuberance and trying not to stand out, which is an equally desirable attribute in their Asian culture. Depending on social or genetic differences, or both, says Posner, "the same behavior of focusing on a dimension of self-control seems to be involved in creating quite different personalities."

Even within a single individual, a biologically based behavioral predisposition doesn't operate in isolation, but in concert with the person's other qualities and environments. As Posner points out, whether their small child's innate temperament is sunny or stormy, parents will intuitively draw the tot's attention to smiles, laughter, and hugs, thus reinforcing the desirability of positive emotion. To help children who are not naturally inclined to focus on their schoolwork—or on life's little pleasures—he and Rothbart have developed exercises that significantly improve the executive attentional skills of four- and six-year-olds. Such training could help the millions of schoolchildren who struggle with attention, mood, and self-control problems.

Nature and nurture have combined forces to give you a characteristic way of focusing that's part of who you are, but research on the brain's neuroplasticity, or ability to reorganize itself by forming new neural connections throughout life, proves that your identity isn't written in stone. Posner is speaking of the children he works with, but his observation increasingly seems to apply to people of any age: "Kids have strong genetic make-ups, but you can also shape them through experience."

CHAPTER 5

Nurture: This Is Your
Brain on Attention

Who you are—Chuck Yeager or Rudolf Nureyev—affects what attracts your rapt attention (jets or jetés), but what you focus on also affects who you are. New research on its recently unimagined neuroplasticity shows that what you pay attention to, and how, can actually change your brain and thus your behavior. This extraordinarily practical scientific breakthrough shows that like physical fitness, the mental sort that sustains the focused life can be cultivated.

For a story called "Pearls Before Breakfast," the *Washington Post* staged a clever experiment that unwittingly illustrates how what you habitually attend to affects your identity. Posing as a musician playing for donations, the violin virtuoso Joshua Bell performed breathtaking classical works on his $3.5 million Stradivarius during morning rush hour at a D.C. subway stop, and the reporter Gene Weingarten observed the public's response. The *Post*'s stated objective was an exploration of "context, perception and priorities—as well as an unblinking assessment of public taste: In a banal setting at an inconvenient time, would beauty transcend?" From a different perspective, however, the experiment demonstrates the way attention shapes not just your immediate experience, but also your individuality.

Early speculation about Bell's incognito concert included fears that the handsome young star would be mobbed, and that police would be needed to manage the crowds. In the event, however, sixty-three people passed by before anyone even paused to listen. After forty-five minutes, 1,070 people had paid no attention at all to the glorious music, and just seven had actually stopped to listen. Accustomed to earning up to a thousand dollars per minute, Bell made a total of thirty-two dollars and said he felt "oddly grateful" when someone threw in a bill instead of change.

Of more than a thousand people, only two had really focused on the sublime music. One was a classical aficionado who had once studied the violin with a view of becoming a professional. He gave five dollars. The other was a concertgoer and the only person to recognize Bell, having seen him in a more customary venue. She gave twenty dollars. In short, the people who paid attention to the celebrated maestro and the Bach chaconne weren't run-of-the-mill commuters, but serious music lovers whose lifelong focus on the great works of the classical canon had become, as the saying aptly puts it, "part of them."

IN ONE MUCH-PUBLICIZED early demonstration of the adult brain's unsuspected malleability, fMRI studies showed that the experience of navigating London's vast tangle of streets actually causes the brains of its taxi drivers to develop an enlarged hippocampus, which is involved in spatial processing and memory. A similar experiment showed that although they often can't say why, archaeologists on digs just get better and better at locating artifacts; imaging studies support their claim by distinguishing the veterans' neurophysiology from that of novices. In short, it seems that simply going about your business, whether it's driving a taxi or spotting pottery shards, teaches your brain what to attend to and customizes your nervous system to suit your experience and modify who you are.

Using sophisticated EEG (electroencephalography) and fMRI scanning, the University of Wisconsin neuroscientist Richard Davidson is a pioneer in showing how experience in general and attention in particular affect your brain and behavior. This physiological as well as psychological shift sounds dramatic, he says, but shouldn't be so surprising, because your nervous system is built to respond to your experience: "That's what learning is. Anything that changes behavior changes the brain."

Along with conducting basic research on how experience affects neurophysiology, Davidson is exploring ways in which individuals can use focus to change problematic attentional, cognitive, and emotional patterns. The mental-fitness regimens that he and colleagues in a half-dozen labs around the world are working with are based on meditation, which boils down to an exercise in paying rapt attention to a target for a certain period of time. Various Eastern and Western religions have used it over the past 2,500 years to enhance spiritual practice, but meditation is easily stripped of sectarian overtones to its behavioral essence of deliberate, targeted concentration that invites a calm, steady psychophysiological state.

The point of a secular attentional workout is not spiritual experience but the enhancement of the ability to focus, emotional balance, or both. In the "mindfulness meditation" that's the most widely used form, you sit silently for forty-five minutes and attend to your breath: inhale, exhale, inhale, exhale. When thoughts arise, as they inevitably do, you just shift your awareness back to breathing, right here and now, without distraction from the tape loops usually running in your head. As Davidson says, "A complete atheist can use these procedures and derive as much benefit from them as an ardent believer."

Research that reveals what's going on in the black box shows that different types of attentional training affect the brain and behavior in different ways. Practices that feature neutral, single-pointed concentration, such as mindfulness meditation, particularly improve your ability to focus as you go about your daily life. "Attentional blink" experiments suggest why. If you're shown two letters flashed a half-second apart in a series of twenty numbers, for example, you'll almost certainly see the first letter but miss the second one. The glitch is caused by "sticky" attention, which keeps you glued to the first cue, preventing you from catching it the next time. After three months of breath-centered meditation, however, you're able to "let go" of the first letter quickly and be ready to focus on the second.

No mere psych-lab curiosity, the blink research, which offers yet more proof that the world you experience is much more subjective than you assume, has important real-life implications. Even when you think you're focused on what's going on, these data show, you miss things that occur in quick succession, including fleeting facial and vocal cues. As Davidson says, "Sensitive attention is a key substrate of successful social interactions, and the consequences of missing that kind of information can be quite significant." Indeed, research done by Paul Ekman, a psychologist at the University of California at San Francisco, shows that slight, rapid changes in a person's expression are highly meaningful, if unspoken, indications of what's really on his or her mind. Most people don't read these cues very well, he finds, but attentional training can greatly improve this interpretive ability.

Because the blink phenomenon has long been regarded as relatively fixed, the fact that it can be modified helps prove that attention is indeed a trainable skill. That's particularly good news for the many people who have difficulty focusing, including the 5 percent of American children who struggle with ADHD. Although he doesn't conduct research on the problem per se, Davidson thinks that regimens derived from one-pointed meditation could help: "It's worth trying, both in hopes of reducing the children's medication and making a real difference in their behavior, particularly because there are very few if any negative side effects."

In another area of research, Davidson explores the way in which temperamental features, such as an inclination toward positive or negative emotionality, affect and even drive attention—an interaction that is vitally important to the quality of your experience. As he says, "One of life's challenges is to maintain your focus despite the continual distracting emotional stimuli that can capture it." Certain lucky individuals are born with an affective temperament that naturally inclines them toward an upbeat, proactive focus, but research increasingly shows that others can move in that direction through attentional training.

Chances are that you've seen some of the striking, brightly colored fMRI images from Davidson's investigation of the brain-activity patterns associated with various emotions and dispositions and of how those patterns interact with attention. Unfortunately, he says, these pictures are often used to support cartoonish generalizations about the functions of the left and right brain and the "happy" or "unhappy," "logical" or "artistic" sorts of people dominated by one or the other hemisphere.

Popular wisdom has it that the brain is neatly divided into the analytical, verbal left hemisphere and the intuitive, creative right hemisphere, and that some individuals' behavior is more influenced by one side than the other. Up to a point, there's some truth to these notions, but research on so-called brain lateralization quickly becomes more complicated. The more difficult your task, for example, the more both hemispheres are likely to get involved. Moreover, advances in brain imaging mean that it's no longer enough to say that a function is located in the right or left brain. To be accurate and meaningful, information must distinguish exactly *where* within a hemisphere the activity in question occurs.

Describing his nuanced findings, Davidson says that although many other regions of the brain are also involved, "people who have greater activation in very specific left prefrontal regions—not the whole hemisphere—report and display more of a certain positive emotion—not simply 'happiness'—that's associated with moving toward your goals and taking an active approach to life."

Their rigorous practice of rapt attention over many years has created particularly striking differences in the neurophysiology and daily experience of some of Davidson's most accomplished subjects: Tibetan Buddhist monks who have each spent at least ten thousand hours in meditation. Even when they are not engaged in the practice, Davidson suspects that the regions in their left prefrontal cortexes that are associated with positive emotionality are much more active than those of control subjects or novice meditators, and he's currently investigating that thesis. Moreover, average subjects who had completed an eight-week meditation course showed significantly increased activity in the left prefrontal regions that are linked to this optimistic, goal-oriented orientation.

The discovery that a focusing regimen can have profound impacts not only on a person's ability to concentrate but also on his or her basic emotional disposition is particularly significant, because temperament has traditionally been regarded as highly stable and resistant to change. In Davidson's view, however, the genes you inherit "set very coarse boundaries" for your identity and behavior, but they don't *determine* it. What really counts, he says, is your epigenetics, or the way in which your genes are expressed in the real world; this function can be strongly modified by your experience, which in turn greatly depends on how you direct your attention. As Davidson says, "*That's* the process that ultimately determines who you are and what you do."

Not only *how* you focus, but also *what* you focus on can have important neurophysiological and behavioral consequences. Just as one-pointed concentration on a neutral target, such as your breath, particularly strengthens certain of the brain's attentional systems, meditation on a specific emotion—unconditional love—seems to tune up certain of its affective networks. In experiments, when monks who are focusing on this feeling of pure compassion are exposed to emotional sounds, brain activity increases in the insula, a region involved in visceral perception and empathy, and in the right temporo-parietal junction, an area implicated in inferring and empathizing with others' mental states. These data complement research done by Barbara Fredrickson and others showing that concentration on positive emotions improves your affect and expands your focus. Davidson speculates that deliberately focusing on feelings such as compassion, joy, and gratitude may strengthen neurons in the left prefrontal cortex and inhibit disturbing messages from the fear-oriented amygdala.

Training your brain to pay more attention to compassion for others and less to the self's narcissistic preoccupations would be a giant step toward a better, more enjoyable life. When you aren't doing anything in particular but are just "at rest," your brain's so-called default mode kicks in. This baseline mental state often leads to inward-looking, negative ruminations that tend to be, as Davidson puts it, "all about my, me, and mine." Before long, you find yourself thinking, "I actually don't feel so great," or "Maybe the boss doesn't really like me." Davidson is investigating whether the brain areas associated with this "self-referential processing" may be much less active in the monks, whether they're meditating or not; indeed, he speculates that superadvanced practitioners may perceive little or no difference in the two states.

Research increasingly shows that just as regular physical exercise can transform the proverbial 110-pound weakling into an athlete, focusing workouts can make you more focused, engaged with life, and perhaps even kinder. "My strong intuition is that attentional training is very much like the sports or musical kinds," says Davidson. "It's not something you can just do for a couple of weeks or years, then enjoy lifelong benefits. To maintain an optimum level of any complex skill takes work, and like great athletes and virtuosos, great meditators continue to drill intensively."

Just as a good gym routine includes both upper- and lower-body exercises, an ideal attentional regimen would target both cognitive and affective fitness with a combination of exercises that strengthen concentration and benignity. Just as they now gauge your body mass index or core strength, professionals will someday be able to assess your attentional and emotional style, says Davidson, then help you select the right training method. Meanwhile, "just as you have to search for the right kind of physical exercise program that meshes with who you are, you might have to spend some time finding out which of the hundreds of kinds of meditation you really enjoy and can commit to."

Meditation is not the only way in which you can use attention to change your neurophysiology and experience, but at present, these practices are the best understood, most accessible, and most clearly beneficial regimens. "It may well be that fly-fishing, say, engages a similar kind of focus," says Davidson, "but you probably don't get to do that very often. Most people could meditate daily, and the more you practice, the better you get. Our data directly correlate the number of hours spent with the magnitude of the changes in the brain signals."

When he tells the monks that William James observed that a person can't focus steadily on an object for more than three or four seconds, "they just laugh," says Davidson. "They can't believe that someone I hold in such high regard would say something so stupid, so inconceivable. They think that controlling your attention is within the inherent capability of all human beings, and that it's foolish not to develop that capacity."

NOT JUST YOUR temperament and personal experience but also your culture affects the relationship between your attention and identity. It increasingly seems that the "smart baby" theorists of the past twenty years were wrong and the Swiss developmental psychologist Jean Piaget was right: infants are born ignorant. Except for a few hard-wired instincts, such as an attraction to human faces, babies have to construct knowledge from experience and learn what to attend to. Much depends on who is doing the teaching, and where.

As election-year politics invariably make plain, even in a single country or community, individuals from different social backgrounds confronting the same situation often attend to very different realities. In *The Big Sort*, Bill Bishop and Robert Cushing argue that in a polarized red-versus-blue America, you're likely to know only people who share your worldview and focus on the same issues: gay rights or right to life, greenhouse gases or the price of gas.

In his research on how cultural experience influences what you pay attention to, the University of Michigan psychologist Richard Nisbett found that in America's once Wild West and South, a disproportionate number of males are still reared in an old-fashioned "honor culture," which trains them to focus on whether they're being treated rudely or well in any situation and to zero in on the hint of an insult. For most other Americans, a cheating spouse or misplaced property fence is a legal matter to be settled by lawyers, but for them, such occurrences are overt manifestations of disrespect and egregious affronts that must be personally countered or avenged.

The choleric honor ethos that still prevails in much of the South and West is rooted in the old Scots-Irish and Hispanic herding cultures, whose descendants have settled much of those areas. (Exhibit A: the former secretary of the navy and now Virginia senator Jim Webb's *Born Fighting: How the Scots-Irish Formed America*.) "Herders are tough, because they can lose their cattle or sheep—everything—in an instant," says Nisbett. "So for them, it's 'Don't mess with me!'" Reared in this bellicose tradition, "many men from these regions feel they must respond directly with violence or the threat of it to any insult or infraction, especially if it concerns home and family."

The extent to which your cultural experience helps select what you pay attention to and shape who you are is vividly illustrated by research that contrasts how Westerners perceive the world compared to East Asians—and basically, the rest of the human race. In one of Nisbett's studies, some Americans and Japanese are shown an underwater scene for twenty seconds, and then are asked what they saw. The Americans say something like, "There were three big blue fish swimming off to the left. They had pink stipples on the belly and big back fins." The Japanese, however, respond this way: "It looked like a stream. The water was green. There were rocks on the bottom, and some plants and fish." In other words, the two groups looked at the same scene, but they attended to very different realities. The Westerners zeroed in on what seemed like the most important thing, but the Asians focused on the relationships between things.

The different attentional styles of the West and most of the world are underscored by an experiment in which some Americans and Japanese first looked at pictures of some familiar everyday objects. Then they were shown certain of those things in the same context and others in a new setting. The Americans recognized the objects when they were presented in a different milieu, but the Japanese didn't. "The change in setting just throws them," says Nisbett. "Americans don't attend to context anyway, so the difference doesn't matter."

After a dozen years of investigation, Nisbett is convinced that *Homo sapiens'* natural inclination is to attend to and think about the world in a holistic way, as East Asians do. Instead of focusing in on the environment's most significant feature, such as those three bright, centrally located tropical fish, in the Western fashion, our species evolved to take in the big picture: the entire aquatic context, of which the fish are just a part. By nature, human beings are also inclined to consider each situation on a case-by-case basis, as Asians do, rather than to sort things according to the laws of logic and categorization, like Westerners. As Nisbett puts it simply, "In most of the world, people's range of focus is much broader than ours."

The human being's naturally expansive, relational focus on reality was radically altered in the West when the ancient Greeks came up with a new, artificial, analytical way of attending to the world. Ever since, Western children have learned to focus on objects or subjects in an evaluative, logical way. We scan a situation, quickly seize on what seems most significant, label it, then apply categorical rules to explain it or make predictions about it, says Nisbett, "and all with a view of controlling it."

The attentional habit of sizing up a situation in a way that prepares you to take charge of it is a cornerstone of Western individualism. This master-of-my-fate ethic and the categorical, logical focusing style that supports it confer many advantages. It was the Greeks, after all, who invented science, which is all about thinking in terms of types and rules rather than individual circumstances. Where the drawbacks are concerned, as Nisbett says, "Many Westerners don't look to the left or the right to see what other people might want or need. After I give a lecture, an American will just say, 'Swell talk!' But a Japanese person might say, 'You seemed nervous.' "

Similarly, Asians' focus on context and relationships supports their more collectivist ethic. Compared to individualistic Westerners, East Asians are generally better at picking up social cues and affective nuances and at functioning cooperatively. This attentiveness to their wider social and physical context reflects their long historical experience in densely populated, highly interdependent societies. To function efficiently in such circumstances, you need very clear roles and rules about relationships. "Asians almost never act in an autonomous Western way," says Nisbett. "In order to get things done, they have to coordinate with others much more than we do. So they look at the world through a wide-angle lens."

To illustrate this vast East-West difference in attending to social cues, Nisbett describes an experiment in which some members of the two groups are shown drawings of a cartoon character who looks irate, puzzled, or joyful and is flanked by other such figures. Then the subjects are asked, "What's the expression on the central guy's face?" The Westerners simply look at the character and reply, "Angry" or "Happy." Because they also take in the surrounding faces, however, the Asians make comments like, "He looks happy, but the people around him don't, so maybe he's not really happy." As Nisbett says, "Asians just aren't capable of ignoring the social context."

Not infrequently, these broad cultural differences in attention are reflected in East-West clashes in world events. In the run-up to the 2008 Olympics in Beijing, the Chinese public on the one hand and Americans and Europeans on the other were locked in mutual incomprehension regarding Tibetans' violent struggle for independence. The former focused on the threat to collective harmony and a unified motherland, and the latter on the Tibetans' right to autonomy and freedom. A few years before, the clashing worldviews fueled a crisis when an American spy plane was damaged by a Chinese jet fighter and forced to land on Chinese territory. The Chinese refused to send the American crew back until the United States apologized. The American government's response was, "Why should we? The Chinese pilot's carelessness caused the accident." But to the Chinese, says Nisbett, "that was a bizarre explanation, because we had been spying on China and had invaded their airspace. Because we throw away that kind of context, to us, all that had happened was that their plane struck our plane."

Bringing his observations about culture and attention back home to America once more, Nisbett raises the fraught subject of race and academic achievement. "You focus on what your culture tells you to focus on," he says. "Black culture traditionally hasn't told you to be smart in school and to work hard, because your effort would benefit the slave-owner, not you." Times have changed, and over the past thirty years of increasing racial justice, the average black IQ has already risen five points. Moreover, blacks now rank first in surveys of the importance various ethnic groups ascribe to education. Nevertheless, compared to other groups, blacks still do a fraction of the homework, which suggests that these students aren't highly focused on scholastics as yet. In contrast, Asian students actually achieve much more than their IQs would seem to predict, because they work so hard in school. Thanks to their culture's stress on academic achievement and not shaming the family, says Nisbett, "a Chinese-American with an IQ of 100 achieves at the level of a white American with an IQ of 120."

After much study, Nisbett concludes that neither the systematic Western nor holistic Eastern way of attending to reality is right or wrong, good or bad, per se. It's just that, as Kaiping Peng, the Chinese graduate student who first inspired him to look into these cultural differences, once said to him, "You and I think about the world completely differently. You think it's a line, and I think it's a circle."

RESEARCH FROM FIELDS as different as neuroscience and anthropology shows that what you pay attention to shapes your brain and behavior in surprising ways that would have been hard to imagine even at the turn of this young century. Whether you've paid rapt attention to classical music, like Joshua Bell, or compassion, like the Tibetan monks; focused on the big picture, like a Japanese, or the one big thing, like an ancient Greek; perceived the world as a line, like the American professor, or as a circle, like his Chinese protégé—such differences have helped to make you who you are. The good news, however, is that attention's ability to change your brain and transform your experience isn't limited to childhood but prevails throughout life.

CHAPTER 6

Relationships: Attending to Different Worlds

Attention, from the Latin for "reach toward," is the most basic ingredient in any relationship, from a casual friendship to a lifelong marriage. Giving and receiving the undivided sort, however briefly, is the least that one person can do for another and sometimes the most. In *Death of a Salesman*, Arthur Miller describes the final courtesy that even the failed, deluded, doomed Willy Loman deserves, because "he's a human being, and a terrible thing is happening to him. So attention must be paid."

Because it's impossible to communicate, much less bond, with someone who can't or won't focus on you, that capacity is crucial even to exchanges between people and the interactive robots designed to do their bidding. For that reason, MIT's Rodney Brooks, founder of iRobot, is particularly proud of Mertz, a mechanical grandchild created by his former student Lijin Aryananda, because the fetching machine adeptly expresses "beingness" by paying attention to you and engaging your attention to . . . it? Her?

Mertz's most distinctive features are the big, blinking eyes, emphasized by strong brows, that dominate its childlike, Kewpie doll head. Behind

these baby blues are camera sensors programmed to recognize and respond to human faces. When you interact, Mertz locks eyes with you, sig-
naling the robotic version of rapt attention, then chats about what you
want it to do. This personable machine once enjoyed an active social life
on the MIT campus, where it would tune in on and interact with
passersby whom it had learned to identify visually as individuals. As you
approached, says Brooks fondly, "Mertz would say to itself, 'There's
P327,' even if you wore different clothes or changed your hair style. Ideally, it would learn to recognize your voice, too."

In principle, Brooks believes that robots are capable not only of paying and receiving attention but also of "all the aspects of humanness and
beingness. Whether today's machines have them or whether we're smart
enough to build them are different questions." He once defined artificial
beingness as inherent in a machine that could affect us "sort of like children," but he now says, "a robot can be a being with a lot less than that.
After all, we regard animals as beings."

Intrigued by the "monkey see, monkey do" antics of his macaques,
the University of Parma neuroscientist Giacomo Rizzolatti traced that
copycat behavior to the "mirror neurons" that help forge the close connection between attention and social behavior. When animal A merely
watches animal B doing a task, these nerve cells are activated in the same
way as if A itself were doing the chore. In human beings, mirror neurons
are thought to help us understand others' behavior and to foster empathy, appropriate facial expressions, and language. Evolution seems to have
designed us to pay attention to others not just so that we can do what they
do, but also to feel what they feel.

Because the capacities are crucial to beingness, interactive robots are
designed to portray both attending and being attended to. Long before
Mertz, the humanoid robot Cog used eye movements and head tilts—two
major indications of focus for machines and people alike—to indicate
that it had zeroed in on something you had shown it. You know such a

robot is paying attention to you when it bats its eyes and cocks its head, and it responds to similar cues from you. "As you check his eyes, he's also checking yours," says Brooks. "Without words, you can use your gaze or gestures to indicate your attention and direct his." Thus, if you're show-ing the robot how to do a task, "you continually glance at his eyes to see if he's watching and if he 'gets it,' just as you would with a person. If he's not looking, you chastise him—'Pay attention!'"

Just as it suggests beingness in general, attention conveys a capacity for emotion in particular, which fosters a sense of bonding. For this rea-son, intelligent robots are surprisingly good at wearing their hearts on their sleeves. Brooks recalls a sociable machine called Kismet, which could detect approval or disapproval in your voice, react internally, then display the appropriate affective response with her puppetlike face, voice, and head movements.

The "Bicentennial Man" of the eponymous movie is Brooks's fa-vorite celebrobot, but far less sophisticated machines than R2D2 and C3PO can engage your attention and emotions. A prime example is Brooks's Roomba, that cunning little vacuum cleaner with a mind of its own, which now has 2 million enthusiasts, some of whom name their gadgets and even buy special clothes for them. Young army troops simi-larly name and bond with the little tanks that iRobot designed to detect deadly roadside IEDs in Iraq, where they've significantly cut casualties. If their mechanical protector gets damaged, says Brooks, "the soldiers will bring it in to the repair shop and wait for it to get fixed, like you would for a friend in an ER, rather than just take another machine." This strong attachment particularly interests him, because unlike Mertz, Cog, Kismet, and their ilk, these martial robots don't have eyes or faces. On the other hand, on behalf of their humans, the machines pay keen attention of a lifesaving sort.

No one could have imagined, even twenty-five years ago, how much machines have increased our ability to crunch information, and it's not far-fetched to think that they could also improve our capacity for attention, which is, after all, the neurological gatekeeper of data. "The trouble about the future is that you don't know it," says Brooks, "but some things could certainly change the way attention happens." Right in his own home, he's tracking one such attentional development that could have profound future implications for our relationships. An electronic communications gap has been widening among his four children. Compared to her three older siblings, who range in age to a ripe old twenty-three, Brooks's youngest child, eighteen, spends much more time instant-messaging multiple friends and SMS-ing on her phone. She has also more or less jettisoned e-mail in favor of Facebook.

The young lady's dad, who's no slouch in the electronics department, is struck by her ease at attending to many simultaneous interactions, which he partly attributes to the fluid switching promoted by a computer screen that separates bits of input both temporally and spatially. "That computer's capacity to time-slice allows her to focus on many more conversations than I'd be happy with!" he says, "but people under twenty can adapt to that kind of technological development. That machine is an example of an external device that has already changed our species' ability to attend."

LEAVING ASIDE THE question of whether focusing on multiple electronic communications seemingly at once is a good thing, lots of research shows that simply paying attention to someone else—the essence of bonding—is highly beneficial for both parties. Indeed, having social ties is the single best predictor of a longer, healthier, more satisfying life.

At the very least, paying attention to someone else confers the big psychological benefits of structuring your experience and distracting you from the self-referential rumination that so often takes a negative cast. Then too, like youths who fixate on sports heroes or other role models, you can direct your focus to a certain person in order to influence the way you currently regard yourself. Research by the Canadian psychologist Joanne Wood shows that if you want to feel better about who you are, you should concentrate on someone of lower status, but if you're trying to get motivated, you should fix on a person who outranks you.

Attending to others also invites interaction and feedback, which help you feel useful and connected to the larger world. When employees focus on how their efforts affect other people, rather than just on the details of their tasks, their sense of relationship boosts both their satisfaction and their productivity. Thus, cafeteria line workers who can see their satisfied customers are more contented than employees buried back in the kitchen, and fund-raisers who first spend ten minutes with scholarship students drum up twice as much money for their schools.

Paying attention is an individual effort, but it's also a kind of social cement that holds groups together and helps them feel part of something greater than themselves. When they're focused on either a social activity or a task, the moods of even fragile or stressed people, including breast-cancer patients, bulimics, and chronic depressives, are no different from those of average subjects in control groups but drop precipitously when they're alone or have nothing to attend to.

Simple socializing is good, but as Wordsworth and Coleridge, Jefferson and Madison, and Butch and Sundance knew, hanging out with a kindred spirit who focuses not just on you but also on the same hopes and dreams is even better. As well-matched tennis partners, chess players, book-group members, and spouses can attest, along with the benefits of bonding, such relationships provide a benign stimulus to be, as the marines put it, "the best you can be."

The message that paying attention to the other guy often helps you more than him is not one that you often hear from the therapy and psychopharmacology industries. In their different ways, each encourages you to look inward, whether psychologically or biologically, for answers to a better life. Yet at least one author of best sellers on happiness, who's a Nobel Peace Prize winner to boot, is all about others. As the Dalai Lama puts it, "My religion is kindness."

IT'S NOT A coincidence that the Dalai Lama and his worldview are rooted in the traditions of other-directed, interdependent Asian village life, variations of which still obtain in much of the world. An anthropologist, linguist, winner of the MacArthur "genius" award, and director of UCLA's Center on Everyday Lives of Families, Elinor Ochs has studied how children are socialized and learn language in parts of the developing world as well as in white middle-class America. After defining attention as "a focus on a point of orientation that can be at once perceptual, conceptual, and social," she identifies two broad cultural variations in the way it affects family relationships.

In it-takes-a-village societies such as Samoa, people are encouraged from very early life to direct their attention outward to others. Children are cared for by friends and relatives as well as parents and are actively taught to notice other people and their needs. When carried, babies are held outward on the hip or perched so they can peep over the caregiver's shoulder. Even before they can talk, these tots are primed to attend to what others are doing and feeling. As Ochs says, "In their culture, the priority is to be relational and person-oriented."

In contrast to the outward, other-directed focus that prevails in much of the world, people in the highly individualistic West are encouraged early on to concentrate on their own needs and desires. Instead of mostly being carried, babies are held at arm's length in strollers, high chairs, car seats, or other devices; they sleep in their own cribs and even rooms, which would be unthinkable elsewhere. During the preschool years, the child's social circle is often limited to parents, perhaps a babysitter, and a few others. As if to reinforce their highly personalized experience, Western children are encouraged to pay lots of attention to objects. "Even little babies have toys," says Ochs, "and they're taught to pay attention to their shapes and colors." (Despite the claims made for products marketed to hopeful parents, one study showed that rather than creating infant geniuses, focusing babies aged eight to sixteen months on "educational" videos actually impedes their verbal development; each hour of viewing per day correlated with a child's knowing six to eight fewer words than unwired peers.)

These big cultural differences in what children are trained to attend to and the consequences for relationships come across in the very different expectations of small children in "the West and the rest," as it's sometimes baldly put. By the age of four, for example, Samoan children contribute to society, helping to care for younger siblings and carrying messages for adults. That tots should work for the commonweal sounds like abuse to most Westerners, who assume that young children either can't or shouldn't have to respond to others' needs.

The ways in which American culture's individualistic, object-oriented focus affects its social life often surface in the UCLA center's research on families. To provide in-depth information about what our fast-changing domestic experience is really like, its team of twenty-one scientists from different disciplines has spent four years minutely observing and analyzing—right down to the stress chemicals in their saliva samples—the lives of thirty-two families from across the socioeconomic spectrum. In one illuminating study, they examined a seemingly important moment in the day—the parents' homecoming in the evening—and found that the overriding dynamic was the children's continued focus on their own little worlds, often electronic. For that matter, spouses paid little more attention to each other than their kids did to them. A child might briefly tune in on a returning mother. Over 80 percent of the time, however, fathers were either ignored or treated as a "secondary focus," perhaps meriting a wave or a high five. The bottom line, says Ochs, is that it's "rare" for a child to get up and say to a returning parent, "How are you?"

If there's one hallowed, Norman Rockwell moment in which family members are supposed to pay attention to one another, it's dinnertime. Yet the UCLA team found a stark contrast between the reverent lip service paid to the ritual and the widespread avoidance of the actual experience. On one hand, Ochs says, Americans assert that gathering the family around the table every night is very important and that not doing so is "the reason for drugs, delinquency, obesity—everything!" On the other hand, the families in the study dine together only 17 percent of the time, *even if everyone is at home.*

To put it mildly, as Ochs says, the postmodern dinner is "no longer about 'Let's all sit down and say grace together.'" Rather than focusing family members on each other around the groaning board, the new custom is a "staggered meal" that occurs at different times, in different rooms, and with different participants. On a typical evening, two people might eat take-out chicken in the kitchen. Someone else wanders in and joins, then one person leaves. Upstairs, yet another member nibbles on pizza while working on a computer.

Interestingly, when asked why they don't dine together more often, families answer with the ubiquitous "busy-busy" lament that other unavoidable commitments—to jobs, meetings, lessons, sports—have forced them to cut back on time for domestic togetherness. Crocodile tears notwithstanding, the researchers discovered surprisingly little objective support for this assertion. Instead, says Ochs, "We simply found that some families make dinner together a priority, and most don't."

The UCLA team finds that, even when they make the effort to eat together, families often undermine the desired feeling of fellowship by focusing on the wrong things. Once at table, a dramatic shift occurs, and all eyes are trained on the hitherto-ignored paterfamilias. Suddenly, he becomes what Ochs calls "the Supreme Lord—or the High Executioner," who's in charge of evaluating the day's events. Mothers tend to pick the subject—"Tell Dad what happened at school"—and fathers provide the judgment: "That's a very good grade" or "You should have practiced harder." Fathers almost never focus on their own daily experience, however, and when they do, their narrative style doesn't encourage feedback. In contrast to the moms' and kids' open-ended, participatory approach—"How should I deal with this situation?"—the men go for "Here's how I'm handling it."

As if to compound the chilling effect of dinnertime's judicial focus, parents also concentrate on prying information from their suddenly mute progeny, which of course drives the kids to escape a.s.a.p. In a typical scenario, Dad grills teenaged Susie about the boy who has been hanging around lately, then criticizes him: "Has he ever been to a barber? He looks like he does drugs." Susie is outraged, even Mother gets upset, and suddenly the table turns into what Ochs calls "a battleground."

In a more perfect world, instead of acting like the Supreme Court or the FBI at dinnertime, parents would focus everyone on nonconfrontational conversation. They'd encourage anyone so inclined to raise a topic and invite feedback, and also accept "just listening." If Johnny brings up his dismal math grade, Dad will stifle the urge to issue a verdict and ask why his son thinks he did poorly on the test. Does he need some tutoring? Mom might wonder if it would be a good idea to do his math homework before rather than after dinner, when the house is quiet and Johnny's not so tired. Susie might recall having the same trouble with plane geometry and getting extra help from the teacher. By focusing together on an everyday issue in a nonjudgmental way, says Ochs, "a family can exchange information, air different viewpoints, and test out new strategies, which not only solves problems but also cements relationships."

When he watches his UCLA team's videotapes, the psychologist Thomas Bradbury sometimes notices a new kind of parental hyperattention to children's résumés, which makes him "feel uncomfortable, because that's my life, too." As husband, father, and professional observer of how relationships develop, he thinks that this newly vigilant parental focus reflects the conflict between America's venerable ethic of upward mobility and its increasingly downwardly mobile socioeconomic conditions. Higher education was once a guarantee of prosperity, but for the first time in the nation's history, job stability for a college graduate is the same as a high school graduate's. "We want our kids to do better than we've done," says Bradbury, "but there's a growing divide between the haves and have-nots. Middle-class parents fear that for their kids, it could go either way. The only control we have is to make sure they get those violin lessons and test-prep classes. We invest more time and energy in the kids so they can make their way, which also means they stay dependent on us for a longer time."

A companion study conducted in Rome allows the UCLA project to make some revealing cross-cultural comparisons of what American and Italian families focus on. "The American model is to be very hard-driving," says Bradbury. "We only take fourteen holidays a year, and some Europeans take thirty-nine. So the big question for us might be 'Are we concentrating enough on where the kids will go to college?' versus 'Are we paying enough attention to the quality of life?' Romans may live in tiny apartments, but they have a lightness and harmony about them that we don't have."

IN "THE SOUL selects her own Society," Emily Dickinson describes the exclusive, rapt focus that marks your closest ties:

> I've known her—from an ample nation—
> Choose One—
> Then—close the Valves of her attention—
> Like Stone—

The relationship most associated with such intimacy, or the intense attachment that's rooted in each partner's special concentration on the other, has traditionally been considered integral to the good life, yet marriage seems increasingly endangered. In sharp contrast to a dramatic increase in cohabitation, the number of wedded couples is falling. Because informal domestic relationships tend to be less stable and more conflicted, this big change poses obvious cultural and socioeconomic risks, particularly for the women and children who end up as single-parent families. Yet as the director of the UCLA family project's "marriage lab," Bradbury is equally concerned about the implications for adults' well-being, because "marriage seems like the last bastion of relationships in which people are still committed to attending to one another."

A profound focus on your partner is, was, and always will be the distinguishing characteristic of an intimate bond such as marriage—at least, that's the theory, says Bradbury. "Nevertheless, I'm continually impressed by the inconsistency of sustained attention in relationships. Partners complain about this all the time, and kids probably would, too, if they could. We've evolved with the capacity to attend to each other, but it's not exactly dominant in our lives. Imagine a world where it was!"

In that ideal realm, you not only would pay particular attention to your partner but would do so in an especially constructive way. In fact, research shows that contented spouses see each other through rose-colored glasses, holding an even more favorable view than their partners have of themselves. That's nice, but in her studies of these "positive illusions," Sandra Murray, a psychologist at the State University of New York at Buffalo, finds evidence of something even better: over time, each person actually *becomes* more like the mate's benignly biased vision.

A study with the seemingly counterintuitive title of "Will You Be There for Me When Things Go Right?" highlights more benefits of maintaining a positive focus on your beloved—and vice versa. Shelly Gable, a psychologist at the University of California at Santa Barbara, asked partners to share a piece of personal good fortune with their mate, and then to evaluate his or her reaction. Rather than addressing the positive event in the abstract—"A raise? Nice goin', hon!"—the responders who got gold stars focused on the good news as an expression or consequence of the partner's own best or authentic self: "You got that raise because only someone with your guts and ingenuity could have won that big account!" Such affirmative reactions aren't just flattering, but also let the other guy relive the experience, thus increasing its pleasure quotient. Popular wisdom aside, says Gable, the way in which a couple attends to the good things that happen in both of their lives actually correlates more closely with their well-being than the way they deal with the tough stuff.

Along with paying especially solicitous attention to each other, each party in a relationship must also try to focus on the world through the other person's eyes. Such attentional flexibility is difficult, but a particularly creative experiment conducted back in the 1970s shows that it's not impossible. First, half of the subjects were told they were "home-buyers," and the other half that they were "burglars." Then, both groups were asked to read the same description of a house. When quizzed later, the buyers had understandably focused on the house's layout, rooms, and dimensions, and the burglars on the locations of the valuables; neither group's members could recall much else about the home. Next, the researchers told their subjects to change roles. Suddenly, the new burglars remembered the expensive possessions and their whereabouts, while the new buyers recalled the floor plan, room sizes, and window placement.

In real life, however, even a devoted couple can find sharing another's focus from day to day to be a formidable challenge. Shaped by your nature and nurture, your particular way of paying attention contributes to your unique perspective, which by definition complicates seeing things from someone else's. Yet particularly when you live with someone, it's easy to assume you share the same reality. By way of illustration, Bradbury recalls counseling a young man and woman who were contemplating wed-lock during one mad-hot Midwestern summer. Finally, he says, the woman grew very upset and said, "'I really don't think we should marry. Things have changed. In fact, we barely make love anymore.' The guy looked at her and said, 'I thought we weren't having sex because the air conditioner is broken.'"

As this illuminating anecdote suggests, attention's selective nature guarantees that even in a close relationship, two partners often focus on different realities. In what Bradbury calls "a watershed study," spouses were given a long checklist of events and activities and asked to tick off the ones that had occurred over the course of a week: candlelit dinners, fights, lovemaking, problems with a child—marriage's whole nine yards. When the data were analyzed, the percentage of agreement between husbands and wives was at the level of mere chance. "It's not just that we have different feelings and experiences," Bradbury says. "My wife is at-tending to a totally different world than I am. She has to try to share her world with me, because I don't have access to it. That's why communica-tion matters so much."

Something of the importance of the ability to share a focus and com-municate comes across in a UCLA study of housework. Videotapes of how couples divide up chores revealed two basic approaches. Partners in one camp concentrate together on a list of routine tasks, figure out a scheme for handling them—he washes the dishes, she cooks, or vice versa—then mostly stick to the plan and mind their own business. Cou-ples in the other group have a very different way of focusing on even reg-ularly occurring chores, such as taking out the trash and doing the laundry. They treat each occasion as if it were the first time, which means they continually negotiate who's responsible. If Joey has to get to his piano lesson every Wednesday, a simple errand that could have easily been scheduled for a whole year becomes a weekly wrangle that drains both partners' finite supplies of attention and good humor. In a healthy relationship, says Bradbury, "you work out a lot of things so that you don't have to keep attending to and talking about them."

According to conventional wisdom, gender is a major reason why spouses attend to two different worlds—Mars and Venus, for example—and have trouble bridging the gap. Women are generally thought to be "better" at relationships because they focus on others more than men typically do. In one exercise conducted by Bradbury and his colleague Benjamin Karney, partners are asked to identify something about themselves that they'd like to change—to become better organized, say, or to exercise more. Then their spouses are asked to be supportive of that goal. In the UCLA lab, men and women are equally enthusiastic about the idea of cheerleading, but the diaries they keep at home show that the wives are likelier to follow through. Rather than attributing this greater attentiveness to female nature, however, Bradbury looks to a dynamic that's more complicated than gender per se: the balance of power.

In any relationship, from student and teacher to boss and worker, the person of lower status benefits by paying careful attention to the person with more clout. In modern marriages, some wives now have equal or higher socioeconomic standing than their husbands, but many still don't. Thus, says Bradbury, "For the time being, women are likelier than men to say, 'Honey, how was your day?'"

When there's trouble in a relationship, men and women exercise equal rights regarding the conviction that it's the other person's fault. The resulting clash of divergent realities invariably animates the first three hours of marriage counseling. "It's all about finger-pointing," says Bradbury. "'He's the problem,' and 'She's the problem.'" The risk is that as time passes, the rift between those parallel universes can grow: "That's why you have to make the effort to come together and process your experiences jointly, so you really are paying attention to the same world."

Often, the all-too-natural tendency to see things only from your own point of view and to blame the other guy first can be traced to a "fundamental attribution error," which undermines the common focus required to solve problems. Once you're in the thrall of such a self-protective distortion, you see your mate's behavior in terms of what kind of person he or she is. When you think of your own behavior, however, you see it in a larger, explicatory context. If *you* have a car accident, you rationalize: "I was caught in a terrible downpour," or "My coffee cup started leaking." If your partner has a crash, however, you think, or even say, "A maniac behind the wheel! Always tailgating!" As Bradbury puts it, "For you, the problem resulted from a situation that anyone would have responded to in that same way. But the other driver has no business being on the road."

Domestic life offers numerous opportunites to succumb to fundamental attribution errors. When your mate acts grouchy after dinner, you might silently or vociferously react thus: "Moody again! That's just who you are. How did I ever end up with *you*?" A better plan, suggests Bradbury, would be to take a deep breath, then ask him about his day. He gets to vent about colleagues who haven't been doing their fair share of the work, and you get to focus on the situation from his perspective, grasp the circumstances that constrain his behavior, and respond in a way that benefits you both.

Then too, even in strong couples, partners are sometimes in different moods, which manifest as clashing views of what would seem to be the same world. Because thoughts and feelings go hand in glove, you process information in a way that jibes with your current emotional state. If you're feeling fried because you just lost your wallet, that edginess casts a pall over your focus on a neutral or even positive situation. Bradbury imagines an evening when you hear your partner return from a business trip. "If you're feeling lousy, you might think, 'He slammed that door just to bug me!'" he says. "If you're in a good frame of mind, you say, 'Gee, it must be really windy.'"

"Happy families are all alike," wrote Tolstoy, "but every unhappy family is unhappy in its own way." Despite his assertion, research highlights certain commonalities in the lives of troubled as well as contented couples, including some big differences in how they deploy attention. The most important such distinction is the happy pairs' resolute focus on the positive. In a good relationship, says Bradbury, "when your partner brings home flowers, you say, 'How thoughtful! A symbol of our love! We'll enjoy them all during dinner!' In a poor relationship, you say, 'Did you do something wrong? Were flowers on sale? Daisies make me sneeze.'"

In a maladaptive version of the Punch-and-Judy dynamic called the "demand-withdraw pattern," some unhappy partners forgo a shared reality to focus on their own stale, gripe-based, finger-pointing scripts. One partner, often female, chronically complains about the emotional detachment of the other, usually male: "You don't care." He responds by becoming even colder and more remote: "Nothing I do satisfies you anyway." Once this vicious circle gets established, refocusing on other views of life and ways of communicating takes real effort.

Differences in self-esteem also influence how couples attend to and interpret their romantic partners and relationships. Sandra Murray finds that people who have a strong sense of their own worth trust that their mates also respect and admire them; they don't brood about being overly dependent or getting rejected. When their partners compliment their strengths, the positive attention is pleasant enough but doesn't change their feeling of commitment and security within the relationship one way or the other. In contrast, people who have low self-esteem assume that their mates share their own poor opinion, so being praised *does* ease anxiety about rejection. However, because they also fear that their partners are "out of their league," they don't return the compliments; instead, hoping to make themselves feel more secure, they harp on their mates' flaws. By paying more attention to guarding against possible pain than to building the pleasures of intimacy, they end up undermining the very bond they're afraid of losing.

No matter what problem might arise in a relationship, the first step toward solving it generally involves redirecting your attention—usually outward to the other person. "That's part of the deal," says Bradbury, "but it's not always easy." One reason is that focusing on an emotional issue can be painful and involves being vulnerable. Once you realize that that's true for both of you, however, it becomes easier to accept that you have to pick up on certain cues that your partner throws off, because they signal a situation that requires your attention. Once again, says Bradbury, practice makes perfect: "The more I know that my partner's interests run with my own, the less I feel threatened by differences, even in arguments, and the more we can forge a common view of reality and focus on each other."

By way of illustration, let's say it's Saturday morning, and instead of sharing your focus on the usual walk followed by brunch, your mate acts withdrawn and refuses to go. This behavior is neither perverse nor accidental, says Bradbury, but a reflection of something that your partner may not feel able to express or even be aware of. Your initial reaction might be to say, "Wow, you're so crabby! We all had a tough week at the office. What makes you so special?" However, he suggests a wiser response: "You *do* seem a little tired. You relax, and I'll bring back some fresh muffins." Every time you respond thus unselfishly to your partner, he says, "your generosity of spirit makes the fabric of your relationship one stitch stronger."

Finally, it's important for both partners in a relationship to stay focused on the kind of behavior that brought them together in the first place and to keep it alive. This is hardly news to anyone who has ever glanced at a breakfast show or a women's magazine, yet the incidence of candlelit dinners, bouquets, and romantic poems drops steeply after the first year or two of marriage, just when such niceties are really needed. Once your relationship stabilizes, the positives—his looks, her charm, their shared sense of humor—become less positive, says Bradbury, "but the negatives don't necessarily become less negative." Avoiding this pitfall requires paying attention to the little things and imposing strategies, like the good old Friday-night date, especially one that features a fresh, highly engaging activity. "Seeing a movie is okay," says Bradbury, "but square dancing is better, because that kind of situation, like travel, means you really have to interact. A relationship takes work, and you have to focus on its maintenance."

ATTENTION FEELS SO internal and personal that it's easy to overlook its tremendous role in social life. Nevertheless, the first step toward any relationship is focusing on someone who returns the favor. If the bond is to become intimate, both parties must commit not only to paying rapt attention to the other, but also to the effort of seeing that person's often very different world, which entails lots of communication.

The home would seem to be the one place where people focus on each other and share the same reality. Yet some sobering research shows that, pulled into their own little worlds by an individualistic me-first culture and accelerating demands on their attention, American couples and families often fall short in this regard.

Particularly in times of social and economic turmoil, we're reminded that not only as individuals but also as members of a society we choose to focus on certain targets and suppress others: risky profits or steady savings; McMansions or "green" homes; multilateralism or unilateralism; SUVs or mass transit; celebrity or character. As the nation faces crises in the economy, the environment, international affairs, and other vital areas, we can no longer afford to indulge in the kind of collective ADHD that's symbolized by President Ronald Reagan's removal of the solar panels that President Jimmy Carter had installed in the White House during an energy crisis thirty years ago. In short, it has perhaps never been more important for Americans to join together in choosing our goals wisely and staying focused on them over time.

CHAPTER 7

Productivity: Work Zone

As Freud said, "Love and work . . . work and love, that's all there is," and attention is as essential to productivity as it is to relationships. By actively choosing endeavors that demand your total focus and skillfully using attention to make even inevitable rote chores more engaging, you can blur the distinction between work and play—a hallmark of the focused life.

Over the past hundred years, psychologists have tried to deconstruct what makes something interesting enough to attract and hold your focus, and their various formulas have much in common. To William James, rapt attention requires a target that offers just the right combination of novelty and familiarity. Imagine, for example, that after a long, grey winter, your bleary eye lights on the red breast of the year's first robin. Then, your attentional system kicks in with a memory to add meaning to the new feathered stimulus: robins come in the spring, which has always been your favorite season. Suddenly, you're not just glancing at some humdrum bird but focused on a winged Mercury come to herald good times.

The most important dimension of this equation for drawing and retaining your interest is that neither the familiar nor the novel is captivating in itself. Like a robin in July, writes James, "the absolutely old is insipid." Similarly, because you'd have no associations with some drab little bird you've never noticed before, "the absolutely new makes no appeal at all." It's the *convergence* of the robin's unexpected appearance and its cognitive and affective resonance that makes its debut the stuff of poetry.

Tracey Burke's professional life, which centers on ranching, developed from this powerful alchemy of the familiar and the fresh. Her graduate school was a remote Wyoming cattle spread, whose cowboy owner hired the young Eastern greenhorn, who'd recently given up teaching for the ski slopes of Jackson Hole, to help out during the summer, when he hosted guests. With a laugh, Burke recalls, "He said, 'You can cook, ride a horse, and do all that stuff, right?' I couldn't, but I was young, so I said okay!"

Born and raised in mild Maryland, Burke was no cowgirl, so ranching offered plenty of novelty. On the other hand, she had a math teacher's problem-solving mind and a strong, athletic body developed over years of competitive swimming and gymnastics, so she felt comfortable with work that called for ingenuity and physical skill. "How to bake from scratch, handle the horses, get along without electricity . . . I just had to figure things out," she says. "Those three years of learning were great."

With her employer-turned-husband, Renny Burke, Tracey now runs the eight-thousand-acre EA Ranch. After you turn off the main road, you still have a rough-and-tumble ten-minute drive to the house and outbuildings, set spectacularly between a trout stream and the blood-red foothills of the Absaroka Range. Cattle and horses graze in the meadows, and you might catch sight of a moose, elk, bear, osprey, or even a grey wolf.

Particularly in the summer, when outdoor chores abound and guests must be cosseted and fed three homegrown gourmet meals a day, her share of running the EA would be a full-time job for most people, but not for Burke. She also raises sheep for meat and hides, trains prizewinning herding dogs, gardens, competes in dressage riding, cooks professionally, and teaches yoga. Until recently, when she took up legal mediation, she was also a ski instructor in Jackson Hole, where she founded the resort's twice-yearly women-only program. In short, this tall, slender, mild-mannered middle-aged woman who lives and works way off the bicoastal power grids makes Jack Welch and Carly Fiorina look like one-trick ponies.

The American dream is no longer just to get rich quick, but also to enjoy doing it, and new captains of industry offer various best-selling decalogues for achieving this goal. Their tips range from the philosophical (learn from your failures) to the practical (never handle the same piece of paper twice). There's one insight into both productivity and satisfaction that they inevitably share, however: the importance of laserlike attention to your goal, be it building a better mousetrap or raising cattle.

Unless you can concentrate on what you want to do and suppress distractions, it's hard to accomplish anything, period. Whether she's herding sheep in the high alpine desert or negotiating a settlement in a law office, Burke is right *there*, as attentive as a bird dog. According to the underappreciated mid-twentieth-century psychologist Nicholas Hobbs, the way to ensure this calm but heightened attention to the matter at hand is to choose activities that push you so close to the edge of your competence that they demand your absolute focus. In a variation on James's recipe for interesting experience—the familiar leavened by the novel—Hobbs's "art of choosing difficulties" requires selecting projects that are *"just manageable."* If an activity is too easy, you lose focus and get bored. If it's too hard, you become anxious, overwhelmed, and unable to concentrate. Tellingly, one group is distinguished by its zeal for the kind of work that requires you to give it all you've got: high achievers particularly relish taking on risky projects that have only a 50/50 chance of success.

Considering the daunting range of skills that have devolved from her embrace of challenges, it's comforting to learn that it took Burke, like many of us, quite a while to find her vocation. After college and a stint of teaching that she found "mentally and emotionally draining," she went through a "transitional period," joining the gang of young ski bums, cowboys, and mountaineers in the Tetons who paid for their food, shelter, and lift tickets by wearing many hats. This immersion in outdoors thrills and chills and catch-as-catch-can employment provided Burke with a valuable crash course in the rancher's hardscrabble, just-manageable way of life to come.

THE INSIGHTS INTO rapt attention's role in human behavior in general and productivity in particular first contributed by James, Hobbs, and Abraham Maslow, who studied "peak experience," have been greatly expanded by the more recent research on "flow" conducted by the Claremont psychologist Mihály Csíkszentmihályi. This state of "optimal human experience" kicks in when you're completely focused on doing something that's both enjoyable and challenging enough to be just manageable. Either attention or motivation—the drive that impels you toward a goal—can jump-start flow, but both of these major psychological processes must converge to sustain it.

Like James, Csíkszentmihályi has taken the study of daily life to a new level and occupies a place in the pantheon of American psychology. He also shares his predecessor's strong feelings about the importance of attention, which he regards as nothing less than "psychology's bottom line. Any complex behavioral issue has attention at its core." (His attitude is no accident, considering that he spent most of his career at the University of Chicago, where the psychology department was long presided over by the philosophically minded Carl Rogers and Heinz Kohut, who, like James, regarded reality as an intentional, first-person experience that you construct from the material of attention.) He stresses that like other kinds of power, this "psychic energy" is both necessary to make things happen and finite in supply. In fact, according to his calculations, you can only attend to about 110 bits of information per second (listening to someone speak, for example, requires processing about 40 bits per second), or about 173 billion bits over an average life span. Even other researchers' higher estimates underscore the fact that this valuable resource is distinctly limited.

Gleaning accurate information about daily life as it's actually lived isn't easy. Historically, such research has been retrospective and based on getting subjects to fill out questionnaires: "On a scale of 1 to 5, how much do you enjoy your work? How important is your family?" To investigate the individual's intentional and attentional reality with new rigor, Csíkszentmihályi developed a technique, called the Experience Sampling Method, that's a major innovation in psychological research. Instead of filling out the traditional questionnaires, subjects in ESM studies wear pagers or watches that beep randomly during two-hour intervals over a period of several weeks as they go about daily life. When signaled, they record the most important details of their situation: location, activity, thoughts, feelings, presence or absence of others. This information paints a much more detailed picture of how a person or a group, such as teenagers or single parents, actually experiences real life, compared to what they say about it later.

Over the past thirty years, ESM studies conducted with tens of thousands of people have yielded some stunning insights into what makes for a high-quality experience, including its parameters in the workplace, which is one of Csíkszentmihályi's recent particular interests. Whether you're selling real estate or training a horse, removing an appendix or cutting hair, you're in flow if you're so focused on your work that time flies, your ego drops away, and you act intuitively. You think along the lines of "I was born for this" or "This is what it's all about." You know you're in the right business if you feel that you'd work "for the sheer pleasure": an intrinsic reward that's far more satisfying than extrinsic ones such as a big salary and professional recognition, which depend on comparisons with others.

When asked what kind of work most engages her focus and produces rewarding experience, Burke gives an answer unlikely to be heard in Wall Street or Silicon Valley: "Something that combines physical activity and problem-solving!" As she discusses her varied career, this theme surfaces again and again, whether she's talking about irrigating a hay field, preparing elk steaks for guests, or teaching yoga. In class, if need be, Burke can pick up an aspiring yogi like one of her sheep and just plain put the person in the right pose, which occasions much mirth. However, what really engrosses her and sends her into flow is figuring out how to help a particular student conquer a demanding asana a quarter-inch at a time. "I really like the process of breaking down a skill," she says, "so that a person can concentrate on getting it in manageable steps."

THE MOST SURPRISING discovery about the kind of focused, fulfilling experience that Burke enjoys when teaching yoga or rounding up cattle is that most people enjoy so little of it. About 20 percent of people flow once or more each day; about 15 percent, never; the great majority, only occasionally. Sadly, many of us spend much of our time oscillating between states of stress and boredom: different but equally unfocused, unproductive, unsatisfying conditions.

We assume that artists such as Julie Taymor, Elmore Leonard, and Bob Dylan are lucky enough to delight in and be absorbed by their work, but surprisingly, so are high achievers in the business world. Citing his research with Yvon Chouinard, founder of Patagonia, Jack Greenberg, CEO of McDonald's, and their ilk, Csíkszentmihályi stresses the tremendous pleasure they derive from what they do. "They all report that it's not enough to be good at the job," he says. "If you want to be really effective, they say, you also have to enjoy your work."

The specifics of flowing at work differ for the scientist and the poet, but no matter what their field, exceptional achievers are characterized as much by their intense focus as their ability. In his research on the subject, Csíkszentmihályi found that in youth, the Nobel physicist John Bardeen, the writer Denise Levertov, and the jazz musician Oscar Peterson were not necessarily more intelligent than other students, but they already exercised more "concentrated attention" on the subjects that interested them. In addition, such paragons of inventiveness also maintain a wide-angle perspective on life that ensures that they will, as Csíkszentmihályi puts it, "be surprised by something every day."

One major reason for the poor quality of much daily experience is that many people simply don't know which activities both provide enjoyment and require total focus. Research conducted by the University of Michigan psychologist Oliver Schultheiss shows that even when taking the important step of choosing a career, individuals often fail to recognize the kind of work that will engage and also satisfy them. A naturally sociable person brought up to value wealth and status, for example, might not realize that she'd be happiest in a "helping" profession such as teaching and therefore end up as a rich yet dissatisfied stockbroker. To avoid such frustrating scenarios, Schultheiss suggests doing visualization exercises in which you "pre-experience" a career or other important goal by imagining yourself pursuing and attaining it, then judge how emotionally satisfying that process would be.

In a stunning example of the kind of mind-set that undermines good daily experience, most people reflexively say that they prefer being at home to being at work. However, flow research shows that on the job, they're much likelier to focus on activities that demand their attention, challenge their abilities, have a clear objective, and elicit timely feedback—conditions that favor optimal experience. Support for these underremarked workplace gratifications is implied by an interesting finding from Arlie Hochschild's study of employees at a Fortune 500 company: despite their grumbling and self-sacrificing talk of improving the family finances, most parents who opted to work overtime did so less for the extra money than because life was just more satisfying at the office.

Interestingly, to say that you're likelier to experience the intensely focused flow state when you're on the job isn't necessarily the same thing as saying that you feel "happier" there. Indeed, during a long conversation about a varied career that she greatly enjoys, Burke never mentions happiness per se. Csíkszentmihályi allows that people may not be whistling while they work, but his research shows that they do report feeling more creative, active, concentrated, and involved than they do in domestic life.

Then too, once you're intently focused on what you're doing, it's hard to think about something extraneous, like whether you're having fun or not. It's often only when you look back on a challenging experience—starting a company, trekking in a developing country, competing in a contest—that you can say, "That was one of the best times in my life, and I want to do something like that again." As Csíkszentmihályi puts it, "If you ask me while I'm playing tennis if I'm happy, I'll say, 'Heck! Wait a minute . . .' Happiness is a later reflection of the flow, rather than the result of the experience at the time."

Where the subject of happiness is concerned, Csíkszentmihályi is among the scientists who are wary of psychology's recent loose talk and generalizations about this poorly defined condition and its purported prevalence. Based on his studies of daily experience conducted over long periods with thousands of subjects, he says, a benign, pleasant state "doesn't seem natural to most people and has to be worked on and developed. Those who learn to control their inner experience will be able to determine the quality of their lives, which is as close as any of us can come to being happy."

Regarding the common assumption that your well-being depends on what happens to you, Csíkszentmihályi observes that this destructive notion permeates culture and language. "German has the same word—

gluck—for happiness and luck," he says, "and in Old English, 'hap,' which is the root of happiness, also meant good luck. It's best to forget that those two things are supposedly intimately related."

ON OCCASION, EVEN the most productive person is hard-pressed to concentrate on the job, much less enjoy it. Burke offers an example of her strategy for coping with such moments: "Draining the flooded driveway doesn't sound so interesting, but it becomes fun if you try to make the water go here or there." Her way of turning chores into play is a good illustration of an important and under-remarked finding from research on the workplace. With some thought, effort, and attention, says Csíkszentmihályi, you can make even an apparently dreary job, such as assembling toasters or packaging tools, much more satisfying. "The trick," he says, "is to turn the work into a kind of game, in which you focus closely on each aspect"—screwing widget A to widget B or the positions of your tools and materials—"and try to figure out how to make it better. That way, you turn a rote activity into an engaging one."

Ironically, some of the most famously productive people face a particular obstacle to flow on the job: having totally mastered a difficult skill, they no longer feel challenged and lose focus. According to the psychologist Gilbert Brim, who's a strong advocate of just-manageable difficulty, high achievers who win the Oscar, MVP award, or corner office can avoid burnout, depression, and even self-destructiveness by "going wide," or focusing on a new vocation or avocation along with their business as usual. When not busy with the demands of the Revolution or the presidency, for example, the highly cerebral Thomas Jefferson delighted in making and designing simple, useful things, such as keys and a plow. By learning to fly-fish or play the violin, the jaded CEO or celebrity becomes a beginner in pursuit of an enjoyable new goal that demands total attention—the ticket to joie de vivre and renewed energy back on the job.

. . .

WE'RE ACCUSTOMED TO thinking of productivity in terms of career, but if you're living the focused life, your free time should be just as generative or even more so—particularly if you don't especially enjoy your work. Despite the lip service we pay to our treasured leisure, however, it's often unsatisfying, largely because we don't devote it to activities that demand focus and skill.

Recollecting that flow requires the convergence of your attention and motivation, consider this common leisure-time scenario: after a hard day at the office, you kick off your shoes and ponder the activities afforded by your living room. You determine that you could either play the piano or watch TV. Compared to the instant gratification of flopping on the couch and focusing on the screen, practicing that Duke Ellington you've been working on will require some mental muscle. Its just-manageable difficulty will demand that you concentrate on your sheet music, struggle with those tricky passages, and make quite an effort before the rewards of flow kick in. In the end, the payoff will be greater, but if you don't summon the motivation to get over the hump of your initial inertia and focus, you'll settle for the temporal equivalent of junk food.

Part of the blame for our lost evenings and weekends lies with evolution, which has primed us to focus on the thrills of life on the savannah but has yet to adapt us to sedentary metropolitan existence. You probably don't have to track predators or gather roots on Saturdays, but you'd derive real satisfaction from a challenging pursuit—playing jazz with friends, say, or tackling a do-it-yourself project. Unless you focus on making it happen, however, it's all too easy to drift into the aimless puttering, chatting, or channel surfing that ultimately leaves you feeling vaguely discontented, annoyed at having wasted free time, and even secretly longing for Monday morning.

Leisure is one of Csíkszentmihályi's special interests, and he has the facts and figures that show how often we lose focus and end up misusing our limited supply. In one illustrative study, his subjects flowed for 44 percent of the time when playing sports and games and 34 percent when doing a hobby, but only 13 percent when watching television. In fact, TV generally provides the lowest quality of experience you can have: a state of entropy that's often neither functional nor really fun. Nevertheless, the subjects spent *four* times longer parked in front of the tube than on the demonstrably superior activities. Summing up, Csíkszentmihályi says, "If left to their own devices and genetic programming, and without a salient external stimulus to attract them, most people go into a mode of low-level information processing in which they worry about things or watch television."

The antidote to leisure-time ennui is to pay as much attention to scheduling a productive evening or weekend as you do to your workday. This can seem counterintuitive, says Csíkszentmihályi, "because you assume that it will be pleasant to decide spontaneously what to do. But that's much more complicated than you think." Saturday may be okay, because you'll do some chores and errands, then go out or see friends at night. However, by Sunday noon—not coincidentally, the unhappiest hour in America—you may have run through your options and wind up slumped on a couch, suffering from the Sabbath existential crisis. It's at just such unfocused, unproductive times, says Csíkszentmihályi, that "people start ruminating and feeling that their lives are wasted and so forth."

If you need some inspiration for avoiding the unfocused sloth-angst syndrome, history offers stirring role models. Before the age of professionalism, the amateur enthusiasts Baruch Spinoza, whose day job was making spectacles, and William Blake, who was a printer by trade, used their free time to advance philosophy and the arts. Countless weekend naturalists have greatly enriched botany, ornithology, and the other life sciences. Csíkszentmihályi sees no reason that you shouldn't plan your leisure time with equally high expectations and care. The idea, he says, is to set goals that are, like redesigning the garden, cooking a new recipe, or painting a watercolor, "fun but also stretch you in some way."

IN THE SHORT term, whether it's writing an epic or building a birdhouse, choosing work and play that call for rapt focus and all of your skill provides satisfying, productive experience. Whenever you squander attention on something that doesn't put your brain through its paces and stimulate change, your mind stagnates a little and life feels dull.

To appreciate the long-term wisdom of making tough choices about what to attend to, you need only look back on your own youth. Let's say that as a poor defenseless child, you were forced by your evil parents to take piano lessons and listen to classical music. You hated it, says Csíkszentmihályi, until one day, "some wonderful Mozart piece intruded itself on your attention, and you said, 'This is kind of great!'" Perhaps that experience even motivated you to listen on your own and to practice more often. Eventually, music became an optimal experience that you'll enjoy for a lifetime.

Similarly, if you're now in the parental shoes, you know how important it is to focus your child on what's important, such as schoolwork, sports, and that piano, and what an often thankless, brutally difficult task that can be, especially with adolescents. By way of illustration, Csíkszentmihályi describes a father who tells his son that on vacation, they're going to go scuba diving in the Caribbean. The parent knows that the boy will ultimately enjoy the wonderful new world of the coral reef. However, the son doesn't seem at all interested—perhaps he's bored or scared by the prospect—and only grudgingly indulges his old man, who supplies the initial motivation. After some dives, however, the boy gets hooked on aquatic flow, and when he heads off to college, he studies marine biology.

Not all children have parents who help them focus on the right pursuits, and when the young are left to their own devices, the consequences for their futures can be dire. In one ESM study, 866 teenagers rated whatever they were doing at various times throughout the day as "more like work, more like play, like both, like neither," then reported how they felt about it. The older the kids were, the less they enjoyed worklike activities, so sixth-graders rated them far more positively than twelfth-graders. Worse, 30 percent of the teens spent significant time on purpose-less activities that were "like neither work nor play"—even though they didn't find it enjoyable.

Research shows that the quality and quantity of the time and attention that many people devote to the families they purport to value more than anything leave much to be desired. Csíkszentmihályi particularly de-cries the widespread belief that domestic life is effortlessly, spontaneously rewarding as a dangerous "cultural myth." Lulled by the nice, traditional ring of "home sweet home," he says, "we assume that everyone will just love each other and be fun to be with. But it's not like that. If you want it to be meaningful and enjoyable, you have to take your family time as se-riously as you take your job. What you pay attention to is not just an in-dividual issue, but a social one."

Conventional wisdom has it that most of the children who lack con-structive parental attention are poor, but research questions that assump-tion. Coming down squarely in favor of both quality and quantity of family time, Csíkszentmihályi cites a large study of one thousand teens that shows that the well-off suburban children of two busy upscale profes-sionals are likely to be significantly unhappier than less-affluent middle-class peers who see more of their parents—and no happier than low-income kids in urban ghettoes.

Regardless of income, teens who spend far more time with their peers than their families end up focusing on significantly fewer of the challeng-ing activities, from studying to sports, that really develop their abilities. In wealthy, hard-driving professionals' families, parental attention often has less to do with the children's needs than with whether they meet their elders' expectations, says Csíkszentmihályi: "The children learn that they don't count unless they have good résumés. In families in which children develop well, parents distribute their attention well."

Over time, a commitment to challenging, focused work and leisure produces not only better daily experience, but also a more complex, interesting person: the long-range benefit of the focused life. As Hobbs puts it, the secret of fulfillment is "to choose trouble for oneself in the direction of what one would like to become." While many other baby boomers are planning their retirement, Burke is tackling the new field of mediation, not just because she likes the work but also because she likes developing a new side of herself in midlife. When she opted for this just-manageable challenge, she had in one way or another mostly worked outdoors or with her hands. But, she says, "As I looked at the big picture of my life, I knew that I could and should move on. I had to carry over some of the confidence I've gained in other sorts of work to this new kind."

Looking back at the evolution of her diverse, satisfying career, Burke says, "The biggest hit on the head for me is to see how, when I start something new, I focus on the big picture, then work towards the smaller, finer details as needed. That's what I sense has held things together for me." Her courageous commitment to keep upping the ante on her expectations of herself is what Hobbs called "the fine-tuning of a life," which brings "zest and joy and deep fulfillment."

HAVING THOUGHT ABOUT attention with great depth, rigor, and ingenuity over decades, Csíkszentmihályi has some particularly well-informed ideas about how it can improve daily life. Stay focused on the moment, he says, even when you're engaged in routine tasks or social encounters. Practice directing and mastering your attention by any enjoyable means. You don't have to go off to a cave to meditate if you find tap-dancing or crewel embroidery a more amiable way to concentrate your mind, he says: "What matters is the control." Because you actually might not know what activities truly engage your attention and satisfy you, he says, it can be helpful to keep a diary of what you do all day and how you feel while doing it. Then, try to do more of what's rewarding, even if it takes an effort, and less of what isn't. Where optimal experience is concerned, he says, "'I just don't have the time' often means 'I just don't have the self-discipline.'"

In *The Evolving Self: A Psychology for the Third Millennium*, Csíkszentmihályi makes the case for using attention to transform experience not only for the individual, but also for the species. Problems ranging from America's obesity epidemic to chronic conflict in the Middle East show that our innate focus on instant gratification and negative emotions such as anger and fear, which once helped us survive, have now become serious menaces. Our future depends on directing our attention to new goals, such as the cooperation that's required to clean up the environment and avoid wars.

Not coincidentally, an important recent discovery in flow research has a social as well as a personal dimension. Once you focus on an activity—ranching or marketing, haiku or horticulture—and start to develop the skills required, you need to take on progressively greater challenges to keep on experiencing flow. In this way, writes Csíkszentmihályi, optimal human experience is a Darwinian dynamic that can slowly transform society and even affect evolution by encouraging activities of ever-greater complexity, countering business-as-usual mind-sets, and offering alternatives to obsolete, destructive behavior.

As to the theory that what you focus on creates your experience and that choosing those targets wisely is the key to the good life, Csíkszentmihályi simply says, "Yes, absolutely."

. . .

THERE ARE DIFFERENT formulas for the fulfilling experience variously described as "interesting," "peak," or "optimal," but rapt focus is central to all of them. Whether the equation's other integers are the novel balanced with the familiar or the challenging with the enjoyable, they add up to the same thing: engagement in activities that arrest your attention and satisfy your soul. If most of the time you're not particularly concerned about whether what you're doing is work or play, or even whether you're happy or not, you know you're living the focused life.

CHAPTER 8

Decisions: Focusing Illusions

Sometimes, really bright people make really foolish choices, from relocating to a beautiful place that will bore them stiff to involving a nation in a needless war. Research in the burgeoning field of behavioral economics shows that such disasters, large and small, are often rooted in an all-too-human tendency to pay attention to the wrong things during the decision-making process.

Looking back, Shannon Howell sees that her transfer from the University of Michigan to Brown University, long her dream destination, was based on her single-minded focus on Ivy League prestige rather than on what kind of college experience would best meet her needs. "My first year in Ann Arbor, I was obsessed with the thought that I wasn't at the school I wanted to be at," she says. "So much so that I refused to see that Michigan actually suited me very well."

Once she got to Brown, Howell found that she attended to the wonder of the hallowed halls of ivy much less than she had imagined. She also belatedly realized how many things she had really liked about Michigan, including friends, festive Big Ten football games, and the fine psychology department. "But I didn't focus on those things when I was there," she says, "because I was so fixated on my initial judgment that Michigan was not the school I wanted to go to."

As Howell's story shows, attention orders but also limits your experience, which can be tricky where big decisions are concerned. Considering the number of fine colleges to choose from, students have to narrow their selection somehow or go mad. On the other hand, by zeroing in on certain criteria—a school's status, say, or geographical location—and ignoring others, they can end up focused on one dimension of an important experience that might not prove to be as vital as they thought.

Early in his long and varied career, the Princeton psychologist Daniel Kahneman wrote a book about attention, and the subject figures prominently in his more recent work on the decision-making process. In 2002, this research brought him the Nobel Prize in economics, yet Kahneman remains every inch a psychologist. His demeanor is that of a certain kind of therapist: not the warm, fuzzy sort but the penetrating, hard-hat type who doesn't miss a thing. Unlike some venerable figures, he doesn't treat an interview as a monologue, but attends closely to his interlocutor's remarks. When a comment questions or differs from his research findings, he says, "Interesting."

As a twenty-year-old psychologist in the Israeli army, Kahneman was already focused on an elegant research technique that would shape his life's work: the art of the question. His military colleagues devised many for the elaborate personality tests they gave to soldiers, yet these extensive queries failed to meet the objective of identifying who would do well or poorly in battle. Looking to the opposite extreme, Kahneman discovered the work of the Columbia University psychologist Walter Mischel, who gained a lot of very useful information about a child's nature with just one brilliantly conceived question: Do you want this small lollipop right now or this big one tomorrow?

When asked if he had ever come up with such a simple, focused question for assessing personality, Kahneman nods: "How many kids would you like to have in your tent when you're camping?" The answer gave some insight into a child's sociability, he says, "but it didn't work as wonderfully as Mischel's." Next, he listens to a visitor's attempt to put a temperament in a nutshell: "Do you want to spend more time today by yourself or with other people?" He considers this, then says, "That's a good one. Although the answer would depend very much on your immediate context—on how much time you're spending with other people now. You'd have to refine the question."

In their work on decision-making, Kahneman and his late partner Amos Tversky made the art of the refined query into a science. "Our research method was to write one question at a time, formulated to make a specific point," he says. "Then we published our questions, answers, and predictions. That is what we did." Of the Nobel, he says, "I got the prize because some economists became convinced that you could do economics in a slightly different way—by being more realistic about psychology."

According to the principle of "bounded rationality," which Kahneman first applied to economic decisions and more recently to choices concerning quality of life, we are reasonable-enough beings but sometimes liable to focus on the wrong things. Our thinking gets befuddled not so much by our emotions as by our "cognitive illusions," or mistaken intuitions, and other flawed, fragmented mental constructs.

Facing a choice, for example, you might focus on the quickest, most accessible solution, rather than taking time to think things through. When making a decision that affects your long-term future, you might mistakenly concentrate on very short-term concerns. "That's why following every detail of your financial situation is a problem, unless you get pleasure from it," says Kahneman. "If you focus too much on each issue separately, considering each loss and gain in isolation, you make mistakes."

If you're pondering a choice that involves risk, you might focus too much on the threat of possible loss, thereby obscuring an even likelier potential benefit. Where this common scenario is concerned, research shows that we aren't so much risk-averse as loss-averse, in that we're generally much more sensitive to what we might have to give up than to what we might gain. Let's say that you're invited to toss a coin. The terms are that if it's tails, you lose twenty dollars; heads, you win a certain amount. If you're then asked how much your winnings would have to be to make you take the chance, you're likely to suggest between forty and fifty dollars. In other words, because we put more weight on the loss than the reward, before taking a 50/50 gamble, most people want to know that they'd win at least twice as much as they'd forfeit.

Economics is concerned with making better decisions about money, but much of Kahneman's current research focuses on making wiser choices about the even more valuable resource of your experience. When you stop to consider your own life, you probably do much the same thing as traditional psychologists do with their questionnaires, asking yourself, "How are things going in my home, job, relationship, commute? Great, good, fair, or awful?" The problem is that this type of abstract evaluation "isn't looking at how people actually *experience* their lives," says Kahneman, "but how they *think* about their lives. That distinction has been my entry into well-being research."

To get closer to what life in the trenches is really like, behavioral scientists increasingly eschew the traditional questionnaires for newer techniques, such as Mihály Csíkszentmihályi's Experience Sampling Method, that provide more-immediate information about everyday experience. For a large study published in the prestigious journal *Science*, Kahneman asked 909 working women to record in a diary everything they had done and how they felt about it on the previous day. He found that presumably major issues, like job security and marital status, had surprisingly little effect on the women's sense of daily satisfaction compared to their choices—and the lack of same—regarding the use of time: the experiential equivalent of money. Most subjects spent most of their waking hours—11.5 on average—doing the things that they least enjoy, such as commuting and housework, as opposed to favored activities, particularly social interactions with friends (rather than family, because the former engage your attention more fully). Although your degree of contentment with life partly depends on genes and early environment, which you can't control, it's also affected by how many hours you spend enjoyably or not, which you can often do something about. As Kahneman says, "You can choose to put yourself in better rather than worse contexts and try to spend more time in the good situations."

How you decide to spend your time and make other choices that affect your quality of life is closely bound up with attention, which "governs how people think about well-being," Kahneman says, "and also governs the experience." To illustrate, he points out two ways in which focusing on the wrong thing can skew your choices about how best to live.

First, there's a gap between your real life and the *stories* you tell yourself about it, and you're apt to fixate on the latter. Stressing the importance of this divide, Kahneman says, "Attention both to what you choose to experience and what you choose to think about it is at the very core of how I approach questions of well-being." He traces this disconnect between reality and your thoughts about it to two different selves that pay attention to different kinds of things.

Your hands-on "experiencing self," which concentrates on just plain being in the here and now, is absorbed in whatever is going on and how you feel about it without doing much analysis. Your evaluative "remembering self," however, looks back on an experience, focuses on its emotional high points and outcomes, then formulates thoughts about it, not always accurately. Much research incontrovertibly shows that memory is biased and unpredictable—more like a patchwork quilt than the seamless tapestry of reality we like to imagine. Indeed, you don't so much recall something that happened as reconstruct a facsimile of it. Moreover, this mental artifact is likely to be either more positive or negative in tone than was the actual event.

The differences in what your experiencing and remembering selves pay attention to may account for some seeming paradoxes in your life, as they do in Kahneman's research. For example, most mothers say that having children is one of life's greatest satisfactions. Yet his subjects' diaries show that actual roll-up-your-sleeves parenting was among the women's least enjoyable activities. This apparent contradiction and others like it are explained by the divergent focuses of a person's two selves. The experiencing self of a tired woman who's contemplating the wreckage of her slovenly adolescent's room might well give mothering a poor rating at that moment. If parenthood comes up later at a party, however, her remembering self zeroes in on its emotional highs and long-term results—that sweet poem on Mother's Day, the soccer trophy, the acceptance letter from Harvard—rather than on momentary vexations like dirty socks and old pizza crusts sprouting life-forms. It's just as well for their progeny that when adults make choices about how to live, they pay more attention to the remembering self's judgmental voice than to the experiencing self's whispers, which say more about their own daily satisfactions.

The key to understanding why you pay more attention to your thoughts about living than to life itself is neatly summed up by what Kahneman proudly calls his "fortune cookie maxim" (a.k.a. the focusing illusion): "Nothing in life is as important as you think it is while you are thinking about it." Why? "Because you're thinking about it!"

In one much-cited illustration of the focusing illusion, Kahneman asked some people if they would be happier if they lived in California. Because the climate is often delightful there, most subjects thought so. For the same reason, even Californians assume they're happier than people who live elsewhere. When Kahneman actually measured their well-being, however, Michiganders and others are just as contented as Californians. The reason is that 99 percent of the stuff of life—relationships, work, home, recreation—is the same no matter where you are, and once you settle in a place, no matter how salubrious, you don't think about its climate very much. If you're prompted to evaluate it, however, the weather immediately looms large, simply because you're paying attention to it. This illusion inclines you to accentuate the difference between Place A and Place B, making it seem to matter much more than it really does, which is marginal.

To test the fortune cookie rule, you have only to ask yourself how happy you are. The question automatically summons your remembering self, which will focus on any recent change in your life—marriage or divorce, new job or home. You'll then think about this novel event, which in turn will increase its import and influence your answer. If you're pleased that you've just left the suburbs for the city, say, you'll decide that life is pretty good. If you regret the move, you'll be dissatisfied in general. Fifteen years on, however, the change that looms so large now will pale next to a more recent event—a career change, perhaps, or becoming a grandparent—which will draw your focus and, simply because you're thinking about it, bias your evaluation of your general well-being.

Because your remembering self pays attention to your thoughts about your life, rather than to the thing itself, it can be difficult to evaluate the quality of your own experience accurately. By way of illustration, Kahneman describes an experiment done by the University of Michigan social psychologist Norbert Schwarz, in which he asked one group of subjects a question: "How much pleasure do you get from your car?" Not surprisingly, there was a significant correlation between an auto's value and its owner's enjoyment, so that the remembering selves of BMW and Lexus drivers were more satisfied than those of people who drove Escorts and Camrys. Next, Schwarz probed the immediate reality of the experiencing self by asking another group of subjects a different question:

"How much pleasure did you get from using your car *today?*" Abruptly, the correlation between the owners' satisfaction and their cars' worth vanished. What determined their answers was not the quality of their vehicles but of their actual commute that very day: whether it was marked by good or bad weather, traffic conditions, or even personal ruminations—in short, the experiencing self's quotidian ups and downs.

The experiencing and remembering selves' different attentional perspectives make for what Kahneman understatedly calls "a complicated story." If you're asked how much pleasure you get from your car, the question summons up your evaluative remembering self, because "when you get pleasure from your car is when you *think* about your car." When queried, you don't stop to consider your most recent driving experience, but flash to "imagining yourself thinking about your car." That complex relationship between your experience and your thoughts about it takes on far more significance when the matter at hand isn't just your ride, but your career, family, friends, or home. The point, says Kahneman, is that "we shouldn't measure our lives on the quality of our memories alone."

Unless you're a Zen sage like Yoda, however, shifting your attention from thinking to being is harder than it might seem at first. For one thing, as soon as you try, you're apt to revert to your remembering self. "That's very complicated," says Kahneman. "When you think about your life, your only natural perspective is retrospective—looking back. So to make a decision because it will affect your experience, even if it's unlikely to have a big effect on your memory, is a deliberate stance that you could take. You might do that when you think about the balance of your life and decide to spend most of your time doing this or doing that."

LIKE FOCUSING TOO much on the opinions of your remembering self, overlooking the effects of adaptation—the process of becoming used to a situation—can obstruct wise decisions about how to live. As Kahneman says, "when planning for the future, we don't consider that we will stop paying attention to a thing."

The tendency to stop focusing on a particular event or experience over time, no matter how wonderful or awful, helps explain why the differences in well-being between groups of people in very different circumstances tend to be surprisingly small—sometimes astoundingly so. The classic examples are paraplegics and lottery winners, who respectively aren't nearly as miserable or happy as you'd think. "That's where attention comes in," says Kahneman. "People think that if they win the lottery, they'll be happy forever. Of course, they will not. For a while, they are happy because of the novelty, and because they think about winning all the time. Then they adapt and stop paying attention to it." Similarly, he says, "Everyone is surprised by how happy paraplegics can be, but they are not paraplegic full-time. They do other things. They enjoy their meals, their friends, the newspaper. It has to do with the allocation of attention."

Like couples who've just fallen in love, professionals starting a career, or children who go to camp for the first time, paraplegics and lottery winners initially pay a lot of attention to their new situation. Then, like everybody else, they get used to it and shift their focus to the next big thing. Their seemingly blasé attitude surprises us, because when we imagine ourselves in their place, we focus on how we'd feel at the moment of becoming paralyzed or wildly rich, when such an event utterly monopolizes one's focus. We forget that we, too, would get used to wealth, a wheelchair, and most other things under the sun, then turn our attention elsewhere.

This attentional myopia is especially problematic when you're trying to make important decisions about the future. Overlooking the fact that a romance's honeymoon novelty must fade, an older man leaves a seemingly comfortable union of many years for a young "trophy wife," only to find that he still faces the demands of marriage and misses the easy family life he shared with his first spouse. An urban couple decides that because they enjoy their country weekends so much, they should move to their rural hamlet for good, then later realize that on a full-time basis, they had rapidly adapted to and outgrown its limited resources. Offering a dizzying reconfiguration of the way we usually think, Kahneman says, "When you anticipate something, what you anticipate is memory more than experience."

Forgetting that you'll eventually stop paying attention to a new thing can skew not just big decisions about the future, but also the small ones that quietly but profoundly affect your present well-being. These "comforts," as distinguished from "pleasures" by the late Stanford economist Tibor Scitovsky, are in fact "pleasures that you've stopped paying attention to," says Kahneman. "The difference between them is clearly one of attention."

Attention's relationship to comforts and pleasures often affects your decisions about consumer goods. The focusing illusion predicts that you'll exaggerate the importance of a thing just by thinking about it, as when you ponder a big purchase. Soon after you buy it, however, you stop noticing the costly pleasure—perhaps a top-of-the-line Sub-Zero fridge or Viking stove—which gets downgraded to a comfort. "That's a very interesting distinction—goods that you attend to when you use them and those that you don't," says Kahneman. "There's probably much less focusing illusion with pleasures like fresh flowers or a glass of wine." Because it gives you more fun and bang for your buck, spending five hundred dollars a year on bouquets or Burgundy is a better investment in your well-being than upgrading a major appliance.

Despite your initial excitement and a high price tag, adaptation guarantees that your focus will soon stray from the wondrous pleasures of your new computer or larger apartment, consigning them to mere comfort status. Rather than bingeing on such big, costly amenities, a better—and cheaper—strategy for boosting your daily satisfaction quotient would be to add many more simple, inexpensive ones: a fine piece of chocolate, an interesting magazine, a great DVD. After all, on any given Monday morning, your comfortable bank balance pales beside a good cup of coffee. These little things in life, which afford what Kahneman calls "experiences that you think about when you're having them," provide a great deal of everyday enjoyment. Because you're apt to pay more attention to your remembering than your experiencing self, however, it's all too easy to forget to indulge yourself in these small but important pleasures on a daily basis, thus depriving yourself of much joy.

BASED ON RECENT research on well-being, Kahneman says, "I can imagine a future in which, just as many of us exercise physically, we'll also exercise mentally for twenty or thirty minutes a day. That's the kind of world 'positive psychology' is looking for. Whether its principles will work or not in the long run, I don't know. All the data aren't in yet. But it's clear that getting people to pay attention to what's good in their lives is a good thing. There's no question about that."

As to the idea that the ability to focus on *this* rather than on *that* gives you control over your experience and well-being, Kahneman says that both the Dalai Lama and the Penn positive psychologist Martin Seligman would agree about the importance of paying attention: "Being able to control it gives you a lot of power, because you know that you don't have to focus on a negative emotion that comes up."

At the end of a discussion of attention and decision-making, Kahneman remarks on research that suggests older people connect more with the experiencing self, which is inclined to pay rapt attention to little everyday delights, like sunbeams dancing on water or music drifting through a window. "That sounds like a survivor's experience," he says. "A survivor appreciates life more. I think that's true of old age, too. There are many small pleasures that I enjoy more now."

.   .   .

FEW THINGS ARE as important to your quality of life as your choices about how to spend the precious resource of your free time, but the different focuses of your experiencing and remembering selves can seriously perturb your decision-making in this regard. Contemplating the prospect of a free evening, your high-minded remembering self directs your attention to that uplifting concert, art exhibit, or play you've been meaning to go to. Or why don't you pick up the phone and arrange to get together with X, Y, or Z, whom you really like and never see? Before you proceed, however, your experiencing self chimes in, whining that you're too stressed and/or tired to do anything more than sprawl on the couch and watch HBO reruns.

Perhaps you've experienced this attentional conflict between the two modes of *me* on a Sunday morning, when you settle down with the newspaper and subject your remembering self to the temptations of the travel and arts sections. As you consider the possible mind-expanding vacations and worthwhile cultural events, you envision a time in a few weeks or months when life won't be as hectic as it is right now. You go ahead and book the airline tickets or the opera series. Then, as the big day approaches, lofty thoughts of expanding your horizons evaporate as your experiencing self fixates on how busy you are, as usual, and how much better off you'd be just staying home.

On the other hand, history has taught you that unless you want to spend all of your free time reading about things that you might but don't do, you must occasionally attend to your remembering self's urging and commit to that ballet subscription or bike trip in the west of Ireland. You know that on the day of the performance or departure, you'll smite your brow and say, "Was I crazy? I can't do this right now!" But you've plunked down your money, so you go, and you're always glad afterward. Once you get to the concert hall or Galway, your experiencing self kicks in to enjoy the moment, and your evaluating self gets a juicy good-life memory to chew over later.

This common type of attentional conflict reminds the Swarthmore psychologist Barry Schwartz of a decision-making dilemma, explored by the New York University psychologist Yaacov Trope, that's peculiar to academics: Why does Professor X agree to contribute a chapter to a colleague's textbook when he knows that when he sits down to write, it's going to be a nightmare? To Schwartz, the answer is that when you first think about a long-term project, you focus on the goal—the finished chapter, cleverly written and beautifully annotated—and barely consider the matter of how you'll get to that point.

As the deadline looms, however, your focus shifts from the rewarding goal to the grueling means. "*That's* when you realize that you're already overextended," says Schwartz, "and that you don't feel like doing the extra work to bone up on the latest developments in your subject." Personal experience has taught him the wisdom of sitting down to consider what a new commitment will mean before he accepts it. Nevertheless, he says, "our natural inclination is to attend to the end product. As a result, we have a lot of regret over our decisions."

Making tough choices about how to spend your time in a busy, busy world is not the only major decision-making quandary that's endemic to life in the twenty-first century. In our age of endlessly proliferating consumer goods, when entire TV shows are devoted to culling jammed closets, drawers, and garages, deciding what sound system or computer to buy can turn into a major research project. After he wrote *The Paradox of Choice*, Schwartz got fervent amens from European governments as well as individual readers for insisting that the management of your focus has become one of decision-laden modernity's major challenges. Many behavioral economists and social psychologists also share his concern about what he calls "the consequences of mis-attention."

In supermarkets and malls, the ever-accelerating explosion of products and services that clamor for your focus can turn once easy decisions—black or brown, Ford or Chevy—into white-knuckled traumas. The focusing illusion is one major culprit in these scenarios. If you have to decide between air conditioner or compact car A and B—to say nothing of W, X, Y, and Z—it seems only reasonable to winnow your list of options by ignoring the products' similarities and zeroing in on the differences. The problem is that by focusing on those often minor variations, you dramatically inflate their real importance. Even trivial distinctions soon loom large enough to obscure the fact that for all practical purposes, the gizmos are nearly identical. Depending on the number under consideration, this process can be a major waste of your time and energy. Doing his bit for the public's well-being, Schwartz has advised the editors of *Consumer Reports* that rating fifty-five washing machines, fifty-three of which are basically fine, is counterproductive. "They make distinctions that really don't matter," he says, "but because there *are* distinctions, you think they *must* matter. So you attend to them and torture yourself over which washer to buy."

Some research suggests that the "sweet spot" for the ideal number of consumer options is between eight and ten—enough to offer variety without being overwhelming. That moderate range suits the mellow folks whom Schwartz calls "satisficers," who are contented with an item that's, well, pretty good. Finicky "maximizers" who have to have "the best," however, are apt to agonize over too many choices.

Even consumers who are determined to protect their finite attentional resources find it's not always easy to fend off unwanted choices. Schwartz describes a colleague who, when buying electronics, always asks for "the second cheapest Sony." Nevertheless, salespeople often insist on dragging him through the other products anyway. They do so because when given a choice between a sound system that has seven features and one that has twenty-one, you're apt to pick the latter, and more expensive, model, even though you won't be able to figure out how most of the features work once you're at home.

When you must choose between a product's usability and capability, you tend to focus on the latter, because you think, "Who knows what I'll want to do with it someday?" If consumers are able to test both sound systems or other products before deciding, however, most will pick the simpler device. Yet as Schwartz says, "This is a very hard lesson to learn. We all have a gadget sitting in a box in a closet somewhere, but we think it's going to be different next time."

Institutions as well as individuals get seduced by too many choices and the focusing illusion into squandering their attention. As a professor, Schwartz's particular peeve is the admissions process at top colleges. Confronted by an embarrassment of riches, the Ivies and other prestigious schools end up fixating on incredibly fine distinctions between many essentially equal applicants. This procedure not only drains their own administrative resources but worse, puts a terrible strain on the kids. Instead of paying attention to important developmental questions—What subjects do I really care about? How am I getting along with others?—many high school students take on activities that they're not even interested in because they look good on their applications. If Schwartz had his way, elite colleges would divide their applicants into those who are good enough to admit and those who aren't, then put the former's names into a hat and pick at random. Instead, he says, "the demand, both for colleges and kids, is that everything matters and has to be focused on. That's a recipe for misery and a model of the attention problems that we face all over."

Even certain places can befuddle us by offering too many potential choices to attend to. Observing that New York City recently appeared at the very bottom of a list of America's happiest cities, Schwartz says that one reason is that its infinite number of options for dining, entertainment, the arts, shopping, and everything else drives people crazy. To the argument that New Yorkers live there *because* of the options, Schwartz patiently responds, "But a lot of research shows that people don't know themselves very well and are characteristically their own worst enemies."

In an age of constant assaults on your attention, sanity requires that you tune out many of them, beginning with those from your own communications devices. However, it's not easy to resist the enticing call of these machines or to protect your experience and relationships from the businesslike expectations they impose. "There's something about the pace of life now that makes you just want the executive summary," says Schwartz, "and an e-mail or voice mail does that, compared to an actual conversation, which is 'messier.' It's as though every one of our interactions has to be instrumental. But when the point of them isn't getting together, but achieving some goal, that's a dramatic diminishment of the quality of life."

Information technology also threatens your limited store of attention with the decidedly mixed blessing of the potentially 24/7 workweek. As Schwartz says, "You now have the opportunity to choose whether to work every minute of every day, no matter where you are. Even if you turn all your machines off, you think about them! The pressure is always on." On recently receiving an auto e-mail that said, "I'll be out of the office for two hours," his initial reaction was, "She must be kidding!" Then he realized that if you're expected to be available all the time, yet decide not to be disturbed at certain times, as many professional women have done, "you may have to pay a price."

Summarizing a major behavioral predicament of the information age, Schwartz says, "On the one hand, you've got to defend your limited cognitive resources so you can attend to what really matters. On the other, you can't just tune out. You need to find a way to be part of society as it is without being weighed down by all the claims on your attention it imposes."

Even maximizers and New Yorkers can husband their finite attention by applying a few of Schwartz's simple principles to decision-making. The next time you face a choice, he says, rely on habit. Instead of fretting over which is the supremo suitcase or cordless drill, buy the same one that you bought last time. When in doubt, let a more knowledgeable friend choose for you. "Don't think about your cell phone or long-distance plan," he says. "Just call the right person and do what he or she says. A group of friends could have a designated expert in investments, restaurants, electronics, and so on."

Finally, don't worry if the choice you made wasn't the absolute best, as long as it meets your needs. Offering the single most important lesson from his research, Schwartz says, "Good enough is almost always good enough. If you have that attitude, many problems about decisions and much paralysis melt away."

FROM "BUYER'S REGRET" to a "crime of passion," many poor decisions spring from focusing on the wrong things. The human condition seems to include tendencies to avoid loss even at the expense of considerable potential gain and to exaggerate something's importance merely because we're thinking about it. We're apt to base choices on our evaluations rather than on our actual experience and to forget that no matter how great or terrible the thing we're focused on today, chances are that we'll soon get used to it. In addition to these age-old problems, our capacity for rapt attention is increasingly under assault from a barrage of goods and services and our own beeping, blinking, ringing electronics. Now as never before, some of our most important decisions concern where to direct our limited supply of attention. Remembering that your life is the sum of what you focus on helps to bring clarity to choices about where to spend that valuable mental money.

CHAPTER 9

Creativity: An Eye for Detail

Looking at Mary Ellen Honsaker's small sketch of a field mouse, portrayed with every whisker and digit just so, brings to mind William James's simple experiment on how to improve your ability to pay attention. First, he says, make a dot on a piece of paper or a wall, then try to stay focused on it. In short order, your mind will wander. Next, start asking yourself questions about the dot: its size, shape, color, and so on. Make associations with it: its existential pathos, perhaps, or the dot as yang to the paper's yin. Once you're engaged in such elaboration, you'll find that you can focus on the negligible mark for quite a while. Observing that this ability to attend to and develop even the humblest subject is a cornerstone of creativity, James says, "This is what the genius does, in whose hands a given topic coruscates and grows."

Not least because she specializes in portraying wildlife, and a field mouse, much less a moose, grizzly, or wolf in nearby Yellowstone is not about to hold a pose, Honsaker uses attention in very particular ways to organize, enhance, and limit aspects of her experience at each step of the creative process. When she sets out to "grow" a picture, she first focuses on the animal in its proper habitat, even if that means a trip to Africa. "I have to see and hear the creature," she says, "really *feel* it, so I can tell its story." While in the field, she concentrates on her subject's most important features, rapidly recording them in quick sketches, photographs, and notes. Back in the studio, she blends these fresh observations with a lifetime's experience with animals and art and focuses on the best way to interpret her subject, often in pastel, an unusual medium of paint pigments formed into crayonlike sticks.

Since the muses of ancient Greece and accounts of Jehovah's invention of the world, creativity has been linked to divinity, and even in modern secular circles, it's often romanticized as mostly talent. Many other qualities are important to it, however, beginning with the capacity for both highly targeted, knowledge-based "convergent" thinking that searches for logical solutions to a problem and especially the freewheeling "divergent" type that ranges far off the grid to find new options. Along with knowledge, motivation, discipline, intelligence, confidence, and risk-taking, creativity calls for attention, from the almost subliminal awareness of a gestating idea to the conscious top-down "Eureka" on its realization.

When we imagine Einstein coming up with $E=MC^2$ or Michelangelo sketching the design for the Sistine ceiling, we envision these protean creators lost in rapt attention to their great breakthroughs. Such *Ahas!*, however, are invariably preceded by long periods of steady concentration on a subject, whether in art or science, business or politics, punctuated by spells of "incubation," when the mind's searchlight seemingly shifts elsewhere. After spending years thinking about the individual's rights and studying the views of the English philosopher John Locke as well as his own august peers, Thomas Jefferson could "dash off" the revolutionary Declaration of Independence in a matter of days.

On the more immediate level, creativity also involves focusing on your target in a way that turns a spark of inspiration into a burst of fireworks. Serious composers including Brahms, Ravel, and Bartók based major orchestral works on phrases from folk or popular music, for example, and like a melody or James's dot, a thought must be developed and embroidered on if it is to achieve its full potential. In a fortuitous circular dynamic, whenever you engage in a creative activity, you boost your level of positive emotion, which in turn literally widens your attentional range, giving you more material to work with. As James says, the generative mind is "full of copious and original associations," so that attending to the germ of an idea soon leads to "all sorts of fascinating consequences."

CONSIDERING HER ANIMATE subject matter, it's not surprising that Honsaker's cozy, agreeably cluttered home, shared with three dogs and a cat, is less like the predictable minimalist artist's loft than a rustic lodge. Even her clock tweets rather than chimes. Seated between a crackling woodstove and a bronze sculpture of two hares, she talks about attention's role in her creative life and inadvertently also describes its effects on experience and well-being.

No one knows exactly what happens inside your head during the creative process. If she's working well, however, Honsaker is aware of paying rapt attention that's "really different" from her everyday experience: "When the art is coming, everything else just disappears. All of my other responsibilities fall away. There's no pressure. I can forget about mealtimes and find that although it's two a.m., I'm not tired. There's a lot of freedom in that kind of concentration."

This association of focusing and freedom recalls an imaginative experiment that suggests that at such moments, the brain releases its brakes, allowing the mind to let loose. The Johns Hopkins Hospital ear, nose, and throat specialist Charles Limb, who's also an amateur jazz saxophonist, asked six pianists to play a keyboard while undergoing fMRI scanning. When they improvised on their own—the keystone of all kinds of creativity—the musicians' brains went into a "dissociated frontal activity state," a.k.a. "being in the zone." Neurological activity associated with self-monitoring and inhibition decreased, which increased their ability to process new stimuli and ideas. When they played a standard tune, however, the musicians' brains didn't respond in this way. Limb suspects that other forms of improvisation, even conversation, involve the same type of brain activity as playing jazz and plans to investigate that possibility with subjects who aren't artists.

The presumably special nature of brains such as Einstein's, Bach's, Shakespeare's, and those of other protean creators has inspired much speculation. Along with their other unparalleled gifts, the sheer *muchness* of their works bespeaks a prodigious capacity for attention. Listening to the sublime trio in the first act of Mozart's *Così Fan Tutte*, called "Soave sia il vento," the density of stimuli—the layers and layers of beauty—makes you wonder that any one mind could attend to so many intricate things at the same time.

In attentional terms, the super-rich, thickety networks of Mozart's brain enabled him to focus on and absorb information effortlessly and to process very complex things that most of us would have to work on sequentially as if they were a single unit. His focal spotlight shone forth in an especially expansive radius, illuminating more "winners" in the competition for his awareness. Because such a brain can simultaneously represent many more things than the average model, it has many more sources of inspiration to elaborate on and can create a bigger, deeper reality for us lesser mortals to wonder at.

CREATIVITY IS MOST commonly associated with the arts, but for more than thirty years, the Harvard psychologist Ellen Langer has applied hers primarily to the study of human behavior. In fact, her inventive approach to research inspired Jennifer Aniston to coproduce and star in an upcoming movie based on an elaborate experiment Langer conducted back in

1979. First, she created a complete environment from the year 1959, right down to its magazines, newspapers, and music. Then she told her subjects, elderly men who had volunteered to live in the setting for seven days, to start thinking, talking, and otherwise acting as they had twenty years before. In a stunning demonstration of the power of mind over matter, after a week of focusing on their salad days, the old men grew visibly younger—not just in their frisky attitude, but even in their physiology. Medical examinations showed that they stood straighter and were more flexible. Even their fingers, which shorten with age, grew longer.

Not many psychologists could envision such an imaginative research project, much less execute it in detail, but Langer is not your average scientist. Long before she started painting a few years ago, she was bringing an artist's fresh perspective to the study of the effects of "mindfulness," or purposeful attention, on learning, health, work, and, most recently, creativity. Like James, she believes that this active, searching way of focusing lies at the very heart of inventiveness.

The term *mindfulness* wouldn't be necessary, says Langer, if most people didn't have such an impoverished, static understanding of what "paying attention" means. Over many years, she has asked children and instructors in very different kinds of schools a simple but telling question: "What does it mean when a teacher asks students to pay attention, focus, concentrate on something?" Invariably, the answer is something like "To hold that thing still." In other words, most people think of attention as a kind of mental camera that you keep rigidly, narrowly focused on a particular subject or object. This realization led Langer to two important conclusions: "When students have trouble paying attention, they're doing what their teachers say they should do. The problem is that it's the wrong instruction."

In contrast to this fixed, tunnel-vision mode of focusing, the creative, mindful attention described in James's dot exercise or deployed by Honsaker when she conjures up a wild animal on paper is an active, probing exploration of a target that becomes more interesting as you search for new facets to consider. "Stare at your finger," says Langer. "The more things you notice about it—a hangnail, a little bit of dirt, whatever—the easier it is to stay attentive."

As the great architect Mies van der Rohe famously said, "God is in the details." That principle keeps Honsaker both absorbed in her work, she says, and able to "bring an animal to life." Because it's the little things that make a creature seem individual and engaging, she says, "I try to get down everything I can. I want to be as familiar with that animal as I am with my dog. And when I pet his head, I recognize every bump!"

Mindful attention helps you work more efficiently and creatively, but it also makes life more fun. When she thinks about the pleasures of intently focusing on a picture, "the word *wholeness* comes to mind," says Honsaker. "I know my art is a gift, and that I'm using something that I'm meant to use. One reason why I sometimes forget to eat when I'm in the studio is because I'm being fed in a different way." Because this kind of positive emotion expands your actual focus, your increased élan vital deepens your concentration on your subject. Underscoring this two-way connection between attention and pleasure, Langer says, "Whatever we engage with becomes engaging. If you say to someone who knows nothing about birds, 'Just listen to that brown thrush,' your words may fall on deaf ears. But an ornithologist will notice many things when she attends to that sound and have a richer experience."

Illustrating the connections among attention, engagement, and affection, Langer says, "Imagine that you've had the same spouse for many years. If you look for a way in which he's different today, you'll find something. That makes him more interesting and, probably, more likable." Similarly, whether or not you care for football, the more you notice various things about a game—"even if it's just the players' rear ends," says Langer—the more you'll like it and be able to focus on it without strain. "If something is enjoyable, you don't need other reasons to do it. Mindfulness feels good, so this way of paying attention reinforces itself."

An early painting of Langer's dog Sparky embodies the links between focus and fun. Although it's executed in a quirky style that's very different from Honsaker's realism, Sparky's picture is engaging, not least because it radiates much of its subject's energy and enthusiasm. The work's originality and immediacy support Langer's assertion that "the footprint of mindfulness is left in whatever you do." Her Sparky may not be conventionally accurate, she says, "but it's lovable and brings a smile to my face. I painted it without any idea of what I was doing, so it reminds me to not hesitate to try new things. That I and others enjoy it reminds me that perfection is silly and doesn't really exist."

The same symbiotic relationships among attention, engagement, and enjoyment come across when Honsaker discusses the evolution of a very different canine portrait. When she began working from photos of Sheena, a local family's beloved dog, she honored the owners' desire to capture their late pet's soulful eyes. As she got more involved with her subject, however, Honsaker added some insights of her own. Sheena's noble carriage was inspired by photographs of a wolf. Because Sheena loved to be outdoors, she decided to portray the dog in a grassy setting. "I pay a lot of attention to an animal's personality—gregarious, fierce, mellow—and to the best way to convey it," she says. "With dogs, one should be shown curled up on the couch, another with a herd of sheep or cattle, and another ready to play with a toy."

Her evolution as a self-taught artist convinces Langer that taking on a creative challenge—learn to build a bookshelf, cook Sicilian cuisine, sail to the Caribbean—is a great way to catapult yourself into a new world of mindful attention. "God knows why I even tried to paint," she says. "There was no reason to think I'd enjoy it, but I just began anyway. Now it's something I do all the time." After all, she says, for most of us, the real reward of deciding to focus on writing poetry, playing classical guitar, or engaging in some other creative activity is not to achieve some official standard of proficiency but to embark on a "personal renaissance."

FROM OUR FIRST years in the educational system, society has ways of discouraging the expansive, questing mode of attention that's essential to creativity and personal rebirth. In one poignant indication of what happens when young children learn to switch off active focusing and just go through the motions, second-graders from different schools were given a problem to solve: "There are twenty-six sheep and ten goats on a ship. How old is the captain?" Nearly 90 percent of students from traditional classrooms answered "Thirty-six." Not one pointed out that the problem didn't make sense, compared to almost a third of the kids from less conventional, more mindful classrooms. As a teacher, Langer tries not to let academe's conventional wisdom stifle her own Harvard students' innovative thinking: "When grading papers, I look for what they're trying to say, rather than what they *should* say."

A clever little study suggests the consequences of mindful and mindless attention where adult creativity is concerned. First, Langer showed her subjects an unfamiliar object. Then, she encouraged one group to accept her definition of it: "This *is* a dog's chew toy." She prompted a second group to consider the thing on their own as well: "This *could be* a dog's chew toy." Next, by Langer's design, the need for an eraser arose. Only the participants in the second group responded by using the "chew toy" for a new purpose. Inventive cooks, for whom a recipe is just a starting point, exemplify this "sideways" learning, which encourages variation on the rules. In contrast, mindlessly following a cookbook's highly specific instructions causes your mind to "snap shut like a clam on ice," says Langer, freezing out inspiration and innovation.

After studying how our capacity for paying active, mindful attention gets stifled by institutions and conventions, Langer has identified several damaging "myths." The first is the notion that there are certain basic laws governing the status quo—the way it is—which you must accept without question until they become second nature. Offering an everyday example of this mindless attitude, she points out that although most people are right-handed, the fork is always put to the left of the plate. In far more important matters, right up to the meaning of life, acquiescence to a single way of understanding something means that you stop attending to reality, go on autopilot, and squelch any fresh ideas about how to do things better, or at least in your own way.

Whether your personal renaissance involves taking up drawing or playing the ukulele, you're bound to confront the stultifying myth that only talented experts know the one right way to do the thing. When she felt frustrated over not being able to paint a conventionally correct horse, Langer did some research in art history and found countless variations on the equine theme. As she says, in painting, gardening, or any other endeavor, "everything is the same until it's not. Either you can do a thing or don't yet know if you can. The question isn't 'Can I?' but 'How to?'"

The tyranny of evaluation is another major roadblock on the intertwined paths of mindful attention and creativity. Instead of focusing on the process of playing the flute or designing your own holiday cards, you can get sandbagged by fears that the result might not be perfect. To Langer, flaws and mistakes are neither bad nor good, but "just things you do." Because it also focuses on assessment rather than experience, she says, "praise is as bad as blame."

Several other mindless wet blankets threaten to smother your creativity. You might assume that forgetting is always a lapse or problem, for example, when in fact it often lets you experience something anew. (Indeed, Paul MacLean, the NIMH's late pioneer of behavioral neuroscience, thought that part of orgasm's charm derives from the fact that for neuroanatomical reasons, the experience can't be fully stored in memory, so that each is something of a pleasant surprise.) Then too, you might accept that single-pointed concentration is always best and distractions are always bad, even though going off on a tangent can lead you to exciting new discoveries. Indeed, becoming exasperated with a project and doing something else for a while allows creativity's non-conscious incubaton phase to advance the process. When her work isn't going so well and she gets frustrated, Honsaker says, "that can be good, too. The next morning, I can usually see what the problem was and try something new."

After forty years, Honsaker has learned to keep focusing on her art and navigating past the obstacles to creativity, but it has been a long process. Although she has always been drawn to wild creatures, while studying art at UCLA, she felt pushed to paint in the era's fashionable abstract style. It was only after graduation that she found her perfect medium in pastel, taught a course in animal art at the San Diego Zoo, and took a job with the Audubon Society, which eventually brought her to the Rockies and the life of the kind of artist she wanted to be. "Picasso and I could both paint a mouse, but we'd focus on capturing different things," she says. "Those mice would look very different!"

THE SEARCHING, ACTIVE ATTENTIVENESS that's second nature to Honsaker in her studio carries over into certain of her other pursuits. Majestic in stature and mien, she's one of those quietly remarkable silver-haired women who are the backbones of America's small towns and rural hamlets. Until recently, she was the children's librarian, renowned for her storytelling and artistic projects. At her log-cabin community church, she started a garden to supplement a food bank for the disadvantaged and inaugurated a green market where local folk can sell their produce. Of the two-hundred-mile round trip each week that stocking the market requires, she says, "That's a creative, focused activity too, and a very important one for someone who spends a lot of time alone in the studio."

In an ideal world, the state of intense focus that obtains when you're painting, dancing, or concocting a new dessert would be your baseline condition: the way you are all the time, not just when you're being "creative." As Langer says, "You'd do whatever you're doing and stay mindful all day." In her view, it's not necessary to take time out to sit and meditate, which is after all a practice that's designed to provoke postmeditative mindfulness. Instead, you can cut to the chase and just practice mindful attention. "This way of 'meditating' is fun, easy, and pleasant," she says, "and its consequence is the essence of being happy, effective, and healthy—no small thing."

Symptoms such as locking the keys in the car, forgetting whether you turned off the oven, or becoming judgmental indicate you've left the attentive, creative state and reverted to autopilot. "Part of the problem is that when you're mindless, you don't realize it," says Langer. "You're not 'here' to know you're not here." To her, mindlessness would make sense only in situations in which it's productive or in which circumstances don't change. Because you can't know either of those things in advance, she says, "it's always better to be mindful. Once you realize that this is the way you should feel all of the time, the moment you don't, a bell goes off that something's not right. You feel the transition to mindlessness, and the more you see it, the more you see it."

Psychologists used to speak of "well-being" rather than "happiness," but no matter what it's called, says Langer, "the way to achieve it is being mindful. So many studies of different kinds now measure its positive changes on affect. I try to resist thinking of mindfulness as a panacea, but I really do believe it's the essence of authenticity, creativity, spirituality, and charisma."

OF CREATIVITY'S MANY integers, attention is one of the most important. Whether your form of expression involves concocting a sauce, decorating a room, or writing a poem, you need both an active, exploratory focus on the matter at hand and the long-term concentration required to gain the knowledge and skills that support true mastery.

The best weapon against the ideas and attitudes—from "the one right way" to "experts know best"—that stifle creativity yet abound in our schools and other institutions is a vigorous, searching, questioning, elaborative style of focusing. When you pay rapt attention, your spirits lift, expanding your cognitive range and creative potential, and perhaps even poising you for that personal renaissance.

CHAPTER 10

Focus Interruptus

All day long, you depend on attention to help you make sense of your external and internal worlds, support your identity, and enable you to love and work. Yet if you've ever assembled a shopping list while driving home from the office, listening to the news, and feeling guilty that you haven't called your aged mother, you know that your focus sometimes seems more like a rickety mental machine designed by Rube Goldberg than a seamless laser beam of concentration. That more people claim to have this distracted experience more of the time reflects a sudden major cultural change, whose effects scientists are still trying to assess, and the anxiety it arouses.

In little more than a decade, computers and the Internet, cell phones and BlackBerries have become surrogate body parts that enable nonstop attention to myriad sources of information and entertainment as well as great numbers of other people. This technological bonanza creates a major expansion of the targets for your focus and a potential drain on its finite resources. Despite the widespread lamentations that our machines are driving us crazy in general and ruining our concentration in particular, the truth is more complicated. A short review of attention's interaction with memory, or the storage and retrieval of information, and learning, which is the acquisition of knowledge and skills, helps put things in the right perspective.

Few people have a better gut-level understanding of this mental ecosystem than Scott Hagwood. For four years running, from his debut in 2001, he won the USA Memory Championship, which involves feats such as memorizing exhaustive lists of names, digits, and even a fifty-line poem. The training regimen for this cognitive Kentucky Derby is based on a simple, stunning fact. By and large, if you want to learn and remember something—a new neighbor's name or the directions to the restaurant—you really have to pay attention to it. If you don't, the information probably won't make it to your short-term much less long-term memory, where what you've learned is stored. As a result, you end up waving a wordless hello and asking again at the next gas station.

Sometimes, paying attention is a process that Hagwood charitably describes as "occurring on lots of levels. For instance, right now, I see the light and hear the soft hum of the computer. I just tasted a little bit of coffee." When he describes his rapt focus when he settles down to work, however, his language becomes literally and figuratively muscular: "I take my powers of attention, move aside all the extraneous stuff, and focus completely on the material. When you become great with memory, you become naturally superfocused. At work, I often become so engrossed that I have to set the alarm clock, so that I remember to stop and do whatever else I have planned that day."

A memory champ's pièce de résistance—locking down the order of an entire deck of shuffled cards in less than one minute—is a textbook illustration of attention's basic mechanism of selecting and enhancing your target and suppressing the competition. To pull it off, says Hagwood, "you can't be distracted," and he's not just talking about turning off your cell phone. Because the world tournaments take place in a room holding some sixty people, the contestants wear earplugs to minimize any sound. To eliminate visual distractions, he says, "the Germans wear these little eyeglasses that have sides on them. Some of them will actually face the wall, so they can't see anything at all other than their own movements. That's how important staying focused is."

The Olympian mental effort that this level of attending, remembering, and learning requires comes across in Hagwood's account of trying to memorize the names of all 106 people in a television show's audience. His tactic was to create a powerful link with the new information by shaking a person's hand while listening to the name, then associating it with someone he already knew. "The thing is," he says, "it got so intense that after a little while, the audience became really quiet. I said to them, 'The silence is palpable. You should see the focus, the attention, you're giving to me. It's kind of frightening.' A woman said, 'Well, you should see the attention you're giving us. It's quite frightening.' They were mirroring what I was doing."

IF SCOTT HAGWOOD is at one end of the attention-learning-memory spectrum, many Americans feel that they're sliding way down toward the other. Their concern notwithstanding, new research increasingly shows that usually, glitches and lapses in attention are not signs of incipient ADHD or Alzheimer's disease, but normal, even sometimes beneficial, mental phenomena.

Everyone who has an intact brain can focus, but some people are much better at it than others. Like every human trait or ability, attention can be plotted on a bell-shaped curve, with many individuals clustered toward the middle and fewer toward each tail. Those at one end are champion focusers, and those at the other are said to suffer from "attention deficit." As Northwestern neurologist Marsel Mesulam observes, we don't know what causes these variations in the capacity to attend, "in the same way that we don't know what makes people math or chess or violin geniuses—or not. The entire issue of human talents and normal variations is very poorly understood. To say that someone has an attention deficit may not be so different from saying he has a musical or poetry deficit. We talk about ADHD because attention is important in Western society. Nobody tests us for singing or hunting ability, but those talents would also be distributed unevenly in the population, with some of us performing very poorly."

When writing about two common attentional styles, William James pictures the mind as an archer's target. Some people, he says, naturally focus on the bull's-eye, "sink into a subject of meditation deeply, and, when interrupted, are 'lost' for a moment before they come back to the outer world." For others, however, the target's outer rings are "filled with something like meteoric showers of images" that flare at random, distracting attention from the bull's-eye and carrying thoughts in various directions. Such persons "find their attention wandering every minute, and must bring it back by a voluntary pull."

It's often assumed that really smart people find it easy to focus, but attention researchers, beginning with James, question that notion. Perhaps thinking of some of his Harvard colleagues, he took pains to make clear that neither the "bull's-eye" nor "meteoric" mode of paying attention is necessarily good or bad per se: "Some of the most efficient workers I know are of the ultra-scatterbrained type." The reason, he says, is that a person's total "mental efficiency" derives from the combination of all his faculties, the most important of which is not attention, but "the strength of his desire and passion." Compared to a more naturally focused but less motivated person, the individual who really cares for a subject "will return to it incessantly from his incessant wanderings, and first and last do more with it, and get more results from it."

Just as there are normal variations in the ability to attend, there are "normal" attentional problems. That proverbial professor is not the only person to suffer from so-called absentmindedness. When you drive past your own freeway exit, it's far less likely to be a symptom of a disorder than an indication that you were too distracted by musing on some juicy gossip or singing along with your favorite golden oldie on the radio to attend properly to your space-time coordinates. If you can't remember where you put your cell phone, the probable reason is that you were focusing on something else when you put it down, so that information either didn't get properly encoded in your memory or can't be retrieved at will. Interestingly, as that professor's erudition suggests, absentmindedness has little or nothing to do with a person's general capacity for memory.

More consolation can be found in research that shows that you often attend to and learn things without even trying. Notwithstanding the importance of "explicit" learning, which requires effortful attention, as when you memorize verb conjugations, you also benefit from plenty of the "implicit" sort, which you seem to pick up by osmosis, as when you "just know" something. If you're given a list of flowers and asked to identify the red ones, later on, you very well might recall as many or even more of the whole list than someone who had been told to memorize it—an explicit task. Implicit learning doesn't mean that you didn't pay attention to the information, but that you processed it without intending to. Indeed, this process underlies the acquisition of many complicated real-life skills, from grammatical speech to playing a sport to pinch-of-this, dab-of-that cooking, as well as exciting "Eureka!" moments.

At first glance, recent research that indicates your brain probably spends even more time wandering than you fear seems like bad news. Studies by Jonathan Schooler, a psychologist at the University of British Columbia in Vancouver, show that even when you're supposedly reading, you're daydreaming about 15 to 20 percent of the time, often without realizing it. Surveys of high school and college students suggest that their minds wander from schoolwork up to about half and a third of the time, respectively.

Common wisdom notwithstanding, there's growing evidence that mind-wandering is a basic mental function that can boost your efficiency, creativity, and well-being. When you're not paying attention to anything in particular, your brain is busily maintaining its still-mysterious "default" state. In this baseline mode, large areas that are relatively quiet when you perform tasks become activated. When you're daydreaming, your baseline network is activated, which supports the educated guess that its function is to accommodate such poorly understood mental processes.

Not focusing on what you're allegedly doing sounds like a big problem, but sometimes it actually makes you more productive. After all, if you're walking, driving, sweeping the floor, or doing anything else that doesn't require your full attention, your thoughts might as well stray to your weekend plans, dinner menu, or that roman à clef you could write about your dysfunctional family. A certain amount of daydreaming at school or the office can even help you solve problems. In contrast to maintaining an unblinking, rigid focus on a dilemma, allowing your thoughts to stray opens you up to fresh perspectives and useful information from seemingly unrelated areas.

Where big breakthroughs are concerned, getting to "That's it!" requires not only the intense focus and explicit learning associated with the furrowed brow of a Thomas Edison or Marie Curie, but also plenty of incubation, mind-wandering, and implicit learning. In a typical scenario, your brain's executive cortex first bears down on the problem du jour with all of its double-barreled top-down concentration, advancing things as far as cognitive processes can. Then you get tired or fed up, shove back your chair, and say to yourself, "Enough of that!"

When you head to the cafeteria or gym and start paying attention to something else, nonconscious parts of your mind slow-cook your earlier insights into the problem and supply associations; the brain's right hemisphere, which has long been associated with so-called holistic reasoning, intuition, and artistry, seems especially involved in this incubation process. Then, walking back to work, you see the solution whole.

This special alchemy of attention and distraction, information and inspiration enabled Einstein, after many years of work, "suddenly" to see the theory of relativity not while bent over his desk, but in a dream: "Like a giant die making an indelible impress, a huge map of the universe outlined itself in one clear vision." On a more quotidian plane of experience, the same combination of cerebration and woolgathering, and even counting sheep, allows you to wrestle with a question all day—should you take the better job in the less desirable city or paint the living room fire-engine red?—then "sleep on it," and awake with the solution.

Finally, not paying attention to anything in particular sometimes just plain feels good. Research conducted by the University of Michigan psychologists Rachel and Stephen Kaplan shows that when you gaze dreamily at drifting clouds, twinkling stars, rippling water, or other natural stimuli, you drift into a soft-focused state of "fascination" that allows your mind to relax and unwind, reduces the incidence of dumb "human errors," and even lowers physiological measures of stress.

SOME SEEMING PROBLEMS, such as reasonable amounts of daydreaming, spacing out, and distraction, are adaptive variations on attention, but others are not. Perhaps you've tried to be more productive by making calls while emptying your in-box or dishwasher, only to forget whom you phoned when she picks up. Yakking away while keeping one eye on your computer, maybe you've hit "Reply" instead of "Forward," thus sending your snarky e-mail comment to the very person you least wanted to receive it. If so, you've experienced multitasking's major effect on your attention.

Thanks to the electronics revolution, the possibility of doing several things at once, which formerly mostly concerned pilots and other techies, has become a major cultural preoccupation. People in the trenches may still be debating its benefits and drawbacks, but science has determined that multitasking is for most practical purposes a myth, and that heeding its siren call leads to inefficiency and even danger.

There are certain situations in which you easily perform two rote functions at once, as when you walk and chew gum at the same time. You also readily combine different forms of perception. At the movies, for example, you seamlessly process the audio and visuals, which "go together" and merge into a single multidimensional entity. When they don't, as in a badly dubbed foreign film, you're soon addled by attending to the conflict between the soundtrack and the actors' faces.

Multitasking's real trouble sets in when you try to focus on two demanding activities simultaneously. The Cornell psychologist Ulric Neisser proved that after an enormous amount of practice, his subjects could learn to take dictation and read at the same time. However, acquiring the skill takes months of drilling and is confined to those particular tasks. For most people most of the time, attempts to combine such "higher order" chores fail or are flawed.

Multitasking's most obvious drawback is inefficiency. In many cases, your ability to do two things simultaneously is impaired because both tasks draw on one or more of the same information-processing systems in the brain. For activities that involve language, such as conversing, watching TV, or simply thinking, for example, there's just one major channel through which you send input and receive output. There are occasional exceptions to the rule, says David Meyer, a cognitive scientist at the University of Michigan in Ann Arbor, but generally, "if you're, say, trying to listen to someone on the phone while typing an e-mail, something has to give."

You may *think* you're multitasking when you're listening to your boss's report while texting your lunch date, but what you're really doing is switching back and forth between activities. Despite your fond hopes, the extra effort involved actually makes you less rather than more productive; your overall performance will be inefficient, error-prone, and more time-consuming than if you had done one thing at a time. As one attention expert ruefully observed after writing a book, "if your train of thought is interrupted even for a second, you have to go back and say, 'Where was I?' There are start-up costs each time as you reload everything into memory. Multitasking exacts a price, and people aren't as good at it as they think they are."

Multitasking not only is inefficient but can also be dangerous, even lethal. Illustrating the risk of operating machinery while engaged in another activity, one scientist recalls that while he was listening to a football game and driving, his car started swerving all over the road; seeing the match in his head conflicted with his visual attention to the reality in front of him. If the traffic worsens or a car swerves into your lane while you're driving, you can turn off the radio or stop chatting with a passenger, but the situation is more difficult if you're talking on the phone— especially if seconds count and you're going 60 miles per hour. Hundreds of thousands of cell-related traffic accidents each year make plain that the car-phone combination is unsafe, potentially deadly, and should be completely illegal.

Anyone who has ever had to read the same paragraph twice understands why the connections among attention, memory, and learning are especially important for students—the very people most attracted to multitasking. Using fMRI imaging, UCLA psychologists found that when you focus on a demanding task, your brain's hippocampus, which is important to memory, is in charge. However, if you try to work while distracted by instant messaging or the like, the striatum, which is involved in rote activities, takes over. As a result, even if you get the job done, your recollection of it will be more fragmented, less adaptable, and harder to retrieve than it would be if you had given it your undivided attention.

American youths spend an average of 6.5 hours per day focused on the electronic world, and many put in much more time there. Stunningly, up to a third say they're involved with more than one medium most of the time. The young seem to enjoy switching their attention from target to target more than older people, but scientists don't yet know what long-range impact this huge new cultural change will have on growing brains and minds.

Of the possible ways in which multitasking can interfere with education, the most obvious is the fact that you can't process information very well if you're attending to something else at the same time. Ideally, children, whose brains are in the most active stages of development, would focus on acquiring the basic knowledge and abilities that will be most important to them later. If they don't get the necessary training and experience at the appropriate stages of growth, their potential mastery is reduced.

Offering a personal example, Meyer says, "I know that learning tennis is best done between the ages of eight and fifteen. The longer you delay, the harder it will be, and your ability to play will suffer—as mine did. This principle applies to all sorts of skills, both physical and mental, including the ability to concentrate, direct your focus at will, and manage your time." Kids also need to work at developing the capacity for the concentrated, sustained attention required to succeed in many endeavors, not just the skill of flitting among them, he says: "Einstein didn't invent the theory of relativity while he was multitasking at the Swiss patent office."

Multitasking also raises serious concerns about the shallow focus on the world that it encourages, reinforced by the flip, casual, rapid-fire style of electronic communications. Eloquent testimony comes from five of Japan's ten best-selling novels in 2007, which were composed on cell phones. Not surprisingly, these romances, which were written by young women in the truncated, text-messaging style, fail to approach the depth of *Anna Karenina* or even *Bridget Jones's Diary*. Intellectuals lament this dubious new art form and blame manga, Japan's ubiquitous comic books, but there have been no complaints from the huge cell-phone industry.

Rather than alienate the young Western and Eastern consumers who drive the market, powerful communications companies increasingly cater to kids' preference for qwik-n-ez information that can be grasped in smaller and smaller bits, encouraging a superficial mentality that's only lightly disguised by keyboard athletics. The young can get away with IM-ing while playing a computer game or the like, but there's a risk: if you grow up assuming that you can pay attention to several things at once, you may not realize that the way in which you process such information is superficial at best. When you're finally forced to confront intellectually demanding situations in high school or college, you may find that you've traded depth of knowledge for breadth and stunted your capacity for serious thought.

Along with the costs to strong learning and deep thinking, hours spent in the thrall of alluring machines exact a toll from your attention to actual human beings. At the very least, time online is subtracted from real world interactions, such as conversation, sharing a meal, or even having sex. (Indeed, in one Italian study, couples who had a TV in the bedroom had intercourse only half as often as those who didn't.) Accustomed to triaging your electronic contacts, you might also find yourself wondering if actually talking to someone just because she's your neighbor or he's your uncle is the best use of your valuable time. The young in particular might fail to consider how many people in their electronic address book really know them and would be there for them if they needed help, as a friend or relative does and would.

ONE NATURAL REACTION to anxiety about feeling distracted and unfocused is to look for a way to improve your capacity to pay attention.

Considering the need, there are surprisingly few simple, effective strategies to date, but encouraging research is under way.

Some of the easiest tricks to improve your focus have been employed
by great teachers since students first wriggled at their desks. As a lifelong
professor of philosophy and psychology, William James knew all too well
that some things are just plain more interesting than others. As Elizabeth
Barrett Browning wrote in a sonnet, "How do I love thee? Let me count
the ways." Yet he argued that even a tedious topic can take on a certain
fascination if you make an effort to look at it afresh: "The subject must
be made to show new aspects of itself; to prompt new questions; in a
word, to change. From an unchanging subject the attention inevitably
wanders away."

Tapping his own store of pedagogical know-how, James urges you to
enliven dull work with "frequent recapitulations, illustrations, examples,
novelty of order, and ruptures of routine." When you write a report or
the like, he says, "If the topic be inhuman, make it figure as part of a story.
If it be difficult, couple its acquisition with some prospect of personal gain.
Above all things, make sure that it shall run through certain inner
changes, since no unvarying object can possibly hold the mental field
for long."

Along with benefiting from liberal dollops of novelty and variation,
James's students probably spiked their ability to focus with a venerable psychoactive substance. In 1600, long after the Muslim world discovered
coffee's lively effect on attention, Pope Clement VIII authorized Christians
to partake of what had hitherto been "Satan's drink." Studies of "sustained
attention" show that coffee and other stimulants, as well as changing conditions, companionship, and music, help you to stay alert if you're, say,
driving across Nebraska on I-80. In one study, subjects were shown a series of capital letters, then asked whether they were the same ones they
had seen two sequences before. Those who had previously drunk some
coffee were significantly better at recalling the letters than those who

hadn't. Because caffeine not only activates brain regions responsible for attentiveness but also seems to increase short-term memory, it's popular with students as well as long-haul truckers.

Newer chemical attention-boosters such as Ritalin and other stimulants can prove more problematic than espressos and lattes. The best seller *Listening to Prozac* first examined the question of whether behavioral drugs designed to treat illnesses, such as depression, should also be used to help healthy people feel better, too. Long before Prozac, however, military personnel and certain high achievers, including William F. Buckley, Jr., had enhanced their ability to focus with drugs that are officially prescribed for people who suffer from ADHD.

In some schools, the use of attention drugs is so widespread that some parents feel pressured into medicating any child who isn't performing well. Significant numbers of normally attentive students already take these agents to write term papers and to study for and take exams. For that matter, as one researcher says, "I have plenty of highly esteemed colleagues who take Ritalin before a speech or when reviewing a grant to improve their ability to concentrate at a very high level." As the quality, variety, and use of psychopharmacological agents increase, it's easy to imagine scenarios in which healthy people working in competitive schools or offices would take an attention-enhancing drug, such as the newer agent modafinil, in order to function at 110 percent, thereby putting unmedicated peers at a disadvantage.

Considering the drawbacks of behavioral drugs, notably their side effects and often uncertain consequences over the long term, the idea of improving attention through some sort of training has a lot of appeal. According to David Meyer, such regimens can work, at least within particular environments: "Air traffic controllers are very good at managing their attentional and multitasking skills in their work setting. But to what extent are they also able to use those same skills in the home or classroom?"

Some new attentional workouts use computer screens as gyms. In their work with young children, University of Oregon psychologists Michael Posner and Mary Rothbart have shown that such exercises can markedly increase the capacity for executive attention, thus improving memory, self-regulation, and the ability to plan and reason. In a study of adults, subjects were presented with from one to five columns of numbers on a screen, then later asked whether the digits had already been displayed. In the first trial, they were much faster with the one-column version. After about seven sessions, however, they could perform as quickly with four columns as with one. In other words, through practice, they had expanded their capacity to focus.

One commercially available computerized mental workout, the Brain Fitness program, uses attention drills to tune up elders' cognitive functioning. Designed by Michael Merzenich, a UCSF neuroscientist who helped develop the cochlear implant for the treatment of deafness, this four-hundred-dollar software operates on the principle that, like your muscles and joints, your brain is subject to the "use it or lose it" rule. For an hour a day over eight weeks, seniors log on to a computer and perform a series of repetitive, progressively demanding exercises. Judging whether tones are rising or falling, say, or distinguishing between "bo" and "do" or "shee" and "chee," requires close attention and puts the brain through its paces. The idea is that the effort builds and strengthens neural pathways, which improves both the brain's ability to crunch information and the user's mood. The scientific jury is still out on the effectiveness of such regimens, but some users report improvement on their performance on the drills and in daily functioning.

Particularly considering the lack of other well-developed, safe, and readily accessible tools to improve attention, some type of meditation, or practice derived from it, looks like the best way to enhance your ability to focus and perhaps enjoy other benefits too, such as improved well-being.

· · ·

HER INVESTIGATION OF training attention to improve daily experience began with what the Penn cognitive neuroscientist Amishi Jha calls a "defining moment" in her own life, albeit one common to a legion of exhausted, harried professional women with families. Juggling the demands of the tenure track, research, teaching, and a husband and small child had jacked up her stress level so high that just before giving an important lecture, she was clenching her jaw and grinding her teeth so much that she lost all feeling in them. "I knew I had to make a choice," she says. "It was change my life or change my mind."

Because its stress-relieving potential is backed by a lot of research, Jha bought a couple of manuals and began to do daily, nonsectarian, breath-focused mindfulness meditation. In attentional parlance, she selected the present moment and made it salient, while suppressing the mind's usual jumble of reactive thoughts and feelings. A month later, Jha felt more relaxed and able to cope. To her surprise, like many of Richard Davidson's subjects, she also felt more focused.

Just as she concentrated on her breath during meditation, Jha found that she could concentrate on her work at the lab or on her family at home, undistracted by her other responsibilities. This increased feeling of control over a demanding life combined with her sophisticated scientific background to produce an epiphany. "I thought, 'I could actually study this!'" she says. "And that's what I'm trying to do in my work. To learn how to harness attention—to transform and improve it through training."

To explore the effectiveness of various attentional regimens, different groups of Jha's subjects learn different types of meditation, which they practice daily. Periodically, they report to her lab, where they're tested on objective focusing tasks. Like other research, her results show that practices that require you to concentrate on a target, such as your breath, strengthen attention's selective orienting system, which increases your ability to focus in real-life situations; she also finds improvement in short-term memory.

Recently, Jha has been investigating another mode of focusing and the type of training that seems to enhance it. Science mostly talks about attention as a restriction and filtering of information, but Jha is interested in the process of actively broadening, rather than narrowing, your focus: a different kind of selection. To illustrate the difference in the single-pointed and expansive ways of attending, she describes an experiment in which she gives her subjects three words—*bull*, *shoe*, *car*—then asks for a fourth term that relates to all of them.

There are two distinct ways of working out answers to such a "compound remote associate" problem, each of which seems to spring from a different way of paying attention. Some people take an analytic approach and actively zero in on the various possibilities in a methodical, winnowing fashion—does this word fit, or that one—until they arrive at *horn*. However, others seem to rely on intuition; they relax and allow their focus to expand. "They explain that they don't have anything in particular in mind," says Jha, "then Boom! The word just comes to them. They simply let it emerge."

Just as there seems to be an open, expansive way of attending, there's a type of meditation that's broader and more receptive than the familiar restrictive, breath-focused sort. In this practice, you simply throw up the windows of your awareness and let the moment, or some sensory dimension of it, flood in. You might focus on the clouds drifting across the sky or the sound of waves or a rushing stream. (This wide-open style of practice brings to mind research on how positive emotions broaden attention, and Jha is investigating that connection with Barbara Fredrickson.) Compared with subjects who use the more selective mindfulness technique and improve their real-life orienting ability, Jha finds that those who practice attending in a broadly receptive state enhance their alerting system, which helps smooth the transitions from one target to another in daily life.

As she continues her research, Jha finds that her definition of attention keeps evolving and expanding. "It's a tool that can be used in many ways, and not just for selecting between relevant and irrelevant information. Where I'd like to go is to regard attention as 'the ability to frame your field of awareness in the way that will be most useful to the task at hand.' You could restrict or broaden your focus according to your cognitive, affective, even somatic context."

As to the power of focus to create experience and generate well-being, Jha says, "You hear it all the time now—'Energy flows where attention goes.' If you can harness your own ability to focus and build that skill into the way you operate, that's going to affect how you handle the stress in your life."

WHETHER YOU'RE A child trying to grasp the rudiments of language or a poet perfecting a sonnet, attention has shaped your identity and experience by enabling you to learn and remember. When distractions interfere with that process, your ability to store information and acquire knowledge and skills suffers. That said, as suggested by the hyperactive title of a recent book—*CrazyBusy: Overstretched, Overbooked, and About to Snap! Strategies for Coping in a World Gone ADD*—it has become almost routine to profess that you're overwhelmed by the demands on your attention and dread an incipient deficit disorder.

Where fears about the ability to focus in the early twenty-first century are concerned, the truth is more complicated than most headlines and sound bites suggest. Many attentional lapses are not only normal but even beneficial. All minds wander sometimes, and they often stray in productive directions. On the other hand, embracing the vogue for multitasking, fueled by seductive electronics, can make you inefficient and even endangered. Inordinate amounts of time spent fixated on various screens and keyboards pose particular risks for young people who should be focused on learning and exact a cost in terms of real-life experience, particularly with other living, breathing people. One crucial fact often gets overlooked in laments about the electronic assault on your ability to focus: your machines are not in charge of what you attend to—you are. When they prove distracting, you have only to turn them off.

Considering attention's importance, it's surprising that coffee and Ritalin are still the most popular if imperfect ways to improve it. After a long lag, however, science has new tools in the pipeline, including not just more-sophisticated drugs but also computer programs, and focusing workouts derived from meditation. These regimens exercise attention as if it were a muscle and show that like other skills, it can be improved with old-fashioned training.

CHAPTER 11

Disordered Attention

If you've ever had trouble sitting patiently in a waiting room or grasping the instructions for a new appliance, you've experienced a tiny taste of the frustration endured day after day, year after year by children struggling with attention-deficit/hyperactivity disorder. Unlike normal hitches such as daydreaming and absentmindedness, ADHD is considered to be a psychiatric problem—the commonest one among the young—that affects as many as 5 percent of American kids and three times more boys than girls.

Particularly in the post-industrial West, a child who has a hard time focusing on schoolwork faces serious short- and long-term disadvantages. By and large, if you don't pay attention to information, you don't learn or remember it, at least not well. Moreover, many such children are also more restless, impulsive, and distractible than is usual for their ages, which makes them prone to behavioral as well as academic troubles.

Despite the prevalence of ADHD and the seriousness of its consequences, there's a stunning lack of basic knowledge about it. Scientists still don't understand exactly what it is, what causes it, or how to test for it objectively, as with a brain scan or blood sample. Doctors and other professionals can treat the disorder's symptoms, but their success varies considerably; guesstimates range from 40 to 80 percent. In fact, to say that someone has ADHD is very much like saying he has a fever: a problem that could have many origins and may or may not respond to an "aspirin" such as Ritalin.

The chasm that has separated attention researchers from clinicians is one obvious obstacle to progress in understanding ADHD. The gap dates to the 1980s, when big advances in neuroscience and psychopharmacology led to increased treatment of behavioral problems in general. Eager to formalize some diagnostic criteria, child psychiatrists devised a set of questions to help parents and teachers evaluate a child's ability to focus and control his or her behavior. While a laudable step toward clarifying the symptoms of a common problem, such information doesn't constitute scientific evidence comparable to professionals' in-depth interviews and observations of children, much less physiological measures, yet the questionnaire remains the basis for a diagnosis of ADHD.

Attention researchers tend to describe the dearth of basic knowledge about ADHD in terms like "astounding" and "appalling." "You would not believe how little work of this kind has been done," says the NIMH's Leslie Ungerleider, "and most of that concerns the hyperactivity aspect of control. There's almost nothing about how children filter distractions. Beginning with primates, we've developed good ways to test that, but none of them has ever been used for clinical assessment." Offering the clinicians' perspective, however, Javier Castellanos, a pediatric neuroscientist and child and adolescent psychiatrist at the New York University Child Study Center, says that "it's only recently, under duress from the NIMH, that many attention scientists have been willing to deign to talk to plebeian clinical investigators, which is what's required for them to appreciate the complexity of the situation, from the children's failures to the parents' desperation."

Outside the groves of academe, the fact that an awful lot of little fellows who were once said to "have ants in their pants" or were labeled "fidgety" or even "typical boys" suddenly seem to have an illness that's treated with powerful psychoactive drugs pushes a lot of cultural buttons. Many parents are understandably uneasy about giving a child daily doses of Ritalin or other agents that affect behavior, resemble abused substances, and have side effects such as moodiness and loss of appetite, as well as possible long-term health risks.

The experience of Jack S. and his parents illustrates some of the ups and downs of life with ADHD and its treatment. After a lot of "snakes and snails and puppy dogs' tails" equivocation and waiting for him to "grow up," Mr. and Mrs. S. finally consulted an educational psychologist about their ten-year-old son's lackluster academic performance. Compared to his friends and siblings, Jack found school a struggle, particularly math and foreign languages, and spent much time cooling his heels in the principal's office. After much testing, the psychologist said that Jack had a florid case of ADHD and referred them to a child psychiatrist who understood the problem and could prescribe an appropriate drug.

Jack's parents were of two minds about the idea of medication. Mrs. S. was hopeful that maybe the pills would help their son settle down and finally achieve his academic potential, but Mr. S. didn't like the idea of "resorting" to medication. Summing up this common family predicament, Ungerleider describes the two views of treating ADHD with drugs: "One way is that whatever helps kids focus on their work is a good thing, because then they won't be constantly frustrated. The other way is that we don't want to give drugs to children if we don't know the long-term effects." However, as she observes, what you attend to largely determines your experience, which in turn influences who you are. Thus, when children aren't paying attention to schoolwork and other important activities, "their brains aren't being remodeled by experience in the ways they should be," she says. "It's a very tricky issue."

After much wrangling, his parents decided that Jack would try medication. A few weeks later, the teachers and his mom thought it had helped him calm down and focus at school and on homework. His dad continued to dislike the idea. Jack said that the pills "made it easier to look at the blackboard," but took away his appetite and made him feel "weird" and, when they wore off, "grouchy."

Toward the end of high school, after years of an anxious, labor-intensive, and expensive combination of private school, math tutors, counselors, and drugs, Jack told his mother, "I don't think I really have ADHD anymore. I only have to take the pills to study for big exams." He still has some trouble with math and foreign languages, but he has just finished his first year of college, got a 3.2 average, and made the hockey team. His parents are thrilled that Jack has come so far and feels so much more in control of his experience. They also regret that he had to struggle long and hard to get where he is today and feel for the tens of thousands of kids and parents who lack the necessary resources for the battle.

NO ONE IS more aware of the discontent over the current state of knowledge about ADHD than Javier Castellanos. First, he squarely addresses the major problem, observing that "we don't have an objective way, like a blood test or genetic marker, of definitively saying 'This person has it or does not,' partly because we don't really understand what it is." Then he moves on to what he and his colleagues are doing to improve the situation, with increasingly encouraging results.

One major discovery—that ADHD isn't a single problem that springs from a single cause—is itself an important, hard-won advance. For ten years while at the NIMH, Castellanos and a multidisciplinary team intensively studied 150 children with attention problems who were enrolled in a special school set up just for them. "We really, really knew those kids," he says, "from the results of their spinal taps and blood tests to their psychological profiles." After searching the young subjects' data for some common denominators, he says, "the big thing I learned was that almost none of the kids were like any others. It was almost as if there were a hundred and fifty types of ADHD."

Just as "epilepsy" turns out to be perhaps two hundred different seizure disorders, ADHD is an umbrella term for a variety of problems that have some symptoms in common. As they did for epilepsy, new tools such as fMRI are helping to identify certain broad categories of attention difficulties, which is the first step toward developing appropriate treatments for each—a big step up from the fever-aspirin approach.

Children may attend poorly for many reasons, from lack of motivation to excessive anxiety, but like most behavior, the unfocused, fidgety sort associated with ADHD usually involves a collaboration between nature and nurture. That it's six times likelier to affect children who have been sexually abused offers tragic proof that experience can cause the disorder. Schools as well as troubled homes can fuel attention problems. According to the "perceptual load" theory, you'll experience more distractions when your task is not very engaging—a circumstance that may often obtain even in an average, much less subpar classroom. Then too, says Castellanos, "As long as a child has the full attention of an adult, he has no attention issues. But our schools are based on the Ford assembly-line model, which means serious trouble if you're not the 'typical kid,' especially in adolescence."

Biology is also involved in many if not most cases of ADHD. (Recalling a medical exam of a pair of identical twins, only one of whom had the disorder, Castellanos says that the affected child had actually had a previously undetected stroke.) According to one theory, the problem may often be rooted more in delayed but normal brain development than in some neurological deficit—a notion supported by the fact that three out of four kids outgrow it. In affected children, the brain in general and the cerebellum in particular tend to be smaller than those of kids who don't have the disorder; the possibility that drugs such as Ritalin are responsible has been ruled out.

That genes often play a role in ADHD is clear from the fact that one obvious risk factor is maleness. (Girls who have the disorder are not only far fewer in number but also rarely as hyperactive and disruptive as the boys; their poor concentration at school is often overlooked or ascribed to daydreaming or "not trying hard enough.") Attention problems also run in some families. About 25 percent of the biological parents of diagnosed kids are affected, compared with 4 percent of adoptive parents. Then too, genes that influence not just attention but also a child's activity level, impulsiveness, and other traits may contribute to ADHD. Thus, a certain student may have trouble focusing on math or Spanish less because of some cognitive deficit than from a thrill-seeking temperamental inclination to tune out what bores him and look for some real action.

Although Castellanos regards the role of genes in ADHD as "incontrovertible," the specifics identified so far are "modest in the extreme." According to one leading theory, the disorder arises from the combined influence of different genes, many of which affect the neurotransmitter dopamine. This chemical messenger, which is boosted by Ritalin, is important not only to attention and cognition, but also to the control of movement, emotion, and the ability to anticipate pleasure and reward as well as pain. If dopamine acts as a kind of chemical carrot that raises your hopes of being rewarded for doing a task—say, algebra homework—and if your brain has trouble storing or deploying the transmitter, you can probably still do the math. However, you won't do it as easily or as well as someone well stoked with dopamine. For this reason, Castellanos calls ADHD a "disorder of efficiency—or inefficiency."

Dopamine's involvement in the brain's reward circuitry may explain why individuals who've been diagnosed with ADHD are also likelier than others to smoke, drink, and use drugs. Combined with an attention

problem, this tendency toward substance abuse suggests that they're perhaps motivated less by the desire to "get high" in a recreational sense
than by the wish to feel and function better—to feel "okay" or "normal,"
if only temporarily.

Recently, the search for what he calls "the splinters that make up different attention problems" has taken Castellanos in a new direction. First,
he explains that your brain is far less concerned with your brilliant ideas
or searing emotions than with its own internal "gyroscopic busyness,"
which consumes 65 percent of its total energy. Every fifty seconds, its
activity fluctuates, causing what he calls a "brownout." No one knows the
purpose of these neurological events, but Castellanos has a thesis: the
clockwork pulses enable the brain's circuits to stay "logged on" and available to communicate with one another, even when they're not being used.
"Imagine you're a cabdriver on your day off," Castellanos says. "You don't
need to use your workday circuits on a Sunday, but to keep those channels
open, your brain sends a *ping* through them every minute or so. The fluctuations are the brain's investment in maintaining its circuits online."

Whatever their neurological raison d'être, Castellanos hopes that the
brain's brownouts will advance the understanding of ADHD. He's looking for correlations between those *ping*s, which are easily measured, and
lapses in attention, which can be gauged by how fast his research subjects
press a button when a cue appears. Those who have the disorder take
longer than normal to push the button. If such lags turn out to be connected to irregularities in the brain's periodic fluctuations, they could
serve as red flags for other differences, too, perhaps in working memory,
motivation, or other functions involved in paying attention.

Waving a book called *Attention, Memory, and Executive Function*, Castellanos summarizes its gist: "All three things are intricately related. Is light
a particle or a wave? Or a wavicle? It all depends on what you're using the
definition for, what your purpose is. Paying attention probably involves a
lot of large-scale reconfiguration of different brain systems."

Despite some breakthroughs, when scientists look at a group of people who have ADHD and try to figure out what they have in common, Castellanos says, "The truth is, we don't know. If there are, say, five broad types of causes, some people will have genetic issues and others cerebellum involvement, thyroid problems, head injury, or something else." Complexity notwithstanding, research at least clearly shows that ADHD "isn't a 'spiritual' problem, but a physical, biochemical one, elements of which we can measure. We're just scratching the surface now."

THAT THERE HAS been increased progress in basic research on ADHD is cold comfort if your child suffers from it right now, or if you're one of the minority of individuals who continue to have trouble concentrating into adulthood. As Castellanos says, "I tell parents and kids that if they can get through adolescence without making irreversible mistakes, or at least minimizing their number, brain maturation is a wonderful thing." That neurological development takes time, however, and kids struggling with ADHD must perform well enough in school and the rest of life, from recreation to relationships, to have desirable options when the time comes to apply to college, look for a job, or form lasting bonds. If they don't stay engaged in the classroom, academic failure can start a sad, well-documented downward spiral, particularly for impulsive young males, into disciplinary problems, and even delinquency, dropping out of school, and crime.

Medications such as Ritalin, Concerta, and Adderall help many kids stay on the right track. Scientists have learned that the drugs enhance the activity of dopamine but still don't know exactly how these stimulants produce their paradoxically calming effect on certain brains. Interestingly, like many psychiatric medications, they were discovered by accident. Looking for a headache remedy back in 1937, Dr. Charles Bradley tested one such drug on some children who had been institutionalized for being uncontrollable, only to be shocked when their teachers reported that the kids suddenly could sit still and learn. Some serious fears about the medications have been ruled out, notably that they somehow shrink the brain. No one disputes that they have short-term side effects and may pose long-term risks, but, says Castellanos, the drugs have been used for a long time now, and, when taken as directed, they appear to be safe.

After weighing the possible costs against the potential benefits, Castellanos favors at least trying medication. If he had a child who had ADHD, he'd do so, but first he'd make sure of the diagnosis and would delay medication until it seemed really necessary. "If treatment is done well," he says, "a child shouldn't notice the drug, but just think the teacher has gotten better. It's like glasses—if they're good, you forget about them."

Bringing a neuroscientist's perspective to evolutionary psychology, Castellanos notes that many kids who have trouble paying attention in school, such as Jack S., peform well on athletic fields or when hunkered over a computer game. This seeming inconsistency reflects the fact that Homo sapiens has evolved both the genetic variation that's associated with ADHD and the variation that protects against it. In our sedentary, school-and-office culture, the tendency to shift focus rapidly and to act first and ask questions later is regarded as a problem. Yet that behavior has persisted in the population because it's a real advantage in certain situations, from NASCAR races to war zones to the floor of the Stock Exchange. Indeed, on the savannah where we evolved, someone who focused too long and hard on a particular bird, flower, or thought could end up as a predator's dinner.

Such grisly prehistoric entrées were likelier to have been girls and women than boys and men. In general, females focus more on social interaction and self-expression, which is better suited to the classroom than the wilds. Males typically focus more readily on action, which serves them better outdoors than in the library. These relationships among gender, environment, and attention help explain not only why more boys have ADHD but also why, so soon after millennia of severe inequity, more women than men already attend college.

Ideally, a child who struggles with ADHD doesn't just take medication but also receives counseling on how best to live with the disorder, including identifying opportunities to enjoy intervals of rapt attention away from the classroom. Whenever you put yourself in circumstances that really suit who you are, whether on a mountaintop or in a museum, your brain releases dopamine: the neurochemical that's affected by stimulants, and is so important to attention, cognition, the ability to anticipate pleasure and reward, and much else. Thus, a child who has a hard time coping in the classroom can derive much satisfaction and encouragement from excelling outdoors or on the basketball court. "A big part of dealing with ADHD is understanding yourself," says Castellanos. "Everyone has problems. The trick is knowing which situations make yours worse and which ones ameliorate them."

For that matter, everyone can learn to attend better. If you really want to focus on something, says Castellanos, the optimum amount of time to spend on it is ninety minutes. "Then change tasks. And watch out for interruptions once you're really concentrating, because it will take you twenty minutes to recover."

Summing up the state-of-the-art knowledge about ADHD, Castellanos says, "We're part of the way into the problem. We know a great deal more than ten years ago but are just starting to step on solid ground in terms of understanding the underlying mechanisms. There will be new, very different drugs and treatments. I'm hugely optimistic, but we have to hurry up, because people are waiting."

CHAPTER 12

Motivation: Eyes on the Prize

If you've ever tried to lose five pounds, you've experienced the interaction between attention and motivation. From the Latin *movere,* meaning "to move," this psychic energy impels you toward the goal you're focused on. Several times a day, for example, you zero in on the feeling of hunger; like thirst, sex, and fatigue, it's a powerful drive, or urgent, instinctual need. If you were an animal, you'd simply gobble whatever you could find. You're a human being, however, so you're able to *choose* your response to those pangs. Depending on your motivation, you may decide to wolf down a piece of pie or stick to your new low-carb diet.

Once you choose your goal, your focus narrows, so that that pie à la mode or fitting into your jeans again dominates your mental landscape. The most dramatic example is addiction, in which the motivation to get high restricts attention to the point that the drug seems like the most important thing in the world.

An inventive experiment using food illustrates the neurological foundations of the close tie between attention and motivation. After his subjects had fasted for eight hours, Northwestern University neuroscientist

Marsel Mesulam scanned their brains while they looked at images of tools and edibles. Then, after feasting on their favorite goodies until full, they went back under the scanner to inspect the same pictures again. When the two sets of scans were compared, it was clear that the amygdala, a brain structure whose functions include gauging whether something is desirable or not, reacted more strongly to the images of foods when the subjects were hungry, but not to those of the tools. In other words, depending on your motivation, certain parts of your brain can respond to the same visual experience in drastically different ways. Thus, says Mesulam, "an item in a pastry shop window that's easily ignored when you're full becomes irresistible when you're hungry."

America's obesity epidemic offers stunning illustrations of what can happen when motivation and attention become disconnected from daily behavior in general and each other in particular. Most reasonable people would say that their nutritional goal is to stay healthy and eat right, yet many simply don't focus on their food and how much they actually consume. In *Mindless Eating,* the Cornell marketing and nutritional scientist Brian Wansink offers numerous examples of how this lack of focusing helps pile on the pounds. As if still motivated by childhood's Clean Plate Award, moviegoers will gobble 53 percent more nasty, stale popcorn if it's presented in a big bucket than they would if given a small one. A third of diners can't remember how much bread they just ate. People who stack up their chicken-wing bones at the table will eat 28 percent fewer than those who clear the evidence away. We'll snack on many more M&Ms if they're arrayed in ten colors rather than seven. We consume 35 percent more food when dining with a friend—and 50 percent more with a big group—than when alone. Considering such statistics, it's not surprising that simply by paying attention to your food and eating it slowly, you can cut 67 calories from each dinner and seven pounds in a year.

To help clients who are among the half of overweight Americans to reinforce the link between motivation and attention, the registered dietitian

Gail Posner suggests that they practice "mindful eating." She describes the strategy as "focusing on your food—on its smell, taste, and feel—which lets your brain know that you will soon feel full and satisfied." Once this sense of satiation registers upstairs, the urge to keep on munching decreases, which makes it easier to stay motivated. "The goal of a healthy diet is to stop eating when you're no longer hungry," says Posner. "If you don't pay attention to what you eat, however, that sense of fullness won't kick in. Some people pick that up, and some never do."

When clients insist that they're motivated to lose weight and don't know why they keep gaining, Posner makes some educated guesses that all center on inattention to what they actually eat. Perhaps they let an empty plate rather than a sense of satiety be the cue to push away from the table. Maybe they haven't noticed that many restaurants now serve double-size portions. They might forget to count the calories from those samples of coffee cake at the supermarket or the mindless nibbling while watching TV, standing in front of the fridge, or traipsing through the kitchen. To help dieters focus on such problematic behavior, Posner offers a low-tech motivational tool: a small notebook. "If they write down what they eat and drink," she says, "they soon realize they're consuming far more than they thought. People who keep a record usually eat up to a third less food than people who don't."

The toughest dieting problem is the overeating that's motivated by using food to fill an emotional hole caused by frustration, anger, or sadness. To focus on what's *really* driving your desire to eat, Posner suggests placing your hands where you're hungry. If you put them on your head, she says, you're upset about something; on your mouth, you just want to taste something; on your stomach, you're actually running on empty.

As the term *workaholic* suggests, the rapt attention and motivation inspired by a goal can resemble an addiction. Offering a benign example, Evan G., who lost seventy-five pounds during five months of high school, describes his experience: "I feel that constantly weighing yourself—being overly compulsive about it—is the key to staying motivated and losing more. When I first started dieting, I would weigh myself six or seven times a day. If the scale says 250, and later it says 248, it makes you feel a lot better. It makes you want to go out there and see a change in yourself. It forces you to do better."

Whatever your motivation—to lose weight, get a graduate degree, learn to ski—attention is the link between your goal and the resources you bring to it. Sometimes your objective is immediate and practical: "I need a snack." Other times it's enduring and abstract: "I will stay fit for life." Yet a still-mysterious interaction between your neurophysiology and your goal obtains on the immediate plane of "I want food now" and the long-term level of "I want a long, healthy life." Attention's selective nature will enhance the value of things that are relevant to your objective, from a doughnut right this minute to maintaining lifetime fitness. The challenge often lies in balancing your focus between your present goal (a snack) and your far-reaching one (fitness) so that you choose an apple.

YOUR MOTIVATIONS—GET THAT promotion, throw the best parties, run for public office—aren't impersonal abstractions but powerfully reflect and affect who you are and what you focus on. An individual's goals figure prominently in the theories of personality first developed by the Harvard psychologist Henry Murray. According to his successor David McClelland, what Friedrich Nietzsche called "the will to power," which he considered the major driving force behind human behavior, is one of the three basic motivations, along with achievement and affiliation, that differentiate us as individuals.

A simple experiment shows how these broad emotional motivations can affect what you pay attention to or ignore on very basic levels. When they examine images of faces that express different kinds of emotion, power-oriented subjects are drawn to nonconfrontational visages, such as "surprise faces," rather than to those that suggest dominance, as "anger faces" do. In contrast, people spurred by affiliation gravitate toward friendly or joyful faces. Despite motivation's impact on behavior, however, some individuals fail to recognize and focus it on the right objective. Thus, a person who has a strong drive toward dominance might be far happier in the military but end up in the ministry, and someone impelled toward achievement could prosper as a CEO yet languish as a homemaker.

Like all behavior, your motivations arise from your heredity and experience. Where genes are concerned, for example, individuals who were born with naturally outgoing, sociable temperaments are apt to be motivated by and focus on affiliation, while those who have naturally aggressive dispositions are likely to be driven by and concentrate on the need to dominate. Temperamentally anxious people can have a hard time staying motivated, period, because their intense focus on their worries distracts them from their goals.

Where nurture's impact is concerned, like your focus, your primary motivation can be influenced by your culture. When University of Michigan psychologist Oliver Schultheiss compared American college students and their German peers, he found that the former are markedly more oriented to achievement than to power, as the latter are. Thus, he concludes, Americans tend to focus more on the goals of innovation and success, and Germans on dominance and status.

Interestingly, much of the conventional wisdom about what to focus on in order to strengthen motivation turns out to be wrong. Since the peace-and-love 1960s, the assumption has been that boosting kids' self-esteem is the best way to inspire them and spur them on to achievement. Recent research, however, shows that telling children they're geniuses has very little effect on their performance, especially compared to the motivation they derive from focusing on their own concrete accomplishments and self-control. To be effective, praise, like criticism, should be precisely targeted: not "You're so great!" but "You did a great job on that report!"

Where motivation is concerned, even lauding children for their intelligence, which 85 percent of parents consider important, is counterproductive. Such generic praise actually inclines kids to focus too much on whether others perceive them as "smart" or "dumb" and to avoid risking failure. In a study of more than four hundred fifth-graders, students honored for their effort were likelier to take on a challenging task than those celebrated for their brains. In another experiment, children designated as "smart" also performed less well than those identified as "hard workers," apparently because the pressure to seem intelligent caused them to clutch.

Locker-room pep talks and bonuses notwithstanding, extrinsic focusing on trouncing the competition or monetary reward can actually decrease your intrinsic motivation to pursue a goal. In one study, for example, college students who were paid to do a puzzle were significantly less motivated than those who worked for free. In another experiment, individuals were asked to work on puzzles side by side. Those told to beat their opponents stopped playing after the researchers left the room; those who were simply asked to complete the puzzle continued to work. Moreover, the people who lost the competition but got positive feedback on their effort proved to be significantly more self-motivated afterward than losers who didn't get such affirmation.

SOME VERY FOCUSED individuals have lots of the stick-to-itiveness, epitomized by heroes from Clint Eastwood to *The Little Engine That Could*, that the Penn psychologist Angela Duckworth simply calls "grit." When it comes to understanding achievement, she believes that our cultural bias toward the idea of innate talent and ability causes us to undervalue this tenacious trait. Grit clearly involves motivation and perseverance in the pursuit of a goal despite setbacks, but its less obvious component is closely bound up with attention: maintaining consistent interest in a project or idea over time.

Given a hard problem to figure out—the nature of gravity, perhaps—most people might think about it for a while, then get tired and forget about it. A genius such as Isaac Newton, however, has enough "mental energy" to pay rapt attention to the same thing for a long time without wavering: "I keep the subject constantly before me and wait until the first dawnings open little by little before me into the full light." His modern successor, Richard Feynman, had a similarly protean absorption in his subject. Upon presenting their presumably new, hard-won theories, his colleagues often found that the legendary physicist had done the math many years before and not even bothered to publish the results. As one peer put it, "Feynman had signed the guest book and already left." Lesser mortals can be very talented and stay enthusiastic for a little while, says Duckworth, "but they can't sustain that kind of interest."

The historical record of the likes of Newton and Feynman in particular first interested Duckworth in taking a serious look at grit's role in accomplishment in general. Biographical analyses showed that with some exceptions, such superachievers have certain things in common. They often find their focus early in life, as did many of the three hundred "Termites," as the brilliant children studied by Stanford's Lewis Terman, the pioneer of IQ testing and the longitudinal study of lives, are called. After homing in on their special interest in youth, most pursued it with tenacious effort and long-term, consistent attention.

Some people are "gritty" and others aren't, but tenacity could be either a heritable trait or a habit established by early experience. People who make a living by doing something that deeply interests them are grittier than those who don't, which suggests that the quality could have developed from their liking what they do. On the other hand, says Duckworth, a gritty person might look harder to find a good vocational fit. "Sometimes a person doesn't seem gritty till he or she finds the right focus."

Respect for the power of perseverance and sustained attention came early to Duckworth, who absorbed it from her parents' Chinese culture.

Even when they're transplanted to America, Asian traditions focus on determination and consistent effort more than those of many other groups. When the Penn team studied children who compete in spelling bees, they found that grittier kids do better, study harder, and come back to try again the next year—no big surprise there. However, all the children who placed first, second, and third in the national finals in 2005 were of Indian ancestry. "Believing that it's all about a person's effort and very little about his fixed ability may be a misguided notion," says Duckworth, "but many Asian parents tend to think that any child can go to Harvard if he works hard enough, which tells you something."

Where the larger society is concerned, grit may help explain why the average IQ has climbed a half-point annually for the past fifty years. (Heredity, which accounts for more than half of a population's IQ differences, can't be the reason, because genes can't alter in such a short time period.) With the spread of democracy, big increases in levels of education, the use of computers and the Internet, and other positive social changes have enabled many more people to find positive motivation and focus and to express their tenacity. As Duckworth says, "We've enriched our world in ways that make us smarter, which in turn inclines us to enhance our environment even more."

Society places great faith in standardized tests as gauges of future accomplishment, but the SAT isn't a reliable predictor of a student's success after graduation. In fact, even your grade point average correlates very weakly with your salary after college. When it comes to getting things done in the real world, grit may be a better augury of achievement. As long ago as the 1950s, the demographer Paul Glick found that high school dropouts were more likely than graduates to be divorced, leading to speculation that people who give up on some hard things, like finishing school, are also unlikely to persevere in other matters, such as working on a marriage. Nevertheless, American culture remains strongly swayed by high IQ and GRE scores and favors "fast learners." As a result, says

Duckworth, "we don't give enough attention to the 'effort' and 'duration' pieces of accomplishment that mean going the distance." A writer who has a certain level of natural ability might need five years to complete a book and another person just a year, she says, but with grit, the former still gets to the finish line: "I believe in the story of the tortoise and the hare."

It remains to be seen if either turtles or rabbits can be tutored in grittiness, because that experiment has yet to be run. Nevertheless, says Duckworth, research has made one thing very clear: "Life is relatively short, so don't labor under the delusion that you can keep switching your focus from goal to goal and get anywhere."

It's often said that the age of thirty is the "new twenty," but the trend for young people to change jobs every year or two in search of the perfect career has costs as well as benefits. "That's how you become a superficial dilettante," says Duckworth. "Do you want to go to a surgeon who has done lots of different interesting operations or the one who specializes in the procedure you need?" She allows that it may be helpful for adolescents to flit from dream to dream as they try to figure out what really interests them. "But if you're forty-five and still haven't found your sweet spot, maybe your expectations about a good fit between you and a job are too high. Perhaps you should settle down with the best thing you've found and focus on it."

DESCRIBING A MOTIVATIONAL dilemma that's endemic to the human condition, St. Paul writes in his oft-quoted letter to the Romans, "For that which I work, I understand not. For I do not that good which I will: but the evil which I hate, that I do." As we might express this sentiment, "Why do I act this way! Instead of doing what I want to do"—eat sensibly, stay sober, pay off the credit card—"I end up doing the opposite!" Scripture also illustrates the oldest strategy for dealing with this problem: shift your focus away from temptation. As Jesus famously told the devil: "Get thee behind me, Satan!"

Behavioral scientists have long brooded over the question of why our control over our impulses is so often erratic. Conventional wisdom has it that if you *really* wanted to, you could save instead of squander, be kind to your impossible in-laws, and run a marathon, yet as Paul plaintively observes, desire alone isn't always enough.

Identifying one reason for seemingly inexplicable behavior, Freud observed that you may be subconsciously attending to a subliminal cue that sparks a hidden motivation. When Truman Capote was a little boy, his mother desperately wanted to be a Park Avenue matron, and she killed herself when her husband thwarted her dream by going bankrupt. Many years later, despite his wealth, success, and celebrity, the author essentially drank himself to death when he was abandoned by his own beloved Park Avenue ladies, whom he had, in astounding opposition to his conscious self-interest, cruelly caricatured in prose. In a less dramatic illustration of a hidden motivation's power, imagine that although you have every intention of living it up with the gang on Friday night, when you arrive at the bar, you feel and act oddly glum and grouchy. Little do you know that a seemingly trivial exchange with a manipulative colleague earlier in the day had subconsciously reminded you of your interactions with a bossy parent and stuck you with a sullen teenager's motivation and manners.

In an ingenious experimental illustration of the consequences of attending to unconscious motivations, the Duke psychologist Tanya Chartrand covertly primed 122 subjects to form impressions of various people based on a short list of characteristics. Then she manipulated whether they would succeed or fail at meeting this subliminal goal by throwing some contradictory traits into the mix. By describing one such target as both "clumsy" and "graceful," for example, she subtly frustrated participants' attempts to come up with a coherent portrait. Afterward, tests showed that her subjects' spirits were lower than those of a control group, although they didn't know why. Because the participants felt the emotional down-shift but weren't aware of the reason, Chartrand calls these states "mystery moods."

By definition, a mystery mood's effects on your behavior are hard to deal with, but some pragmatic research suggests that it's easier to shift your focus from that rich dessert to your goal of losing those five pounds if you practice ahead of time. When you rehearse in your head how you'll react to the lure of the all-you-can-eat buffet or the neighborhood watering hole before you're standing in front of it, you're much likelier to resist temptation than if you trust in your spontaneous response.

Deciding beforehand what you'll focus on when sticking to your goal becomes difficult can even be a better strategy than trying to rev up your motivation. In an experiment on how best to deal with social anxiety, or shyness, Thomas Webb and Paschal Sheeran, psychologists at the University of Sheffield, England, told volunteers to prepare to give a speech, which gives most people the jitters. Then they gave their subjects a list of words and measured how quickly they directed their attention both to anxiety-producing terms, such as *blushing* and *sweating*, and to neutral ones. The volunteers who had been previously told to focus on bland words paid far less attention to the worrisome ones than those who hadn't been prepped. "We know that motivation is a slow, effortful process that has only small effects on behavior, whereas attention is a fast and effortless one," says Sheeran. Therefore, when you're facing a stressful situation, whether you have to give a speech or attend a banquet when you're dieting, "you should plan how you'll act in advance," he says. "Use the format 'if that happens, then I do this!'"

One old-fashioned but effective way to use attention to strengthen motivation calls for a group effort. Concerned about the high incidence of serious infections contracted by intensive-care patients, 1 in 10 of whom died as a result, the Johns Hopkins Hospital anesthesiologist Peter Pronovost designed a simple checklist for doctors and nurses. He found that by performing five easy steps such as hand-washing and donning sterile gowns under a colleague's watchful eyes, an ICU staff can cut the infection rate to nearly zero. All the measures were supposedly standard and utterly familiar, yet medical professionals often succumbed to the temptation to skip them until Pronovost developed a way for team members to enforce one another's motivation.

SOME INTRIGUING NEW RESEARCH on the old-fashioned quality of willpower, conducted by the research psychiatrist George Ainslie, who studies behavioral economics at the Veterans Affairs Medical Center in Coatesville, Pennsylvania, highlights an important reason why we act impulsively or inexplicably and also points to a strategy for staying focused on the right motivation. From his perspective, your life is run not by the highly structured, unified Cranial Central Command that you like to imagine but by a group of bickering agents with different motives. Depending on whose voice captures your attention, you may find yourself engaging in mysterious or seemingly contradictory behavior, from gross overindulgence to acts of surprising heroism. Where sticking to a goal is concerned, you can reduce the conflict by focusing on the most supportive voice and suppressing the distracting, counterproductive ones.

When a little whisper tempts you to stray from your goal of hitting the gym three times a week or staying on your diet, Ainslie finds that you're *temporarily* but strongly inclined to pay attention to and choose the behavior that brings the quickest rewards. Thus, you're powerfully but briefly tempted to watch the tube or eat the pie rather than to persevere in hopes of better but delayed payoffs, such as abs of steel or lower cholesterol. In experiments, for example, subjects will choose a shorter, earlier break from noxious noise instead of longer but later relief only if the shorter reprieve is immediate.

Offering a do-it-yourself experiment, Ainslie says that if you ask a group of friends to choose between an imaginary certified check for $100 that they can cash immediately and a postdated certified check for $200 that they can't cash for three years, more than half of them will opt for the $100 now. However, if you ask them to decide between getting $100 in six years and $200 in nine years—the same choice, but with a much greater delay in reward—they'll all choose the $200. Putting this motivational dynamic in mathematical terms, Ainslie says that we "spontaneously discount the value of expected events in a curve where value is divided approximately by expected delay."

Even pigeons sometimes seem to struggle against this passing preference for making quick if often ultimately unwise choices where rewards are concerned. Like us, the birds will opt for a smaller, earlier payoff (grain, in their case) over a later, larger one when the smaller one is immediate, but not when the food is delayed. Moreover, says Ainslie, some will actually peck a colored key in advance to prevent a later offer from a differently colored key that produces the smaller reward. As these experiments show, he says, "temptation isn't just some human cultural product but a basic behavioral pattern that must have appeared early in evolution."

Heeding the voice that tells the dieter to go ahead and have that slice of fudge cake may not seem important in the grand scheme of things, but that impulsive choice can have serious consequences in terms of what Ainslie unabashedly calls your "willpower." After much investigation of its nature, he defines it "not as an organ of some kind, but as a bargaining situation with your expected future selves, in which the present choice is a test case for a whole category of probable choices in the future. Why not eat the cake? After all, one piece won't show! What you lose isn't that little bit of slimness, however, but your expectation that you'll be able to stick to your diet."

The idea of cultivating willpower—the capacity to choose and follow a course of action despite obstacles—would not have surprised Epictetus,

Augustine, Nietzsche, and other philosophers who have embraced what William James called "the art of replacing one habit for another." Through most of history, gluttony, concupiscence, drunkenness, and sloth were regarded as vices rather than sicknesses, and replacing them with temperance, chastity, sobriety, and enterprise required an act of the will. The sages of old would be amazed to hear modern Americans blame their expanding middles on the genes or habits they inherited from their parents, rather than on their own lack of "self-control"— another anachronistic term. In a culture that increasingly can't just say no, overweight individuals may resort to stomach-stapling surgery, and groups lobby for statutes to make trans fats illegal and tax junk foods.

Offering a historical perspective on the cultural decline of what he regards as an important human faculty, Claremont psychologist Mihály Csíkszentmihályi says that when mid-twentieth-century scientists decided that the stimulus/response dynamic was the foundation of most behavior, will became the baby that got thrown out with the bathwater. If what induces you to act this way or that depends on either positive or negative reinforcement, will is no longer influential in explaining why you do what you do. "It still crops up in a deus ex machina way, he says, "as in 'It's my *will* to do this,' or in the subtler voice of a Skinnerian reinforcement or a drive that you're not even aware of, but the term was essentially obliterated from psychology's lexicon." Nevertheless, the venerable concept sometimes shines through modern research, he says, as when psychologists speak about "'effective motivation,' because there are people who feel motivated to do something but never get around to doing it."

From a neuroscientist's different perspective, Johns Hopkins attention researcher Steve Yantis thinks about will in terms of the ongoing biased competition for your focus. He envisions the huge collection of goals, each of which has value, that's stored in both your long-term and short-term, or "working," memory. They range from lofty aims, such as having a happy family life or a successful career, to quotidian objectives, such as making breakfast or finishing that report. Some goals, such as balancing your checkbook, demand your clear, immediate focus, but you attend to others—say, the Golden Rule—in a diffused way, almost without realizing it.

Will comes into play when a competition arises between two or more conflicting goals and motivations. Driven by your growling stomach, you want to eat something an hour before dinner, but motivated by Weight Watchers, you also want to wait. Many such battles take place below the level of your awareness, but on other occasions, you consider the values you've assigned to the warring goals and willfully bias the competition between them. You may decide that you want a cookie, and you want it now. Or you may figure that yes, you're hungry and would like a cookie or two, but that another objective—zipping up your jeans again—has a higher priority.

The science of genetics has led some academics to discount the very idea of free will, but Yantis calls this "a very pessimistic view that assumes that your choices are hard-wired." Whether it's a microdecision about how to grasp the handle of a teacup or a macrodecision about whether to accept a job offer, he says, "the selection of a course of action is a mechanistic result of an unimaginably complex interaction among biological, genetic, and behavioral factors. At the very lowest level of quantum mechanics, randomness plays a role. But as a human being, I am perfectly comfortable with the idea of being in control of my choices and making rational decisions based on memories, values, and beliefs." That said, the concept of free will has a "mysterious, magical 'black box' quality," says Yantis. "When I consider two competing courses of action and choose one of them, I'm not sure how to think of the ultimate 'me' who makes that decision."

IN THE SHORT term, the interplay of attention and motivation is crucial to taking care of business, and in the long term, it helps to make you who you are. If your high school yearbook described you as "most popular" or "most likely to succeed," it's likely that perhaps in contrast to your hair- or waistline, your deep-seated focus on making friends or running things has remained constant.

Where your immediate as well as lifelong objectives are concerned, focus forges the connection between your goals and your personal resources. Despite our cultural fixation on innate giftedness, the old-fashioned quality of grit may be a better predictor of real-world performance. Attention's mechanics ensure that when you lock on your objective, you enhance that aspiration and suppress things that compete with it, which helps you to stay focused. That rapt dynamic works to your advantage if your goal is positive and productive but, as in addiction, can be deadly if it isn't.

CHAPTER 13

Health: Energy Goes Where
Attention Flows

Where your physical and mental health are concerned, it's hard to exaggerate attention's importance in shaping your immediate experience and securing your long-term well-being. Strengthening your ability to direct your focus away from negative ideas and events when such cogitation serves no purpose and to reframe setbacks as challenges or even opportunities helps you handle stress and approach life as a creation rather than a reaction.

Exhibit A for attention's power to foster well-being might be the Missouri businessman Larry Stewart. His *New York Times* obituary lauded him not so much for his great financial success as for the way he turned one of life's hard knocks into a gift—in his case, a big bag full of them. During every December since 1979, Stewart took to the streets as a Secret Santa who handed out hundred-dollar bills to passersby who looked like they could use a little boost. His Dickensian holiday largesse began one day just a week before Christmas, when he was fired from his job. Parked at a drive-in restaurant, Stewart felt pretty low until he noticed that the carhop in a skimpy coat was shivering in the cold. "I think I've got it bad?" he said to himself, and tipped her twenty dollars. By the time he died, he had not only prospered in business but also anonymously given away $1.3 million to strangers.

The way in which Larry Stewart responded to adversity by directing his attention away from paralyzing gloom and self-pity and toward a big picture that put his loss in perspective and reenergized him could be an anecdote lifted from a textbook on the research of the Penn psychiatrist Aaron Beck. His discovery that attention's selective nature plays a major role in mental illness was a crucial step in his development of cognitive therapy for depression, which has since revolutionized psychiatric treatment, period. Moreover, Beck's insights into the way maladaptive patterns of attention lead to dysfunctional behavior shed light not only on emotional disorders in particular, but on maintaining well-being in general.

Depression is now understood as a complicated problem that has individual biological as well as environmental components, and its treatment may involve medication, psychotherapy, or both. Back in the 1960s, dissatisfied with his patients' lack of progress, Beck looked beyond the psychoanalytical and behaviorist schools that then dominated therapy for a different approach. After combing his patients' case histories in search of a behavioral common denominator, he had a groundbreaking insight: the depressed routinely focus on the negative thoughts and feelings guaranteed to make them feel hopeless and helpless—the cognitive and emotional ingredients of the blues.

Even when asleep, the melancholy tend to focus on futility. In a classic dream, one of Beck's patients saw himself putting coins into a vending machine, then just standing there, waiting for a soda or a refund that never came. The prevalence of this bleak mind-set among the depressed—about 10 percent of Americans in the course of their lifetimes—persuaded Beck that this noirish "selective abstraction" was a crucial element of the disorder. "These individuals would focus on whatever negative experiences they had, to the exclusion of positive ones or the larger context," he says. "Even when looking back into the past, they would recall only negative events."

To succeed in the rough-and-tumble game of life, however, you can't afford to focus on the dark side. In order to keep going up to bat, you have to believe that if you persist, sooner or later you'll hit the ball. Anyone who has ever felt discouraged even briefly knows that it's hard to keep swinging if you're convinced you'll strike out.

To understand attention's role in causing and relieving mental illness, imagine that you, like one of Beck's patients, have been fired from a valued job, failed to find a new one, and fear you'll lose your home and family next. You become depressed and spend all day shuffling around in your bathrobe. When someone finally drags you into treatment, you tell your cognitive therapist, "There's no point in even looking for a job anymore. No one would hire me."

Refocusing the depressed person's attention away from such hopeless and helpless thoughts and feelings toward more positive, productive ones is cognitive therapy's core. In weekly sessions over two to three months, your therapist engages you in Beck's "collaborative empiricism," in which you both test the validity of your knee-jerk negative thoughts against real-life experience. She teaches you how to recognize and counter self-defeating ideas before they can spiral into destructive patterns of behavior. Instead of commiserating over the unjust way your former employer treated you, or over your unhappy childhood, she challenges your self-defeating focus and helps you reinforce new positive insights with practical, demonstrable achievements.

At your first session, the therapist tells you to focus on a single task: be washed, dressed, and breakfasted by eight o'clock each morning of the next week. That's it. You can handle that, so at the next session, she tells you to add reading a newspaper and checking for opportunities on Monster.com to the morning regimen. The following week, she asks you to contact three potential employers from the ads: just send the e-mails or make the calls.

Over the course of therapy, learning to direct your attention away from your old what's-the-use attitude toward can-do behavior inevitably leads to some practical improvements, which help to lift your mood. After all, you do feel better after a shower, some coffee, and plugging into the real world via the newspaper. Moreover, taking real steps toward your goal of employment, from rising at the start of the business day to making those cold calls, greatly increases your chances of getting the break you need. In short, you've acquired both a healthier, less self-absorbed focus on life and a new set of coping skills.

Cognitive therapy has proved to be as effective as drugs in reversing mild to moderate depression, and the approach is now used, often in combination with behavioral therapy and/or medication, to treat many other mental illnesses and several physical ones as well. As Beck says proudly, "The experimental work based on clinical observations concerning attentional deployment in psychiatric problems is as scientific as the work in neuroscience."

The correction of chronically misdirected attention is a public health issue, not just an individual one. Depression costs the American economy about $44 billion a year in lost productivity due to affected employees' reduced ability to concentrate, remember, and make decisions. In addition to their own suffering, millions of untreated depressed parents put their children at increased risk of succumbing to the illness. Citing a study showing that the daughters of such women are apt to share their mothers' dark worldview, Beck says that possible genetic predispositions notwithstanding, a parent's selectively bleak, despairing focus is "certainly a risk factor, and in my view forms the substrate for the negative thinking that occurs in depression."

Maladaptive patterns of attention aren't limited to depression but obtain across the spectrum of behavioral disorders. Just as the melancholy focus on negative information, the anxious and paranoid home in on the threatening sort. Other troubled individuals selectively attend to negative physical rather than psychological cues. Victims of panic disorder fixate on medical catastrophe, hypochondriacs on bodily symptoms, and insomniacs on the consequences of insufficient sleep. As with depression, effective cognitive-behavioral treatments for these disorders aim to correct the distorted attention patterns that underlie them.

Not surprisingly, in Beck's view, William James would be pleased with cognitive therapy for several reasons. First, he says, "because it emphasizes consciousness, which provides many of the clues to understanding psychiatric disorders as well as normal psychology. Secondly, cognitive therapy is pragmatic, and James was a pragmatist." As if speaking of his own philosophy, Beck approvingly quotes James: "The truth is what works."

MEDICAL TREATMENTS THAT harness attention to restore or improve well-being are not limited to mental health. That the ability to control attention and channel it in affirmative directions can improve longevity comes across in an intensive study of a particularly clean-living population: the School Sisters of Notre Dame born before 1917. Researchers at the University of Kentucky found that 9 out of 10 nuns from the quarter of the group who focused most on upbeat thoughts, feelings, and events lived past the age of fifty-eight, but only 1 in 3 of the population's least positively minded quarter survived that long.

One form of directing your focus has been shown to help people cope with diverse, sometimes intractable problems such as stress, cancer, high blood pressure, and gastrointestinal illnesses. As a result, some three hundred health centers across America now offer meditation—the practice of rapt attention—as an adjunct to more conventional medical treatments.

Much of the enthusiasm for using attention to promote health is rooted in the pioneering research of Jon Kabat-Zinn, now an emeritus professor of medicine at the University of Massachusetts Memorial

Medical Center in Worcester. Back in 1979, the former molecular biolo-
gist founded the hospital's "mindfulness-based stress reduction [MBSR]
program," in which participants attend eight weekly classes and perform
breath-focused "mindfulness meditation" for forty-five minutes daily. To
appeal to people of any faith or none at all, Kabat-Zinn peeled away meditation's ancient cultural and religious trappings and stripped it to its behavioral essence: the systematic self-regulation of attention and affect.

On a rainy June afternoon at the Omega Institute for Holistic Studies, in bucolic Rhinebeck, New York, two hundred healthcare professionals move through their Warrior and Downward Dog poses so slowly that
they might be under water. The class is part of Kabat-Zinn's weeklong
training retreat, which is meant to steep participants in two special ways
of focusing: meditation and the mindful state of purposeful, moment-to-
moment, nonjudgmental awareness that it encourages. Yoga classes elsewhere can have a competitive edge, but here the goal is not gymnastic feats
but simply "staying home" in your mind and body by "sinking into the current of your breath." Some people just approximate the postures while
seated in a chair or lying on a mat—a reminder that supermodels in ads
notwithstanding, there are all kinds of bodies, workouts, and ways to
think about health and fitness.

As medical professionals, the Omega participants are all too familiar
with the plight of patients whose health problems, from insomnia to infertility, haven't responded to standard treatments. Many such individuals suffer from chronic pain, which is one of the commonest and
hardest-to-treat of all ailments. Continual headaches, backaches, and the
like feel awful, of course, but they also can take a serious toll on the
body's cardiovascular, endocrine, respiratory, and immune systems—to
say nothing of the economy, to the tune of tens of billions of healthcare
dollars each year. After chronic-pain patients try various treatments without success, doctors often give up on them, writing them off as hopeless
or even "mental" cases, thus compounding their misery.

Sheer desperation motivates many pain patients to try anything that might help, even if it seems as zany or foreign as paying attention to their breath. All MBSR practitioners basically follow the same regimen. "When you put people with all kinds of problems in the same room, you ask, 'Where could you possibly start to help?'" says Kabat-Zinn. "The answer is, 'From where they are.' They all have bodies. They all have minds. Can they pay attention? They all can. To what? It almost doesn't matter. You just ask them to tune in, to befriend their own core of well-being, as opposed to being shredded by life's events."

At the beginning of their attentional training, in a seemingly counter-productive move, chronic-pain patients are asked to focus on their throb-bing heads or rigid necks. Soon, they begin to differentiate between the physiological sensations and their thoughts and feelings about them, which may turn out not to be particularly accurate or important. In the transi-tion from "me in agony" to "how about that twinge," much suffering can evaporate. After eight weeks of classes and daily meditation, half of patients in one study reported that their pain decreased by a third or more—an im-pressive result for a treatment-resistant group. Moreover, most also learned to manage their persistent discomfort better, which enhances the feeling of control that's a major piece of well-being.

Following the yoga session, Kabat-Zinn, who looks more like a sports coach than a scientist, finds a quiet spot to sit down and talk about his re-search, which he describes as "all about the healing power of attention," defined simply as "the capacity to be in a salient relationship with one or another element of your experience for a period of time." Generally, after you focus for a while, he says, you get tired and stop. When you meditate, however, "you bring your attention back online," which increases its capacity, in both duration and depth of perception. Where health is con-cerned, he says, "that kind of disciplined focus has much more potential for rearranging your physiology."

No one knows exactly how paying attention can promote healing.

The best guess is that meditation causes salubrious shifts in the nervous and immune systems. In one study, after people who worked in a highly stressful environment completed the MBSR program, EEG tests showed that the right hemisphere of their brains had quieted down, while activity had increased in the areas of the left prefrontal region that are linked with a zestful approach to life. They also had a stronger reaction to flu vaccine than members of the control group, which supports the thesis that meditation enhances immune function. On the subjective level, the participants reported that after their training, they felt better able to handle unpleasant events and emotions. As Kabat-Zinn observes, "When you feel more comfortable in your own skin, lots of things—outlook, diet, exercise, relationships—may also change, and all of them have profound effects on your health. When you drop in to your own experience and body, you get this sense of belonging, fitting in, coming to terms with things as they are. That's what healing is."

On the most obvious level, the act of focusing can short-circuit the fight-or-flight reaction that's linked to stressful situations. Two impressive studies of psoriasis patients were instigated by dermatologists who were discouraged that so many individuals dropped out of their effective phototherapy treatment. This aversion was understandable, considering that the patients had to stand naked in a kind of phone-booth-style light box, with a pillowcase over their heads and goggles over their eyes, while being irradiated with ultraviolet light. As Kabat-Zinn says, the experience was about as pleasant as "spending time in a toaster oven."

Unlike people who follow an intensive daily meditation regimen, the psoriasis patients paid mindful attention only during phototherapy. Throughout their sessions, given three times per week for three to ten minutes, they listened to an audio that simply asked them to focus on the present without making good-or-bad judgments: Can you feel the warmth? Can you hear the blowers moving the air? Can you be in your body? After four months, when the experiment concluded, their skin had cleared four times faster than that of patients in the control group. Psoriasis is caused by uncontrolled cell proliferation, which inclines Kabat-Zinn to think that the attention exercises somehow accelerated the skin's healing down to the level of gene expression, DNA replication, and cell division.

As is the case with running, weight-training, or other healthful regimens, talking about "just focusing on your breath" for forty-five minutes is much easier than doing it. As Kabat-Zinn says, "If I ask people to 'just pay attention,' they know what to do, but it's hard. Your mind doesn't want to focus on one thing for too long without judging or otherwise reacting to it." On the other hand, a huge 2008 survey from the Pew Foundation shows that a surprising number of people—about 40 percent of Americans of all religious backgrounds, including Evangelical Christians and Muslims—meditate in one way or another at least once a week. For that matter, often without realizing it, everyone has moments of this active, nonjudgmental rapt attention to . . . something. "It really doesn't matter what," says Kabat-Zinn. "Meditation is less about the target than about a state of pure attention that occurs before thinking. A knowing that's more like intuition than cognition." Some practice with a particular focus, often the breath, and others attend to a sunset or the sounds of a stream, albeit without the usual mental commentary. The important thing, says Kabat-Zinn, is that "when your mind goes off on its own tangent, you gently bring it back."

Meditation's rewards include a certain calmness that helps you handle what Kabat-Zinn, in homage to the resilient Zorba the Greek, calls the "full catastrophe" of living. Despite continual romantic, financial, and familial disasters, he says, "Zorba can dance in the present moment, because he knows that stress—the full catastrophe—is not good or bad, but just part of the way life is. You're in it, so how can you best relate to what's happening, both for yourself and for any others involved?"

One way in which meditation ameliorates full-catastrophe living is by making it easier to attend to the reality of the moment rather than your judgments about it. "If things go right, you can be happy; if not, not," says Kabat-Zinn. "That's where we all start out, but most situations are neither all good nor all bad." Until a catastrophe stops you in your tracks, he says, "you may miss a lot of the actuality of things. You're too busy zoning through the moments to get to a better one." Then too, even a serious illness or reversal of fortune is not always as terrible as everyone assumes, because "it can also be very rich. We want things to turn out for the best, but we don't always know what the best is. We go as far as we can in knowing, then we have to rest in not knowing."

After spending three decades teaching sick people how to use attention to "fall awake" and improve their health, Kabat-Zinn concludes that "the knowledge that you're only here for a very short time, plus tender-hearted mindfulness, lets you live inside your experience with freedom and possibility. For many people, much of life is a kind of nightmare. The only way out is waking up—attending to reality."

JUST AS SOME people use the special form of attention called meditation to relieve physical sickness, others use it to ease emotional distress. For nearly twenty years before he began conducting research at UCLA and Harvard, the clinical and health psychologist Lobsang Rapgay was a Tibetan Buddhist monk. As a small child, he fled from Lhasa across the Himalayas on foot with his family when the Chinese invaded the country. After getting a doctorate in Tibetan medicine in India, he came to the United States to pursue a Ph.D. in psychology. His unusual cultural, philosophical, and scientific background led Rapgay to a major research interest: a novel hybrid treatment for anxiety that combines Western psychiatry and Eastern meditation.

People who are diagnosed as having "generalized anxiety disorder" are afflicted by three major problems that many of us experience to a lesser extent from time to time. First and foremost, says Rapgay, the natural human inclination to focus on threats and bad news is strongly amplified in them, so that even significant positive events get suppressed. An inflexible mentality and tendency toward excessive verbalizing make therapeutic intervention a further challenge.

By the time they enroll in one of Rapgay's studies, his subjects' level of anxiety and distress makes normal life impossible. Describing their uncontrollable fixation on fears, he says, "They worry about everything, not just a certain thing." Where work is concerned, for example, such a person might not just fret about performance on the job, but also about the remote possibility of missing the bus, perhaps, and being late. "Many of these patients worry literally all day," he says. "They know it's destructive, but they just can't stop."

In the East-West treatment approach, anxious patients learn to pay less attention to worries and fears in two different ways. Standard cognitive-behavioral therapy techniques identify and correct destructive patterns of thought and emotion. Training in "classical mindfulness," which is based on seated, breath-focused Theravadin Buddhist meditation, helps them sustain a flexible, expansive awareness without relying on verbal or cognitive activity.

For half of each session, the therapist uses a variety of cognitive and behavioral techniques to help the patient free his anxious mind of counterproductive thoughts. He learns to "worry the worry" until it becomes boring, for example, or to stop it in its tracks by substituting another idea. He might also practice challenging a fear, so that "I'll miss the bus to work" yields to "I've never missed it and probably won't tomorrow, either" and ultimately to "If I do, it's not the end of the world."

Even if the person comes to accept that focusing on missing the bus makes no sense—a cognitive advance—he may still have trouble calming his mind and directing his attention more productively. That's where classical mindfulness comes in. In each session, the patient gets instruction in gradually more sophisticated aspects of meditation, with the aim of cultivating what Rapgay calls "an open awareness that's free of preconceptions." Using both approaches is much more effective than either one used alone, he says, because the Western therapy addresses the anxious mind's content—maladaptive thoughts—and Eastern practice its "process"—a churning state of fretful awareness that's rigid, narrow, and focused on worry: "You have to address both content and process, and Western science doesn't have enough nonpharmacological interventions for changing states of mind."

For an anxious person, who struggles with an attentional bias toward threat, a narrow, brittle mind-set, and a tendency toward too much talk, regular immersion in a quiet, relaxed, nonjudgmental, focused state of mind is like time spent in a restorative mental spa. Moreover, the mindfulness cultivated by daily meditation helps the anxious go about their lives calmly, "attending to one thing, then to the next thing, and the next, while disregarding distractions," says Rapgay. "You aren't just mindful when you meditate. Afterward, you can deal with life's many details in a systematic, regulated, less stressful way, rather than having them all jumbled up in your field of consciousness."

This East-West approach to directing attention from worries to calm awareness seems to help the brain's more cognitive cortical region to regulate its more emotional subcortical area which, according to EEG studies, becomes quieter during treatment. The hybrid therapy's effectiveness is supported by some impressive statistics. After a course of fifteen sessions, the average patient's anxiety level, as measured on a test scale of 0 to 50, drops from a jangling high of 42 to a mellow 12. Next, Rapgay plans to study the approach's efficacy in treating obsessive-compulsive and post-traumatic disorders.

As clinician, researcher, and former monk, Rapgay believes that whether you're the anxious type or not, "it's very important to learn to attend to your immediate experience with awareness. This is a state of mind that's open to the spaciousness of consciousness without focusing on any particular content within that spaciousness. The difference between attending and attending with awareness is greater brain stability."

NOT JUST ANXIETY and depression, but also cardiovascular disease and immune dysfunction can be bound up with what you focus on and how. Learning to shift your attention away from unhelpful thoughts and emotions and recast negative events in the most productive light possible is one of the most important of all "health habits" to cultivate. The recognition of the role played by skewed attentional patterns in mental disorders is one of modern psychiatry's greatest advances. As research blurs the distinction between many mind and body problems, increasing numbers of people who suffer from hypertension, infertility, and psoriasis as well as from stress add a regimen of paying rapt attention to their medical treatment, which at the very least increases the feeling of control over one's own experience that's essential to well-being.

CHAPTER 14

Meaning: Attending to
What Matters Most

Of all the subjects that can arrest *Homo sapiens'* rapt attention, among the most distinctive is the fundamental nature of reality and its implications for our lives. For better and sometimes worse, we are the only creatures who focus on questions such as What does it all mean? What's the point of life? What is the right thing to do?

In their different ways, philosophy, religion, and psychology all probe the essential principles of being, knowledge, and behavior, and indeed, for most of history, there was little distinction between the first two systems. Here is Marcus Aurelius, Stoic philosopher and Roman emperor: "One universe made up of all that is; and one God in it all, and one principle of being, and one law, the reason, shared by all thinking creatures, and one truth."

Much has changed since Marcus Aurelius posited ultimate reality's essential oneness in the *Meditations*, yet we too redirect our attention from the daily grind to the contemplation of some deeper, more fundamental truth or reality by any name. Something of this preoccupation's postmodern tenor comes across in a survey of eighteen intellectuals, including Salman Rushdie, Toni Morrison, and Martin Scorsese, who were asked if there is a God. Six said no, five said yes, and seven said maybe, so that even in a seemingly skeptical group, a clear majority thought there is or might be . . . something else. After dismissing the idea of a deity as omnipotent cosmic puppeteer, the writer Jonathan Franzen said, "At the same time, I think there's a reality beneath what we can see with our eyes and experience with our senses. There's ultimately something mysterious and un-materialistic about the world. Something large and awe-inspiring and eternal and unknowable."

Not coincidentally, the disciplines that direct your attention to something large and awe-inspiring, whether called God or universe, consciousness or commonweal, also focus you on the improvement of your self and your world and on the appreciation of life. Indeed, philosophy, religion, and psychology advance many of the same kinds of behavior that account for much of our species' success. At the very least, focusing on values such as altruism and forgiveness that stir positive emotions expands your attentional range, whether trained on your own possibilities or others' needs, which benefits not only you but also the community.

THE IDEA THAT, as the French philosopher and activist-mystic Simone Weil put it, "attentiveness without an object is prayer in its supreme form" has been percolating in American culture since the New England Transcendentalists. Insisting that experiencing reality's true nature, and your own, requires focusing on the present moment, Emerson says, "We are always getting ready to live, but never living." Chiming in, Thoreau says, "As if you could kill time without injuring eternity."

In the 1960s and '70s, some of their philosophical heirs tried to pay rapt attention to ultimate reality with help from a pill. Whether they had good or bad LSD experiences had much to do with the drug's unpredictable effects on attention, so that some trippers got fixated on heaven and others on hell. Certain of these neo-transcendentalists went on to experiment with yoga, Zen, and other forms of Eastern meditation. Among the first of many psychologists to take up the practice was Harvard's Richard Alpert, who went to India and studied with Bhagavan Das, a Californian turned Hindu guru whose autobiography is tellingly called *It's Here Now (Are You?)*. Alpert became Ram Das and wrote his own best-selling *Be Here Now*.

More than a thousand years before Americans started chanting "Om" at the gym and scanning the meditating brain, Buddhism had turned attention into an art and a science. Indeed, like William James, Buddha was a profound psychologist and philosopher whose insights grew out of a dark personal epiphany: no matter who you are, you and everyone you love must endure pain, sickness, aging, and death.

In developing what is arguably less a religion than a philosophy for the relief of human suffering, Buddha recognized the strong bottom-up salience of anger, fear, and sadness, which are rooted in the past or future. The best response, he concluded, is to pay active top-down attention to the present moment and to positive thoughts and feelings, such as kindness and compassion. After a difficult early family life and struggles with depression, James came to a similar conclusion, which he expressed in his pragmatic terms: "I don't sing because I'm happy. I'm happy because I sing."

Dugu Choegyal Rinpoche, a teacher and artist who's based in India and Nepal, is an expert in the Tibetan Buddhist way of paying attention to reality. Indeed, he is a lama in the Kargyu sect, which is famed for its great cave-dwelling hermit-contemplatives such as Milarepa. If you tried to describe the effect of Choegyal's presence, "lighten up" might come to mind. After a little chat with the *rinpoche*—Tibetan for "precious jewel"—you may still have the same problems, but somehow they don't seem so bad.

There's a good chance that you've seen Choegyal or even have his photo stashed somewhere in your home. In 2007, the *rinpoche* materialized on many American coffee tables on the cover of *National Geographic*. In contrast to his timeless monastic robes, his shaved head was completely wired with high-tech sensors for an fMRI study of the brain during meditation. "This work is very, very good," he says, "because it brings knowledge and truth."

Asked to define attention, Choegyal says, "It means mindfulness—just the mind being simple. Whether in meditation or daily life, we try to pay attention to just being present, rather than being caught between hope and fear, which is the mind's usual condition."

Choegyal began to cultivate attention to the moment while still very young. "I realized that there's no escape from death, no matter what," he says. "I saw that before doing anything else, I must see how to deal with that, so I'll know what to do. That became my priority and freed me from many negative things. All my practice was concentrated on seeing what mind really is." Realizing that he has ventured into deep water, he laughs merrily and says, "Mind is not like any other thing, so it's hard to explain. Just as air can't explain fire, or space explain earth."

In the *rinpoche*'s tradition, paying attention is the way to experience true clarity about what is—knowledge that can't be accessed through thinking, but only through *being*. (In the psychologist Daniel Kahneman's terms, this awareness comes from the experiencing rather than the remembering self.) Within Buddhism, someone who sustains this effortless rapt focus on the right here, right now on a continual basis is said to be "enlightened" or "realized." In the *rinpoche*'s Kargyu world, the ranks of these special individuals include elite yogi-monks called *togdens*. One of them, called Amtrin, spent many years meditating alone in desolate mountain caves, attained realization, and became a revered figure in his community. During thunderstorms, people from the local village would say, "That's Amtrin, shaking out his blanket."

During one audience shortly before his death, Amtrin pretty much just sat there on a dais, wearing an Adidas wifebeater, a *togden*'s white robes, and an incipient smile. Nevertheless, the large group of Tibetans and Westerners watched him as intently as if he were Eli Manning throwing the winning pass at the Superbowl. Everyone wanted to know what Antrim knew, so they could be like him, at least a little. As to whether his old friend had still meditated, Choegyal says, "No, no. Eventually that concentrated mindfulness disappears, so that awareness has no boundaries."

In the Buddhist scheme of things, of course, Amtrin's life may be finished, but his mindful attention isn't. By way of explaining reincarnation, the *rinpoche* says that mind's basic nature is "a vibration or energy that over many lifetimes becomes stronger. The good things you learn stay and develop from life to life, giving you a head start. The more clarity you gain, the fewer negative emotions you will have next time."

On the long road to enlightenment, says the *rinpoche*, a person first meditates so that the mind can "get a glimpse of itself. Eventually, you take away the meditative state and free the mind even from that. Then mind can come back to its own nature of attention and awareness without contamination by concepts—even meditation." After visiting five hundred spiritual masters and evaluating their approaches to enlightenment, he says, the Buddha saw that cultivating this "simple mind" is the best strategy: "He didn't really teach 'Buddhism,' but how to let the mind rest in its nature, undisturbed by fear and illusion, or even by meditation."

As an experienced teacher, Choegyal knows that for most people, the mind is a rickety contraption assembled from to-do lists, intimations of the sublime, petty gripes, and thoughts of the next meal. "Some say, 'But the ordinary person has no mindfulness!'" he says. "They're really talking about 'confused mind.' Ordinary mind is basic, clear, and natural. It's *dharma*"—Sanskrit for the universe's underlying order—"but any name spoils it."

Tibetan Buddhism offers many supporting practices, such as the repetition of mantras and the veneration of deities, but meditation's core remains stilling the mind. Research increasingly supports Choegyal's description of two basic ways to achieve this end: the targeted and expansive approaches, which suit two different attentional styles. "One is more structured, one more simple," he says. "The first kind of person thinks, 'We must make an effort! What are the rules for meditation?' For the simple type of person, however, this approach doesn't work. I'm that type. I went through all the monastic training, but I don't take any of that very seriously anymore and just try to be simple and natural. I just try to have ordinary mind. On top of that, you can have concepts, like God, prayer, devotion, meditation, or no concepts. Views or no views. Those things can change. There can be only one truth, however, so that must be the same for everyone."

ECKHART TOLLE WOULD enthusiastically agree. He likes to tell the story of how, as he was preparing to publish his first book—*The Power of Now*, which has since sold millions of copies in thirty-two languages—he shared his ideas about paying attention to the moment with a fellow in a café. The man said, "'Forget it! That's already been done.'"

Even a timeless message requires timely rephrasing, however, and Tolle excels at putting ancient ideas about attention's importance in shaping experience into the nonsectarian Western vernacular. He's described as a "spiritual teacher," but he neither espouses nor rejects any dogmas or rituals, even meditation. The practice he advances is this: shift your focus from the past or the future to pay rapt attention to the present and experience true reality.

In October 2007, the small, unprepossessing man whom his fans simply call Eckhart does a two-day presentation at NYC's Beacon Theatre. The Rolling Stones, Van Morrison, Al Green, Emmylou Harris, and many other musicians have performed here, and like their events, this one has drawn a sold-out crowd of mostly hip-looking youngish and middle-aged adults. One woman says that she has come all the way from Florida, because Eckhart doesn't teach very often, and yes, he changed her life.

Practicing what he preaches, Tolle appears on stage, takes a chair, and just focuses quietly for a few moments. Everyone else settles down, too. Then, with a twinkle, he says, "If you live in New York, this beginning is too slow for you," and illustrates with a typical tourist's anecdote. When he ventured onto Park Avenue that morning, the hard-charging citizens behind him turned what he had intended to be a leisurely stroll into a kind of speed-walk. He was able to go with the flow and enjoy the experience but noticed that his fellow pedestrians didn't seem to. "They were trying to get to the *next* moment," he says, "which they believed would be better than this one. It's a form of collective madness." The first of many bursts of laughter resounds in the big space.

Despite his Hobbit-like mien and droll sense of humor, which inclines him to follow a comment on the meaning of life with a wry, oh-brother eye roll, Tolle is a mystic: someone who, regardless of religious denomination, lives in a state of intense, smell-the-roses attention to the unity and goodness of the ultimate reality that Marcus Aurelius described. Aware that new listeners can focus only on bits and pieces of this very big picture, he reiterates the same few basic concepts throughout his Friday-night and Saturday-afternoon talks.

Whether called consciousness or Now, mind or God, the ultimate reality to which Tolle directs his audience's attention is all that there is: not "up there" to be perceived in some hazy future paradise but experienced "down here," right now, inside you. Seen from this perspective, our customary focus on things temporal and material is the major cause of human misery, because it distracts us from attending to timeless, formless true reality.

In different ways throughout both sessions, Tolle explains how focusing on matters of time and form—stuff, including thoughts—prevents us from apprehending the way things really are. The obsession with time attunes us to the past or future, which makes no sense because the past is, well, past, and "when the future comes, it too is the present," he says. "The clock's hands move, but it's always now." Considering that this moment is all that there is, he says, we might as well pay attention to it: "Can you allow the present to be as it is? Make friends with it?"

Moving from our fixation on time to our focus on thoughts, Tolle says that we believe we could grasp the point of life if we could just read the right book or find the right teacher—in short, by thinking about it. Yet the awareness of true reality is an experience, not an idea, that in fact requires a "radical refusal of thoughts" in favor of a simple state of attending to the moment. "Your purpose—the fullness of life—is just to be here now," he says. "To be the space for whatever happens. Try to do that often throughout the day. The length of time doesn't matter. Always choose now."

ALONG WITH DIRECTING your attention to a deeper reality than the humdrum status quo, philosophy, religion, and psychology focus you on morality and ethics: becoming a better person and creating a better world by cultivating what previous generations unabashedly called virtues. You don't hear that term very often these days, but the University of Michigan psychologist Chris Peterson and some academic peers would like to change that. They've identified six major qualities—wisdom, courage, temperance, justice, humanity (love), and transcendence—and their subcategories as amenable to scientific study. They have a practical motivation for what at first might seem to be a very high-minded pursuit: virtues are robustly associated with well-being.

Despite the traditional emphasis on development as a youthful phenomenon, new studies of the brain's neuroplasticity and of how we acquire certain values, such as honesty or fairness, support the experience of Ebenezer Scrooge: it's never too late to focus on becoming a better person. In fact, says Peterson, "Aristotle taught that you work on developing virtues over your whole life, but you don't really display them until middle age." (Along with more familiar qualities, the sage's list included "magnificence," or making generous gifts to the gods.)

Attention plays a major role in the cultivation of virtue. In fact, in a secular, materialistic culture, the first hurdle in developing such a quality is often simply recognizing it as what it is: not just some random nice thing that you do almost by accident, but the deliberate exercise of a particular ethical or moral strength. Thus, when you stifle a harsh comment or put a problem in the proper perspective, you label it correctly as "self-control" or "wisdom." Unaccustomed to thinking in such terms, many of Peterson's subjects are surprised when he shows them evidence that they're kind, say, or courageous; they'd just never thought of themselves that way.

Once you're clear about what virtues are and which ones you want to cultivate, the next step is to be on the lookout for what Peterson calls "character moments," or everyday opportunities to practice these qualities. "That's a very Jamesian idea," he says. "You deliberately pay attention to your behavior and establish habits that eventually become second nature."

We tend to focus on virtue displayed in heroic circumstances: the bravery of John McCain in an enemy's prison or the justice sought by Martin Luther King in the segregated South. In everyday life, however, most opportunities to build character are modest in scope and easily missed if you're not paying attention. Mother Teresa and Mahatma Gandhi may epitomize the quality of humanity, or unconditional love, but that doesn't stop Peterson from his own pursuit of the virtue on a smaller scale. Offering an example, he says that while rushing home from the psych department one evening, he saw a distraught student clutching a late term paper in the hallway. He could have easily continued on his way, but instead of passing her by, he stopped to reopen the locked office and help her find the faculty mailbox she sought. This small act didn't change the world, but it helped one person and brought another closer to making kindness a habit. "It only required two minutes of my life," he says, "so I took that opportunity and felt a little bit nicer, a little bit better afterwards."

When Emerson wrote, "Make yourself necessary to someone," he anticipated modern research that strongly correlates altruism with well-being. "It's virtually impossible to be happy without good relationships," says Peterson. "That comes out in the research again and again." It's often said that virtue is its own reward, but love and its corollary of kindness confer other major benefits on those who practice them. Whether or not the recipients gain, says Peterson, "we know that the doers do! They're happier and healthier and live longer than people who pursue all the latest toys but never have enough."

The world abounds in kind and hopeful people, but exemplars of what the philosophers sternly called "corrective virtues" are fewer on the ground. Temperance and its habits of modesty, prudence, and avoidance of excess are difficult to develop because they counter stubborn flaws in human nature. As Peterson says, "We're temperate because we're tempted not to be. Are you in control of yourself or are you out of control? It's all about 'self-regulation,' which is a trendy subject in psychology these days. And you become self-regulating by *being* self-regulating, by forgoing or delaying gratification." Because temperance is difficult to develop and requires your deliberate action, he says, "attention plays a particularly important role. We need to *concentrate* on acquiring a trait such as modesty, because we all want to brag about ourselves."

Most parents draw their kids' attention to the importance of developing honesty, fairness, and other virtues, but fewer follow through on the principle that actions speak louder than words. "It's teaching through example," says Peterson. "The parent should label the behavior, whether it's wisdom, courage, or temperance, and also model it." As with adults, the most important virtue for kids to develop in terms of their short- and long-term well-being is love. "When I get up on my soapbox to talk to parents," says Peterson, "I tell them, 'If you want your kids to be happy, don't worry about their GPA, worry about their extracurricular activities. Never stand in the way of their making friends.'"

Data gathered by the Pew Research Center suggest that, in their own self-interest and for the common good, the eighteen- to twenty-five-year-olds who comprise the so-called Generation Next may need to focus on developing concern for others. They're more socially and politically liberal than the Generation Xers who preceded them, but their overriding goal is to become rich and famous. "It's all me, me, me and pleasure, pleasure, pleasure," says Peterson, "but there's lots of evidence that that's what makes people unhappy."

To the poet W. H. Auden, "To pray is to pay attention or, shall we say, to 'listen' to someone or something other than oneself." Most academics are cautious if not negative about discussing religion, and it's with a certain hesitation that Peterson says, "I'm a card-carrying liberal, but politically and religiously conservative people are much more generous. They're responsible for most of the charity in America—not just money, but even blood. Maybe the religious aspect makes them more optimistic and hopeful and not so cynical. They're not so squeamish about focusing on trying to improve their character."

Attending to the pursuit of virtue rather than profit or pleasure may sound positively un-American, but the string of best sellers chronicling the lives of the Founding Fathers suggests otherwise. Flaws and failings notwithstanding, Washington, Jefferson, Adams, and Franklin actively focused on cultivating and projecting good character, which included public service. "Nowadays you don't hear people saying that they're working on becoming a better person," says Peterson, "but once upon a time, they did. Wouldn't it be great if instead of just working out at the gym, we'd go off and focus on doing something that makes us better people?"

. . .

PHILOSOPHY, RELIGION, AND psychology not only focus you on a larger reality and the creation of a better self and world, but also, albeit more recently for psychology, on the often overlooked fact that life is good and meant to be appreciated. As Albert Einstein put it, "There are two ways to live your life. One is as though nothing is a miracle. The other is as though everything is a miracle."

Traditionally, behavioral science has focused less on life's goodness than on its struggles and pain. When Fred Bryant, a psychologist at Chicago's Loyola University, combed his field's archives for research on pleasure, what little information there was suggested that the point of enjoyment is to serve as an occasional "breather" that helps get you through hard times. Dissatisfied with this bleak conclusion, Bryant began to study a form of rapt attention that he calls "savoring," or the mindful, intentional focus on positive feelings: "If you can't say, 'Yes, I was aware of and attended to that pleasure,' it's not savoring."

Research on savoring shows that your sense of satisfaction depends more on your top-down focus, whether it's enjoying the first day of spring or stewing over a bitchy relative's behavior, than on your circumstances, such as whether you're rich or poor, sick or well. In one experiment, Bryant tested his subjects' psychological health, then divided them into three groups. Each was asked to go for a twenty-minute walk every day for a week, but in pursuit of three different top-down goals. One group was told to focus on all the upbeat things they could find—sunshine, flowers, smiling pedestrians. Another was to look for negative stuff— graffiti, litter, frowning faces. The third group was instructed to walk just for the exercise.

At the end of the week, when the walkers' well-being was tested again, those who had deliberately targeted positive cues were happier than before the experiment. The negatively focused subjects were less happy, and the just plain exercisers scored in between. The point, says Bryant, is that "you see what you look for. And you can train yourself to attend to the joy out there waiting to be had, instead of passively waiting for it to come to you."

If you want to savor, you can focus on an internal feeling, as when you thrill with joy, bask in pride, swell with gratitude, or marvel in awe. You can also attend to a sensory pleasure, such as gazing at a rainbow or letting a great piece of chocolate melt in your mouth. Recalling a man who took a special delight in concrete sidewalks, Bryant says, "One person can enjoy something that no one else could. Savoring reveals the tremendous creativity of the human mind."

Whether you're focused on your ice cream cone or your Nobel Prize, the experience's beginning and ending offer the best savoring opportunities. Initially, sheer novelty grabs your attention, as do later cues that something is almost finished. Those first and last few bites of cake, rays of light, or days of vacation prompt you to appreciate what you have and then, are about to lose. "Like the songs put it, you don't know what you had till it's lost," says Bryant. "You want to wring out all the joy that you can from a good experience."

Thanks to your brain's time-traveling capacity, your potential for focusing on life's good things isn't limited to the here-and-now. You can look back at or forward to something nice, of course. Thanks to "anticipated recall," you can also think, while on your honeymoon, perhaps, or at a graduation, about how much you'll enjoy recalling the happy event some day. As Bryant says, "You can even return to the past and remember a happy time when you looked forward to something in the future."

Despite our great potential for attending to life's pleasures, it often remains largely untapped. As Robert Louis Stevenson observed, "There is no duty we so much underrate as the duty of being happy." At one end of the savoring spectrum are people who never relish anything, says Bryant: "They can take a beautiful day and run it into the ground." At the opposite end are the lucky individuals, particularly older people, who take de-light in little things, like pancakes for breakfast or a stupid pet trick.

Despite their generally lower socioeconomic status worldwide, women savor more than men. One reason could be that females usually get more encouragement to feel and express emotion than males, who are generally trained to have a stiff-upper-lip, action-oriented approach to life. As Bryant puts it, "Why would a guy bask in pleasure when there's more work to be done?"

Whatever your age or gender, the great obstacle to enjoying the moment's delights is not paying attention to them. The world's most beautiful garden might as well be an asphalt parking lot if you pound through it while barking into your cell phone. Urgency about time is another major obstacle to savoring. "'If we have to walk through the garden, let's get a move on!'" says Bryant. "'I have stuff to do!'" As he points out, however, "No moment comes twice. If you don't attend to it, you miss it. If you want to smell the roses, you have to *linger.*"

Just as the ancient Greeks feared their pleasure would anger the gods, some people won't focus on the joys of the present lest they jinx the future. Particularly in Japan, Bryant has observed this anxious "yin/yang feeling that if something good happens, something bad will come along to 'make up for it.' The more you hold this view, the more you try to short-circuit savoring and 'calm down.'"

Attending to pleasure is a reward in itself, but savoring also boosts your quotient of positive emotion, which in turn expands your focus and may confer health benefits, such as improved resilience and immune function. During an illness, says Bryant, "you should savor not just for the sheer joy of it, but also to help yourself recover." Then too, he says, "just because something bad is happening doesn't mean lots of good things aren't also. They're two very different phenomena. The joy and meaning you find in life and the current stressor—an illness, a troubled relative, a career setback—are separate concerns, and you can experience both."

The best strategy for savoring is learning to pay rapt attention to carefully chosen top-down targets. To practice this skill, Bryant suggests taking a "daily vacation": spending twenty to thirty minutes focusing on something you enjoy or suspect you might but have never done. Then, at the end of the day, you revisit and relish that pleasurable interlude and plan the next sojourn. After seven days, he says, "most people say, 'What a great week! I wish I could do that all of the time!' Well, why not?"

AFTERWORD

Over the five years since running the psych experiment that led to this book, learning about the nature of attention and how it affects love, work, and everything between has changed my life in some important ways. Actually, I've come to feel that paying rapt attention *is* life, at least at its best.

Focused is how we want to feel. The evidence is all around us, from the calm yet alert faces of athletes "in the zone" to mothers cradling their babies, tradesmen bent over their work, musicians playing their instruments. In *Shine a Light,* Martin Scorsese's documentary on the Rolling Stones, when Keith Richards is asked how he feels when he emerges onstage to confront a hundred thousand screaming fans, he says simply, "I wake up." He's a rocker, not a philosopher, yet his remark echoes those of William James—"Compared to what we ought to be, we are half awake"—and the Buddha: "I am awake." In life's best moments, whether we're writing a book or a letter, making love or dinner, that's how we are, too: awake, focused, *rapt.*

Some of what I've learned about attention has very practical applications. Aware of our limited focusing capacity, I take pains to ensure that electronic media and machines aren't in charge of mine. When I need to learn and remember certain information, do difficult work, or acquire a new skill, I shield myself from such distractions for at least ninety minutes at a stretch. If I tense up over a big decision, I remember the fortune-cookie rule: nothing is as important as I think it is when I'm focusing on it.

Confronted with a seemingly dull chore—say, the laundry—I recall William James's experiment with the dot on the piece of paper and do it a little differently. (One day last summer, when I decided to hang the clothes on the line outdoors instead of just sticking them in the dryer, I saw a double rainbow.) When I can't fathom something that a dear one has just said or done, I try to remember that he or she focuses on a different world and ask for some illumination.

Most important, I've become much more aware of how the way I feel affects what I pay attention to and vice versa. Depending on my emotional state *du jour,* I might barely notice the stack of dirty dishes that someone has dumped in the sink or perceive it as a smoldering Mt. Vesuvius. Should the latter reaction prevail, I've learned that I can ameliorate its consequences for all concerned by refocusing on the situation in a different light—the party responsible is not an awful person but perhaps only distracted by a big project—or by shifting my attention to something else for a while. Simple as it sounds, this strategy is surprisingly effective.

Even in far more difficult situations, I've learned that once any appropriate problem-solving efforts are under way, I needn't stay focused on outrageous fortune's slings and arrows. Tomorrow morning, I'll visit my ninety-four-year-old mother, Winnie, who is becoming very frail in body and mind and is once again in a nursing home. To paraphrase John Milton, "Heaven or hell?" It will depend on what we focus on.

ACKNOWLEDGMENTS

For their contributions to our understanding of attention and for kindly sharing their insights with me, I wish to thank George Ainslie, Marie Banich, Aaron Beck, Marlene Behrmann, George Bonanno, Thomas Bradbury, Rodney Brooks, Bill Brown, Fred Bryant, Laura Carstensen, Javier Castellanos, Tanya Chartrand, Mihály Csíkszentmihályi, Richard Davidson, Edward Deci, Angela Duckworth, Dugu Choegyal Rinpoche, Carol Dweck, Barbara Fredrickson, Howard Gardner, Joseph Giunta, Scott Hagwood, Shannon Howell, Amishi Jha, Jon Kabat-Zinn, Daniel Kahneman, Ellen Langer, Marsel Mesulam, Richard Nisbett, Donald Norman, Elinor Ochs, James Pawelski, Chris Peterson, Gail Posner, Michael Posner, Lobsang Rapgay, Mary Rothbart, Paul Rozin, Oliver Schultheiss, Barry Schwartz, Paschal Sheeran, Ann Treisman, and Leslie Ungerleider.

I also thank Rachel Aviv for research and reporting made possible by the Hertog Fellowship Program at Columbia University's School of the Arts.

For their particular insights and generosity I am especially grateful to Steve Yantis, Auke Tellegen, David Meyer, and Ann-Judith Silverman.

Finally, I thank Ann Godoff, my editor, Kristine Dahl, my agent, and Lindsay Whalen, John McGhee, and the staff of Penguin Press for their erudition, kindness, and hard work on my behalf.

NOTES AND
SUGGESTED READINGS

INTRODUCTION

p.5. **John Milton might have been thinking:** John Milton, *Paradise Lost.* New York: Penguin Classics, 2003.

p.6. **In his masterwork:** William James, *The Principles of Psychology,* Chapter XI: "Attention." Cambridge, Mass.: Harvard University Press, 1981.

p.6. **Despite this kind of gut-level understanding:** Donald Norman, *Memory and Attention.* New York: John Wiley & Sons, 1969.

p.7. **Still unable to penetrate the black box:** E. C. Cherry, "Some Experiments on the Recognition of Speech, with One and with Two Ears." *Journal of the Acoustical Society of America* 23:915–19, 1953.

p.7. **Some theories stressed the stimulus's physical characteristics:** D. E. Broadbent, *Perception and Communication.* London: Pergamon Press, 1958.

p.7. **others its content, such as your own name:** N. Moray, "Attention in Dichotic Listening: Affective Cues and the Influence of Instructions." *Quarterly Journal of Experimental Psychology* 11, 1959.

p.7. **and still others both:** A. Treisman and G. Gelade, "A Feature Integration Theory of Attention." *Cognitive Psychology* 12, 1980.

p.7. **Their efforts were so vague:** H. Egeth and W. Bevan, "Attention," in B. B. Wollman (ed.), *Handbook of General Psychology.* Englewood Cliffs, N.J.: Prentice-Hall, 1973.

p.8. **There's no tidy "attention center":** Michael Posner, *The Cognitive Neuroscience of Attention.* New York: Guilford, 2004.

p.9. **Neuroscience's truly groundbreaking insight:** Robert Desimone and John Duncan, "Neural Mechanisms of Selective Visual Attention." *Annual Review of Neuroscience* 18, March 1995.

p.12. **Even in the hell of the Nazi**

death camps: Viktor E. Frankl, *Man's Search for Meaning*. Boston: Beacon Press, 2006.

p.12. **The rates of psychological problems:** Peter Suedfeld, "Stressful levels of environmental stimulation," in I. G. Sarason and C. D. Spielberger (eds.), *Stress and Anxiety*, Halstead, 1979.

CHAPTER 1: PAY ATTENTION

p.17. **Many extraordinary achievers are fueled:** David Lykken, "Mental Energy." *Intelligence* 33, 2005.

p.18. **Even the *New York Times*'s psychologically savvy:** David Brooks, "The Neural Buddhists." *New York Times*, July 13, 2008.

p.19. **An amusing experiment on "change blindness":** Daniel J. Simons and Christopher F. Chabris, "Gorillas in Our Midst: Sustained Inattentional Blindness for Dynamic Events." *Perception* 28, 1999.

p.20. **A little knowledge about this neurological "biased competition":** Robert Desimone and John Duncan, "Neural Mechanisms of Selective Visual Attention." *Annual Review of Neuroscience* 18, March 1995.

p.20. **According to the Johns Hopkins neuroscientist:** Steven Yantis, "To See Is to Attend." *Science*, January 2003.

p.21. **If you're told to concentrate on a spot:** S. Kastner, Leslie Ungerleider et al., "Increased Activity in Human Visual Cortex during Directed Attention in the Absence of Visual Stimulation." *Neuron* 22, 1999; Leslie Ungerleider and S. Kast-

ner, "Mechanisms of Visual Attention in the Human Cortex." *Annual Review of Neuroscience* 23, 2000.

p.23. **Unlike peers who see a dichotomy:** M. Behrmann and J. J. Geng, "Attention," in E. E. Smith and S. M. Kosslyn (eds.), *Cognitive Psychology: Mind and Brain*. New York: Prentice-Hall, 2006; J. Duncan, "Eps Mid-Career Award 2004: Brain Mechanisms of Attention." *Quarterly Journal of Experimental Psychology* 59, 2006.

p.24. **subjects who focused on a task while researchers flashed images:** Alan J. Parkin, John M. Gardiner, and Rebecca Rosser, "Functional Aspects of Recollective Experience in Face Recognition." *Consciousness and Cognition*, December 1995.

p. 24. **As the poet John Ashbery observes:** John Ashbery, *Rivers and Mountains*. New York: Holt, Rinehart & Winston, 1966.

p.25. **As research on the "beauty bias" shows:** Ingrid Olson, "Facial Attractiveness Is Appraised in a Glance." *Emotion* 5, 2005.

p.26. **After much research on binding:** A. Treisman, "Search, Similarity and the Integration of Features Between and Within Dimensions." *Journal of Experimental Psychology: Human Perception and Performance* 27, 1991.

CHAPTER 2: INSIDE OUT

p.30. **The painting's subject matter reflects:** Edmund Burke, *A Philosophical Enquiry into the Origin of Our Ideas of the Sublime and Beautiful*. New York: Oxford University Press, 1998.

p.31. **Scientists as well as artists:** J. A. Easterbrook, "The Effect of Emotion on Cue Utilization and the Organization of Behavior." *Psychological Review* 66, 1959.

As Charles Darwin wrote . . . Charles Darwin. *Expression of the Emotions in Man and Animals.* Philosophical Library, 1955.

p.32. **In August 2007:** www.this americanlife.org/Radio_episode.aspx?sch ed=1203.

p.32. **In a survey of which topics:** Roy Baumeister, Ellen Bratslavsky, Catrin Finkenauer, and Kathleen D. Vohs, "Bad Is Stronger Than Good." *Review of General Psychology*, 2001.

p.32. **You'll spot an angry face:** Christine Hansen and Ranald Hansen, "Finding the Face in the Crowd." *Journal of Personality and Social Psychology*, 1988.

p.33. **You'll process and remember negative material:** Kyle Smith et al., "Being Bad Isn't Always Good: Affective Context Moderates the Attention Bias Toward Negative Information." *Journal of Personality and Social Psychology*, 2006.

p.33. **react to critical words:** M. Inaba, M. Nomura, and H. Ohira, "Neural Evidence of Effects of Emotional Valence on Word Recognition." *International Journal of Psychophysiology,* 2005.

p.33. **focus on printed adjectives that describe personality:** Felicia Pratto and Oliver P. John, "Automatic Vigilance: The Attention-Grabbing Power of Negative Social Information." *Journal of Personality and Social Psychology*, 1991.

p.33. **You'll listen longer to complaints:** W. G. Graziano et al., "Attention, Attraction, and Individual Differences in Response to Criticism" (1980), cited in Smith et al., "Being Bad Isn't Always Good."

p.33. **Even when you sleep:** Natalie Angier, "In the Dreamscape of Nightmares, Clues to Why We Dream at All." *New York Times*, October 23, 2007.

p.33. **Here's the icing on the cake:** "Chances of Heart Attack Are Greatest on Birthday." *New York Times*, March 19, 1993.

p.33. **Looking at the dark side of things:** Emine Kapcli et al., "Judgement of Control Revisited: Are the Depressed Realistic or Pessimistic?" *Counselling Psychology Quarterly* 12: 1, March 1999.

p.35. **In fact, some research asserts that most people feel "mildly pleased":** Daniel Kahneman et al., "A Survey Method for Characterizing Daily Life Experience: The Day Reconstruction Method." *Science*, December 3, 2004.

p.35. **According to complementary studies, you'll tend to:** Richard Walker, Rodney Vogl, and Charles Thompson, "Autobiographical Memory: Unpleasantness Fades Faster Than Pleasantness Over Time." *Applied Cognitive Psychology,* 1997.

p.35. **There are as many nights as days:** Carl Jung, *Memories, Dreams, Reflections.* New York: Vintage, 1989.

p.35. **Based on objective lab tests that measure vision:** Barbara Fredrickson, *Positivity: Groundbreaking Research Reveals How to Embrace the Hidden Strength of Positive Emotions, Overcome Negativity, and Thrive.* New York: Crown, 2009.

p.36. **the "weapons effect":** Michael Wilson, "After 50 Witnesses in Trial Over Police Killing, Still No Clear View of 50 Shots." *New York Times,* April 5, 2008.

p.36. **Just as bad feelings constrict your attention:** Barbara Fredrickson and Thomas Joiner, "Positive Emotions

Trigger Upward Spirals Toward Emotional Well-Being." *Psychological Science,* 2002.

p.37. **Here's Prince Andrei in *War and Peace:*** Leo Tolstoy, *War and Peace,* translated by Richard Pevear and Larissa Volokhonsky. New York: Knopf, 2007.

p.37. **The type of complex inner experience:** Donald A. Norman, *Emotional Design: Why We Love (or Hate) Everyday Things.* New York: Basic Books, 2004.

p.38. **The influential Dutch psychologist:** A. Dijksterhuis et al., "Of Men and Mackerels: Attention and Automatic Behavior," in Herbert Bless and Joseph P. Forgas (eds.), *The Message Within.* Philadelphia: Psychology Press, 2000.

p.40. **Research on a fascinating group of brain-injured patients:** Marlene Behrmann and J. J. Geng, "Attention," in Smith and Kosslyn (eds.), *Cognitive Psychology.* New York: Prentice-Hall, 2006.

p.40. **In one much-cited experiment, a man is shown a picture:** John C. Marshall and Peter W. Halligan, "Blindsight and Insight in Visuo-Spatial Neglect." *Nature* 336, December 29, 1988.

CHAPTER 3: OUTSIDE IN

p.43. **As the poet:** W. H. Auden, *A Certain World.* London: Faber and Faber, 1982.

p.44. **Fortunately, all cultures try to help you bias:** Paul Rozin and C. Nemeroff, "Sympathetic Magical Thinking: The Contagion and Similarity 'Heuristics,'" in T. Gilovich, D. Griffin, and D. Kahneman, *Heuristics and Biases: The Psychology of Intuitive Judgment.* Cambridge: Cambridge University Press, 2002.

p.44. **"Disgust is the basic emotion":** P. Rozin, J. Haidt, and C. R. McCauley, "Disgust," in M. Lewis and J. Haviland (eds.), *Handbook of Emotions,* 2nd ed. New York: Guilford, 2000.

p.48. **In one large, rigorous study of 941 Dutch subjects over ten years:** Erik J. Giltay et al., "Dispositional Optimism and the Risk of Cardiovascular Death: The Zutphen Elderly Study." *Archives of Internal Medicine* 166, February 27, 2006.

p.48. **Because your reaction to any event:** B. L. Fredrickson and C. Branigan, "Positive Emotions Broaden the Scope of Attention and Thought-Action Repertoires," *Cognition and Emotion* 19, 2005.

p.50. **Compared with the young, the old experience:** Laura Carstensen and J. A. Mikels, "At the Intersection of Emotion and Cognition: Aging and the Positively Effect." *Current Directions in Psychological Science* 14, 2005.

p.51. **The differences in what young and old people:** Laura Carstensen, "The Influence of a Sense of Time on Human Development." *Science* 312, 2006.

p.52. **Debriefing-style counseling after a trauma:** Sharon Begley, "Get Shrunk at Your Own Risk." *Newsweek,* June 18, 2007.

p.52. **Even when you're reeling from a severe blow:** G. Bonanno and K. Coifman, "Does Repressive Coping Promote Resilience?: Affective-Autonomic Response Discrepancy During Bereavement." *Journal of Personality and Social Psychology,* April 2007.

p.52. **The idea that directing your attention away:** Anthony Papa et al., "Grief Processing and Deliberate Grief Avoidance: A Prospective Comparison of Bereaved Spouses and Parents in the United States and the People's Republic of China." *Journal of Consulting & Clinical Psychology* 73, 2005.

p.53. **Individuals of sanguine temperament:** G. Bonanno and H. Siddique, "Emotional Dissociation, Self-Deception, and Psychotherapy," in Jefferson A. Singer and Peter Salovey (eds.), *At Play in the Fields of Consciousness.* Mahwah, N.J.: Lawrence Erlbaum Associates, 1999.

p.63. **Similarly, physiological differences in tongues and taste buds:** L. M. Bartoshuk, V. B. Duffy, and I. J. Miller, "PTC/PROP Tasting: Anatomy, Psychophysics, and Sex Effects." *Physiology & Behavior* 56, 1994.

p.64. **He describes its alerting, orienting, and executive networks:** Michael Posner, *The Cognitive Neuroscience of Attention.* New York: Guilford, 2004.

p.64. **With the University of Oregon psychologist Mary Rothbart:** Michael Posner and Mary Rothbart, *Educating the Human Brain.* Washington, D.C.: American Psychological Association Books, 2006.

CHAPTER 4: NATURE

p.56. **When discussing his favorite targets:** Winifred Gallagher, *Just the Way You Are.* New York: Random House, 1996.

p.57. **Among these temperamentally unhappy campers are "reactant" personalities:** Allison Van Dusen, "Don't Like Being Nagged?" Forbes.com, April 22, 2007.

p.57. **A particularly interesting example of how:** Lorraine and J. Clayton Lafferty, *Perfectionism: A Sure Cure for Happiness.* Chicago: Human Synergistics, 1997.

p.57. **Because they consistently pay too much attention to the wrong things:** Clayton Lafferty, *Perfectionism: A Sure Cure for Happiness.* Chatsworth, Calif.: Wilshire Books, 1997.

p.59. **A person's attentional style:** Auke Tellegen, *Multidimensional Personality Questionnaire.* Minneapolis: University of Minnesota Press, 1993.

CHAPTER 5: NURTURE

p.67. **For a story called:** Gene Weingarten, "Pearls Before Breakfast." *Washington Post*, April 8, 2007.

p.68. **In one much-publicized early demonstration of the adult brain's unsuspected malleability:** E. A. Maguire et al., "Navigation-Related Structural Changes in the Hippocampi of Taxi Drivers." *Proceedings of the National Academy of Sciences* 97, 2000.

p.69. **Using sophisticated EEG (electroencephalography) and fMRI scanning:** R. J. Davidson and A. Lutz, "Buddha's Brain: Neuroplasticity and Meditation." *IEEE Signal Processing* 25, 2008.

p.70. **Indeed, research done by Paul Ekman:** D. Keltner et al., "Facial Expression of Emotion," in R. J. Davidson, K. R. Scherer, and H. H. Goldsmith (eds.), *Handbook of Affective Sciences.* New York: Oxford University Press, 2003.

p.75. **In *The Big Sort*:** Bill Bishop and Robert Cushing, *The Big Sort*. New York: Houghton Mifflin, 2008.

p.75. **In his research on how cultural experience influences:** R. E. Nisbett, *The Geography of Thought: How Asians and Westerners Think Differently . . . and Why.* New York: The Free Press, 2003.

CHAPTER 6: RELATIONSHIPS

p.82. **Because it's impossible to communicate:** Rodney A. Brooks, *Flesh and Machines: How Robots Will Change Us.* New York: Pantheon, 2003.

p.82. **Intrigued by the "monkey see, monkey do" antics:** Marco Iacoboni et al., "Cortical Mechanisms of Human Imitation." *Science* 286, 1999; Marco Iacoboni, *Mirroring People: The New Science of How We Connect with Others.* New York: Farrar, Straus and Giroux, 2008.

p.82. **Evolution seems to have designed us:** Daniel Goleman, *Social Intelligence.* New York: Bantam, 2007.

p.84. **Indeed, having social ties is the single best predictor:** Ronald Kessler et al., *How Healthy Are We?* Chicago: University of Chicago Press, 2004.

p.85. **Research by the Canadian psychologist Joanne Wood shows:** J. V. Wood et al., "Downward Comparison in Everyday Life: Reconciling Self-Enhancement Models With the Mood-Cognition Priming Model." *Journal of Personality and Social Psychology* 79, 2000.

p.85. **When employees focus on how their efforts:** Adam Grant and Elizabeth Campbell, "Doing Good, Doing Harm, Being Well, and Burning Out: The Interactions of Perceived Prosocial and Antisocial Impact in Service Work." *Journal of Occupational & Organizational Psychology* 80 (4), December 2007.

p.85. **When they're focused on either a social activity or a task:** Mihály Csíkszentmihályi, *Flow: The Psychology of Optimal Experience.* New York: Harper, 1991.

p.86. **An anthropologist, linguist, winner of the MacArthur "genius" award:** Elinor Ochs, *Living Narrative: Creating Lives in Everyday Storytelling.* Boston: Harvard University Press, 2002.

p.87. **Despite the claims made for products:** Alice Park, "Baby Einsteins: Not So Smart After All." *Time,* August 6, 2007.

p.91. **Yet as the director of the UCLA family project's "marriage lab":** T. N. Bradbury and B. R. Karney, "Understanding and Altering the Longitudinal Course of Marriage." *Journal of Marriage and the Family* 66, 2004; T. N. Bradbury et al., "Problem-solving Skills and Affective Expressions as Predictors of Change in Marital Satisfaction." *Journal of Consulting and Clinical Psychology* 73, 2005.

p.91. **In fact, research shows that contented spouses see each other:** Sandra Murray et al., "Putting the Partner Within Reach: A Dyadic Perspective on Felt Security in Close Relationships." *Journal of Personality and Social Psychology* 88, 2005.

p.91. **A study with the seemingly counterintuitive title:** Shelly Gable et al., "Will You Be There for Me When Things Go Right? Supportive Responses to Positive Event Disclosures." *Journal of Personality and Social Psychology* 91, 2006.

p.92. **First, half of the subjects were told they were "home-buyers":** J. D. Bransford and M. K. Johnson, "Contextual Prerequisites for Understanding: Some Investigations of Comprehension and Recall." *Journal of Verbal Learning and Verbal Behavior* 11, 1972.

p.93. **spouses were given a long checklist:** Patti L. Johnson and K. Daniel O'Leary, "Behavioral Components of Marital Satisfaction: An Individualized Assessment Approach." *Journal of Consulting and Clinical Psychology* 64, 1996.

p.96. **In a maladaptive version of the Punch-and-Judy dynamic:** Jee Burgeon, Charles Berger, and Vincent Waldron, "Mindfulness and Interpersonal Communication." *Journal of Social Issues* 56, 2000.

p.96. **Differences in self-esteem also influence:** Sandra Murray, "Regulating the Risks of Closeness." *Current Directions in Psychological Science* 14, 2005.

p.98. **the good old Friday-night date, especially one that features:** A. Aron et al., "Couples' Shared Participation in Novel and Arousing Activities and Experienced Relationship Quality." *Journal of Personality and Social Psychology* 72, 2000.

CHAPTER 7: PRODUCTIVITY

p.99. **To William James, rapt attention requires:** William James, *The Principles of Psychology,* Chapter XI: "Attention." Cambridge, Mass.: Harvard University Press, 1981.

p.101. **According to the underappreciated mid-twentieth-century psychologist Nicholas Hobbs:** Nicholas Hobbs, "A Natural History of an Idea: Project Re-Ed," in J. M. Kaufman and C. D. Lewis (eds.), *Teaching Children with Behavioral Disorders.* Columbus, Ohio: Charles E. Merrill, 1974.

p.101. **Tellingly, one group is distinguished by its zeal:** David C. McClelland, *The Achieving Society.* New York: The Free Press, 1967.

p.102. **The insights into rapt attention's role in human behavior in general:** Mihály Csíkszentmihályi, *Flow: The Psychology of Optimal Experience.* New York: Harper, 1991; *Good Business: Leadership, Flow, and the Making of Meaning.* New York: Viking, 2003; and *Creativity: Flow and the Psychology of Discovery and Invention.* New York: Harper, 1997.

p.105. **Research conducted by the University of Michigan psychologist Oliver Schultheiss:** Oliver Schultheiss and Joachim C. Brunstein, "Goal Imagery: Bridging the Gap Between Implicit Motives and Explicit Goals." *Journal of Personality* 67, 1999.

p.105. **Support for these underremarked workplace gratifications:** Arlie Russell Hochschild, *The Commercialization of Intimate Life: Notes from Home and Work.* Berkeley: University of California Press, 2003.

p.107. **According to the psychologist Gilbert Brim:** Gilbert Brim, *Ambition.* New York: Basic Books, 1992.

p.111. **In one ESM study, 866 teenagers:** Jennifer Schmidt and Rich Grant, "Images of Work and Play," in

Mihály Csíkszentmihályi and Barbara Schneider (eds.), *Becoming Adult: How Teenagers Prepare for the World of Work.* New York: Basic Books, 2000.
p. 113. **In *The Evolving Self: A Psychology for the Third Millennium:*** Mihály Csíkszentmihályi, *The Evolving Self.* New York: Harper Perennial, 1994.

CHAPTER 8: DECISIONS

p. 116. **Early in his long and varied career:** Daniel Kahneman, *Attention and Effort.* Englewood Cliffs, N.J.: Prentice-Hall, 1973.
p. 119. **He traces this disconnect:** D. Kahneman and J. Riis, "Living, and Thinking About It: Two Perspectives on Life," in F. A. Huppert, N. Baylis, and B. Keverne (eds.), *The Science of Well-being.* Oxford: Oxford University Press, 2005.
p. 120. **In one much-cited illustration of the focusing illusion:** D. Schkade and D. Kahneman, "Does Living in California Make People Happy? A Focusing Illusion in Judgments of Life Satisfaction." *Psychological Science* 9, 1998.
p. 127. **In our age of endlessly proliferating consumer goods:** Barry Schwartz, *The Paradox of Choice.* New York: Harper, 2005.

CHAPTER 9: CREATIVITY

p. 133. **William James's simple experiment on how to improve:** William James, *The Principles of Psychology,* Chapter XI: "Attention." Cambridge, Mass.: Harvard University Press, 1981.

p. 134. **Since the muses of ancient Greece:** J. P. Guilford, "The Traits of Creativity," in H. H. Anderson (ed.), *Creativity and Its Cultivation.* New York: Harper & Row, 1959.
p. 135. **This association of focusing and freedom:** Susan Stamberg, "Jazz Improv Cranks Up Creativity." *Weekend Edition*, National Public Radio, March 22, 2008.
p. 136. **Creativity is most commonly associated with the arts, but:** Ellen Langer, *Mindfulness.* Reading, Mass.: Addison Wesley, 1989; "Mindful Learning," *Current Directions in Psychological Science* 9, 2002; *On Becoming an Artist: Reinventing Yourself Through Mindful Creativity.* New York: Ballantine, 2006.
p. 140. **In one poignant indication of what happens when young children:** Constance Kamii and Barbara Anne Lewis, in Ron Ritchhart and David N. Perkins, "Life in the Mindful Classroom: Nurturing the Disposition of Mindfulness." *Journal of Social Issues* 56, 2000.

CHAPTER 10: FOCUS INTERRUPTUS

p. 148. **When writing about two common attentional styles:** William James, *The Principles of Psychology*, Chapter XI: "Attention." Cambridge, Mass.: Harvard University Press, 1981.
p. 148. **That proverbial professor is not the only person:** Daniel Schachter, "The Sin of Absent-mindedness." *The Seven Sins of Memory.* New York: Houghton Mifflin, 2001.
p. 149. **Notwithstanding the importance of "explicit" learning:** D. L.

Schachter, "Implicit Memory: History and Current Status." *Journal of Experimental Psychology: Learning, Memory, and Cognition* 13, 1987.

p. 149. **At first glance, recent research that indicates:** Jonathan Smallwood, Daniel Fishman, and Jonathan Schooler, "Counting the Cost of an Absent Mind." *Psychonomic Bulletin & Review* 14, 2007.

p. 150. **When you head to the cafeteria or gym:** Edward M. Bowden et al., "New Approaches to Demystifying Insight." *Trends in Cognitive Sciences* 9, July 2005.

p. 151. **Finally, not paying attention to anything in particular:** Rachel Kaplan and Stephen Kaplan, *The Experience of Nature.* New York: Cambridge University Press, 1989.

p. 152. **after an enormous amount of practice:** Ulric Neisser, *Cognition and Reality.* San Francisco: Freeman, 1976.

p. 152. **Multitasking's most obvious drawback:** David Meyer, "Précis to a Practical Unified Theory of Executive Cognitive Processes and Multiple-Task Performance," in D. Gopher and A. Koriat (eds.), *Attention and Performance XVII.* Cambridge: MIT Press, 1999.

p. 153. **Using fMRI imaging, UCLA psychologists found:** Peter N. Steinmetz, "Alternate Task Inhibits Single-neuron Category-selective Responses in the Human Hippocampus while Preserving Selectivity in the Amygdala." *Journal of Cognitive Neuroscience,* 2008.

p. 153. **American youths spend an average of 6.5 hours per day:** Claudia Wallis, "The Multitasking Generation." *Time,* March 19, 2006.

p. 154. **Eloquent testimony comes**

from five of Japan's ten best-selling novels: Norimitsu Onishi, "Thumbs Race as Japan's Best Sellers Go Cellular." *New York Times,* January 20, 2008.

p. 156. **if you're, say, driving across Nebraska on I-80:** N. H. Mackworth, "Researches on the Measurement of Human Performance." *Medical Research Council Special Report 268.* London: Her Majesty's Stationery Office, 1950.

p. 157. **In their work with young children:** M. Rosario Rueda, Mary Rothbart, and Michael Posner, "Training, Maturation, and Genetic Influences on the Development of Executive Attention." *Proceedings of the National Academy of Sciences* 102, 2005.

p. 158. **In a study of adults, subjects were presented with from one to five columns:** Paul Verhaeghen, John Cerella, and Basak Chandramallika, "Working Memory Workout: How to Expand the Focus of Serial Attention from One to Four Items in 10 Hours or Less." *Journal of Experimental Psychology: Learning, Memory, and Cognition* 30, 2004.

p. 159. **Her investigation of training attention to improve daily experience:** A. P. Jha, J. Krompinger, and M. J. Baime, "Mindfulness Training Modifies Subsystems of Attention." *Cognitive, Affective & Behavioral Neuroscience* 7, 2007; K. K. Sreenivasan and A. P. Jha, "Selective Attention Supports Working Memory Maintenance by Modulating Perceptual Processing of Distractors." *Journal of Cognitive Neuroscience* 19, 2007.

p. 161. **as suggested by the hyperactive title of a recent book:** Edward Hallowell, *CrazyBusy: Overstretched, Over-*

booked, and About to Snap! Strategies for Coping in a World Gone ADD. New York: Ballantine, 2007.

CHAPTER 11: DISORDERED ATTENTION

p.166. **No one is more aware of the discontent over the current state of knowledge:** F. X. Castellanos et al., "Developmental Trajectories of Brain Volume Abnormalities in Children and Adolescents with Attention-Deficit/-Hyperactivity Disorder," *Journal of the American Medical Association* 288, 2002; "Cingulate-Precuneus Interactions: A New Locus of Dysfunction in Adult Attention-Deficit/Hyperactivity Disorder," *Biological Psychiatry* 63, 2008; F. X. Castellanos and R. Tannock, "Neuroscience of Attention-Deficit Hyperactivity Disorder: The Search for Endophenotypes," *Nature Reviews Neuroscience* 3, 2002.

p.167. **That it's six times likelier to affect children:** R. C. Herrenkohl, B. P. Egolf, and E. C. Herrenkohl, "Preschool Antecedents of Adolescent Assaultive Behavior: A Longitudinal Study." *American Journal of Orthopsychiatry* 67, 1997.

p.168. **About 25 percent of the biological parents of diagnosed kids:** P. C. Kendall and C. Hammen, *Abnormal Psychology.* Boston: Houghton Mifflin, 1995.

p.169. **Waving a book called *Attention, Memory, and Executive Function:*** G. Reid Lyon and Norman A. Krasnegor (eds.). *Attention, Memory, and Executive Function.* Baltimore: Paul H. Brookes, 1996.

CHAPTER 12: MOTIVATION

p.173. **After his subjects had fasted for eight hours:** M.-M. Mesulam, "Spatial Attention and Neglect: Parietal, Frontal and Cingulate Contributions to the Mental Representation and Attentional Targeting of Salient Extrapersonal Targets." *Philosophical Transactions of the Royal Society B: Biological Sciences*, 1999.

p.174. **many simply don't focus on their food:** Brian Wansink, *Mindless Eating.* New York: Bantam, 2007.

p.176. **According to his successor:** David C. McClelland, *The Achieving Society.* New York: The Free Press, 1967.

p.176. **When they examine images of faces:** Oliver C. Schultheiss and Jessica A. Hale, "Implicit Motives Modulate Attentional Orienting to Perceived Facial Expressions of Emotion." *Motivation and Emotion*, 31, 2007.

p.177. **Temperamentally anxious people can have a hard time staying motivated:** Georgia Panayiotou and Scott Vrana, "The Role of Self-Focus, Task Difficulty, Task Self-Relevance, and Evaluation Anxiety in Reaction Time Performance." *Motivation and Emotion* 28, June 2004.

p.177. **Where nurture's impact is concerned:** J. S. Pang and O. C. Schultheiss, "Assessing Implicit Motives in U.S. College Students: Effects of Picture Type and Position, Gender and Ethnicity, and Cross-Cultural Comparisons." *Journal of Personality Assessment* 85, 2005.

p.177. **Interestingly, much of the conventional wisdom:** Carol Dweck, "Caution—Praise Can Be Dangerous." *American Educator*, Spring 1999; *Mindset: The New Psychology of Success.* New York: Ballantine, 2007.

p.178. **Locker-room pep talks and bonuses notwithstanding:** Edward Deci and Maarten Vansteenkiste, "Competitively Contingent Rewards and Intrinsic Motivation: Can Losers Remain Motivated?" *Motivation and Emotion*, October 2003; Edward Deci and Richard Ryan, "The Initiation and Regulation of Intrinsically Motivated Learning and Achievement," in Ann Boggiano and Thane Pittman (eds.), *Achievement and Motivation*. New York: Cambridge University Press, 1992.

p.178. **Why some very focused individuals have lots of the stick-to-it-iveness:** A. L. Duckworth et al., "Grit: Perseverance and Passion for Long-Term Goals." *Journal of Personality and Social Psychology* 92, 2007.

p.179. **A genius such as Isaac Newton, however, has enough "mental energy":** David Lykken, "Mental Energy." *Intelligence* 33, 2005.

p.182. **In a less dramatic illustration of a hidden motivation's power:** Gráinne M. Fitzsimons and John A. Bargh, "Thinking of You: Nonconscious Pursuit of Interpersonal Goals Associated with Relationship Partners." *Journal of Personality and Social Psychology* 84, January 2003.

p.182. **In an ingenious experimental illustration:** Tanya Chartrand et al., "Consequences of Nonconscious Goal Activation." To appear in J. Shah and W. Gardner (eds.), *Handbook of Motivation Science*. New York: Guilford, 2007.

p.183. **In an experiment on how best to deal:** T. L. Webb and P. Sheeran, "How Do Implementation Intentions Promote Goal Attainment? A Test of Component Processes." *Journal of Experimental Social Psychology* 43, 2007.

p.183. **Concerned about the high incidence:** Atul Gawande, "The Checklist." *The New Yorker*, December 10, 2007.

p.184. **Some intriguing new research:** George Ainslie, *Breakdown of Will*. New York: Cambridge University Press, 2001.

CHAPTER 13: HEALTH

p.189. **Exhibit A for attention's power:** "Larry Stewart, a Businessman Known for a Santa-Size Generosity, Dies at 58." Associated Press, January 15, 2007.

p.190. **His discovery that attention's selective nature:** Aaron T. Beck et al., *Cognitive Therapy of Depression*. New York: Guilford, 1987; David A. Clark, Aaron T. Beck, and Brad A. Alford, *Scientific Foundations of Cognitive Theory and Therapy of Depression*. New York: Wiley, 1999.

p.192. **Depression costs the American economy:** Walter Stewart et al., "Cost of Lost Productive Work Time Among US Workers with Depression." *Journal of the American Medical Association*, June 2003.

p.193. **That the ability to control attention:** Suzanne Tyas et al., "Transitions to Mild Cognitive Impairments, Dementia, and Death: Findings from the Nun Study." *American Journal of Epidemiology*, June 2007.

p.193. **Much of the enthusiasm for using attention:** Jon Kabat-Zinn, *Coming to Our Senses: Healing Ourselves and the World Through Mindfulness*. New York: Hyperion, 2005.

p.195. **After eight weeks of classes and daily meditation:** Jon Kabat-Zinn, "An Outpatient Program in Behavioral Medicine Chronic Pain Patients Based on the Practice of Mindfulness Meditation." *General Hospital Psychiatry,* 1982.

p.196. **Two impressive studies of psoriasis patients:** Jon Kabat-Zinn et al., "Influence of a Mindfulness Meditation-Based Stress Reduction Intervention on Rates of Skin Clearing in Patients with Moderate to Severe Psoriasis Undergoing Photo Therapy (UVB) and Photochemotherapy." *Psychosomatic Medicine* 60, 1998.

p.197. **On the other hand, a huge 2008 survey from the Pew Foundation:** The U.S. Religious Landscape Survey, February 25, 2008; www.pewforum.com.

p.198. **His unusual cultural, philosophical, and scientific background:** R. A. Baer, "Mindfulness Training as a Clinical Intervention." *Clinical Psychology* 10, Summer 2003.

CHAPTER 14: MEANING

p.203. **Here is Marcus Aurelius:** Martin Hammond (ed.), *Meditations.* New York: Penguin, 2006.

p.203. **Something of this preoccupation's postmodern tenor:** Antonio Monda, *Do You Believe? Questions on God and Religion.* New York: Vintage, 2007.

p.205. **a Californian turned Hindu guru:** Bhagavan Das, *It's Here Now (Are You?).* New York: Broadway Books, 1998.

p.205. **Alpert became Ram Das:** Ram Das, *Remember, Be Here Now.* San Cristobal, N.M.: Lama Foundation, 1971.

p.208. **He likes to tell the story:** Eckhart Tolle, *The Power of Now.* Novato, Calif.: New World Library, 2004.

p.210. **You don't hear that term very often:** Chris Peterson, *A Primer in Positive Psychology.* New York: Oxford University Press, 2006.

p.213. **To the poet:** W. H. Auden, *The Dyer's Hand.* New York: Vintage, 1990.

p.214. **Dissatisfied with this bleak conclusion:** Fred B. Bryant and Joseph Veroff, *Savoring.* Mahwah, N.J.: Lawrence Erlbaum Associates, 2006.

INDEX